P9-CKO-585

## DATE DUE

| | | |
|---|---|---|
| AG 31 '95 | | |
| JE 19 '97 | | |
| AP 2 6 01 | | |
| JE 11 '02 | | |
| | | |
| | | |
| | | |
| | | |
| | | |
| | | |
| | | |
| | | |
| | | |
| | | |
| | | |
| | | |

DEMCO 38-296

# NEW PARADIGMS
# FOR GOVERNMENT

# Patricia W. Ingraham
# Barbara S. Romzek
# and Associates

# NEW PARADIGMS FOR GOVERNMENT

## Issues for the Changing Public Service

Jossey-Bass Publishers • San Francisco

Substantial discounts on bulk quantities of Jossey-Bass books
are available to corporations, professional associations, and other
organizations. For details and discount information, contact the
special sales department at Jossey-Bass Inc., Publishers.
(415) 433-1740; Fax (415) 433-0499.

Manufactured in the United States of America. Nearly all Jossey-Bass
books and jackets are printed on recycled paper containing at least
10 percent postconsumer waste, and many are printed with either soy-
or vegetable-based ink, which emits fewer volatile organic compounds
during the printing process than petroleum-based ink.

**Library of Congress Cataloging-in-Publication Data**

New paradigms for government : issues for the changing public service
/ Patricia W. Ingraham, Barbara S. Romzek, and associates. — 1st
ed.
    p.  cm. — (The Jossey-Bass public administration series)
    Includes bibliographical references and indexes.
    ISBN 1-55542-656-5
    1. Organizational change.  2. Public administration.
I. Ingraham, Patricia W.  II. Romzek, Barbara S.  III. Series.
JF1525.073N493  1994
350—dc20                                           94-15872
                                                     CIP

**FIRST EDITION**
*HB Printing*   10  9  8  7  6  5  4  3  2  1                *Code 9451*

# The Jossey-Bass
# Public Administration Series

## Consulting Editor
## Public Management and Administration

James L. Perry
*Indiana University*

# Contents

Preface                                                              xiii

The Authors                                                           xix

Introduction: Issues Raised by Current Reform
Efforts                                                                 1
   *Patricia W. Ingraham, Barbara S. Romzek*

    **Part One: Understanding the Activities of
       Government Organizations and
          the Challenges of Change**         **15**

1.  Managing on the Frontiers of Knowledge: The
    Learning Organization                                              19
    *Donald F. Kettl*

2.  Implications of Contracting Out: New Roles for
    the Hollow State                                          41
    *H. Brinton Milward*

3.  Creating Government That Encourages
    Innovation                                                63
    *Paul C. Light*

4.  Reinvention and Employee Rights: The Role of
    the Courts                                                90
    *Phillip J. Cooper*

5.  Rethinking Public Personnel Administration        115
    *Hal G. Rainey*

    **Part Two: Managing Change
    Effectively in Public Organizations        141**

6.  Administrative Theory, Political Power, and
    Government Reform                                       145
    *David H. Rosenbloom, Bernard H. Ross*

7.  The Expanding Partnership Between Personnel
    Management and the Courts                          168
    *Rosemary O'Leary*

8.  Revitalizing Employee Ties with Public
    Organizations                                             191
    *James L. Perry*

9.  Reinventing the Senior Executive Service        215
    *Ronald P. Sanders*

10. Rethinking Public Employment Structures and
    Strategies                                                239
    *Lois Recascino Wise*

# Contents

**Part Three: Governance and the Public Service** 259

11. Issues of Accountability in Flexible Personnel
    Systems
    *Barbara S. Romzek, Melvin J. Dubnick*                          263

12. New Visions of Government and the Public
    Service
    *B. Guy Peters*                                                 295

    Conclusion: The Challenges Facing American
    Public Service
    *Barbara S. Romzek, Patricia W. Ingraham*                       322

    Name Index                                                      335

    Subject Index                                                   343

# *Preface*

In the 1980s, the United States and many other countries cast a skeptical and disapproving eye on government and its many activities. There were many efforts at reform; both structural and performance-oriented changes were widespread. National, state, and local governments have continued these efforts in the 1990s, in a slightly different form. Additional reductions in the size of government, continued privatization, and new kinds of flexibility in management are common items on the reform agenda.

In the United States, the work of Osborne and Gaebler and its emphasis on reinventing government informed the 1992 presidential election. Despite the Clinton victory and the current administration's emphasis on government as a problem solver, clearly it will not be business as usual for the public service and its members. *Reinventing* means fundamental redesign of the systems of government; the civil service system, with its years of accumulated rules and regulations, is a primary target.

Nevertheless, much of the prescriptive content of the reforms in the United States and elsewhere has not flowed from research or systematic analysis of public organizations. Rather, it has emerged from advocates of private sector change models or from the experience of a limited number of case studies, most of them focused on local government. Further, many of the proposed reforms advocate a role for the public service and its members that is in conflict with much of the history of public administration in the United States. As a result, proposed reforms have posed significant theoretical issues, which have not been addressed in reform debates. Academic research with the potential to shed light on some of the unresolved issues has also been left out of most discussions. The problems posed for reforms and the public service alike have been severe: without a clear understanding of the potential for effective change and of the obstacles to achieving it, expectations for outcomes and understanding of their reality are distorted in important ways.

## Background and Audience

In March 1993, following the presidential election and the new emphasis on reform in the United States, Dean John Palmer and Vice Chancellor Ben Ware of Syracuse University provided funds for a research conference at the university's center in Washington, D.C. The title of the conference was "Rethinking the Research Agenda for Public Sector Change." All the participants were either academics who had conducted research relevant to effective change or senior executives in government who had successfully managed change in their organizations. The chapters in this book were first presented at that conference. They have been revised to reflect developments since March 1993 and to focus specifically on the components of a coherent research and policy agenda that can provide constructive guidance for effective change.

The issues raised here are important to public managers, elected officials, and academics. The academic audience to which

the book is most specifically directed is composed of graduate
students and others concerned with the theory and practical reality of changing public organizations, but the book also addresses
students of public management more generally.

## Overview of the Contents

*New Paradigms for Government* is organized into three major parts.
The book begins with an introductory chapter — by Patricia W.
Ingraham and Barbara S. Romzek — that provides an overview of the changing nature of government work, the changing demands on government, and the increasing intensity of
calls for reform. We examine issues raised by the latest reform
proposals — those associated with reinventing government — in
the context of public organizations. Part One explores the emerging realities of government work. The five chapters in this section represent a serious effort to move beyond the bureaucratic
paradigm to a more accurate understanding of the complex,
problem-solving activities of many public organizations. In
Chapters One through Four, Donald F. Kettl, H. Brinton Milward, Paul C. Light, and Phillip J. Cooper, respectively, focus
on the changing nature of public tasks and functions and on
the nature of service delivery. Their discussions of learning organizations, innovation, risk, and uncertainty clarify the extent
to which effective reform must be based not only on what public organizations really do but also on what they are likely to
do in the future, however far removed that is from much of our
contemporary understanding. Hal G. Rainey's analysis in Chapter Five of what can be learned from the existing literature underscores that point.

   Part Two explores issues raised by the political environment, the courts, and internal organizational influences. In
Chapter Six, David H. Rosenbloom and Bernard H. Ross
clearly describe the intricate relationship between politics and
administrative mechanisms that characterizes American public administration. Their admonition — that viewing reforms
primarily from a presidential perspective simplifies both the role
of Congress and the real role of the public service in gover-

nance—is important. Rosemary O'Leary provides a perspective
in Chapter Seven on the role of the courts: noting that the courts
both prescribe and proscribe change efforts, she says that they
create a management constraint that is too often overlooked.
In Chapters Eight through Ten, James L. Perry, Ronald P.
Sanders, and Lois Recascino Wise, respectively, examine issues
related to investing in public leadership and to creating management systems that are both equitable and able to meet emerging challenges in the areas of knowledge, skills, and flexibility.

Part Three focuses on accountability and governance. In
Chapter Eleven, Barbara S. Romzek and Melvin J. Dubnick
present alternative accountability mechanisms and structures,
as well as their relationship to change and reform. The particular problems caused by the removal of rules and regulations,
without a clear view of what accountability means in their absence, are also discussed. In Chapter Twelve, B. Guy Peters
ends Part Three by providing alternative visions of reform and
discussing fundamental differences in public organizations and
contingent influences on change. His rich presentation of the
complexities inherent in redesigning and reinventing public organizations is an apt capstone for the arguments in the preceding chapters.

The concluding chapter, by Barbara S. Romzek and
Patricia W. Ingraham, returns to the themes and assumptions
of reform initiatives, such as reinventing government, and contrasts them with the complexity and reality of change in public
sector organizations. Change is clearly necessary, we argue, but
it must be carefully designed and should consider the issues
raised in this book.

## Acknowledgments

We are grateful to the contributors for their consistently excellent work and for their enthusiasm about *New Paradigms for
Government*. We are also grateful to the conference participants
who did not write papers but whose experience and analysis were
invaluable in creating the final product. In the United States,
Sally K. Marshall of the U.S. Office of Personnel Management,

Rosslyn Kleeman of the White House Personnel Office, and Barbara Dyer of the National Academy of Public Administration were enormously helpful. Maria Maguire of the Public Management Service of the Organization for Economic Cooperation and Development, in Paris, and Kees Breed of the Netherlands Ministry of Home Affairs provided superb insights into other national experiences and issues, and we thank them very much.

We also thank the staff of Syracuse University's Greenberg House, Mary Agnagost and Dugan Gillis, for providing a delightful conference setting and staff assistance. James Thompson from the Maxwell School also provided excellent assistance.

We sincerely hope that this book will inform the debate about reinvention and redesign in a way that keeps the unique qualities of public organizations and managers central while still exploring the real potential for positive and effective change. These issues are among the most significant now confronting the entire public management community. We cannot abdicate our responsibility for their careful discussion.

*March 1994* PATRICIA W. INGRAHAM
*Syracuse, New York*

BARBARA S. ROMZEK
*Lawrence, Kansas*

# The Authors

PATRICIA W. INGRAHAM is professor of public administration at the Maxwell School of Citizenship and Public Affairs, Syracuse University. She received her B.A. degree (1964) from Macalester College, her M.A. degree (1965) from Michigan State University, and her Ph.D. degree (1979) from the State University of New York at Binghamton, all in political science.

Ingraham served as associate professor of political science and director of the master's program in policy and administration at the State University of New York at Binghamton. She worked as project director of the Task Force on Recruitment and Retention for the National Commission on the Public Service (the Volcker Commission). She has testified before both the U.S. House of Representatives and the U.S. Senate on issues related to recruiting and managing a high-quality federal work force. She was elected a fellow of the National Academy of Public Administration in 1990.

Ingraham is coeditor of three books: *Legislating Bureaucratic Change: The Civil Service Reform Act of 1978* (1984, with C. Ban); *The Promise and Paradox of Bureaucratic Reform* (1992, with D. Rosenbloom); and *Agenda for Excellence: Public Service in America* (1992, with D. Kettl). She is also author of many articles dealing with civil service reform, public management, and the relationship between the president and the career civil service.

BARBARA S. ROMZEK is associate professor in the Department of Public Administration at the University of Kansas. She received her B.A. degree (1970) from Oakland University in Rochester, Michigan, her M.A. degree (1972) from Western Michigan University, and her Ph.D. degree (1979) from the University of Texas at Austin, all in political science. Her research and teaching interests are in public management, organizational psychology, and personnel policy. Her research emphases include the dynamics of accountability, employee commitment, patterns of employee accommodation to work and nonwork involvements, and intergovernmental relations. Her work has been published in various social science journals. She is also coauthor of *American Public Administration: Politics and the Management of Expectations* (1991, with M. Dubnick).

Romzek is listed in *Who's Who of American Women,* and she received the Mosher Award from the American Society for Public Administration for the best article by an academician. She has been a member of the governing board of the National Association of Schools of Public Affairs and served for one term as department chair at the University of Kansas. She currently serves on the Council of the American Political Science Association, on the executive committee of the Public and Nonprofit Division of the Academy of Management, and on various committees of the American Society for Public Administration and the International City Management Association. She has served on the editorial boards of five scholarly journals.

*Phillip J. Cooper* is chair of the Department of Public Administration at the University of Kansas. He received his Ph.D. degree

(1978) in political science from the Maxwell School of Citizenship and Public Affairs, Syracuse University. He is the author of numerous books and articles in the field of law and public administration.

*Melvin J. Dubnick* is professor of public administration and political science at Rutgers University. He received his Ph.D. degree (1974) in political science from the University of Colorado at Boulder. He has authored or coauthored books and articles on a wide range of topics, with special emphasis on issues related to accountability and reform in public administration. He is coauthor of *American Public Administration: Politics and the Management of Expectations* (1991, with B. S. Romzek). Since 1991, he has served as managing editor of *Public Administration Review*.

*Donald F. Kettl* is professor of public affairs and political science at the University of Wisconsin, Madison. He received his Ph.D. degree (1979) in political science from Yale University. A student of public policy and public management, he is author of *Government by Proxy* (1988), *The Politics of the Administrative Process* (1991, with J. W. Fesler), *Deficit Politics* (1992), *Improving Government Performance: An Owner's Manual* (1993, with J. J. DiIulio, Jr., and G. Garvey), and *Sharing Power: Public Governance and Private Markets* (1993). He has consulted for a broad array of public organizations and has served as a member of the U.S. Secretary of Energy Advisory Board's Task Force on Radioactive Waste Management.

*Paul C. Light* received his Ph.D. degree (1980) in political science from the University of Michigan. He is currently professor of planning and public affairs at the Hubert Humphrey Institute of Public Affairs, University of Minnesota, and director of the Surviving Innovation project at the Humphrey Institute. Before joining the Humphrey Institute, he served as senior adviser to and drafted the final report of the National Commission on the Public Service (the Volcker Commission) and served in a similar role with the National Commission on the State and Local Public Service. He has written six books, including *Vice Presidential Power* (1984), *Artful Work: The Politics of Social*

*Security Reform* (1985), *The President's Agenda* (1991), and *Monitoring Government: Inspectors General and the Search for Accountability* (1993).

*H. Brinton Milward* is director of the School of Public Administration and Policy and serves as associate dean of the College of Business and Public Administration at the University of Arizona. He received his Ph.D. degree (1978) in public administration from the School of Public Policy and Management at Ohio State University. He and Keith Provan hold a major research grant from the National Institute of Mental Health to study the relationship between service implementation networks and clinical outcomes among the seriously mentally ill. He is also conducting research on the institutional design of market-like arrangements for delivering human services. In addition, he is interested in the relationship between policy ideas, interest groups, and agenda setting. He is the author of numerous articles and chapters in contributed collections.

*Rosemary O'Leary* is assistant professor in the Department of Public Administration at the Maxwell School of Citizenship and Public Affairs, Syracuse University, where she received her Ph.D. degree (1988) in public administration. She and Charles Wise were the joint recipients of the 1991 and 1992 William E. Mosher and Frederick C. Mosher Awards for best article by an academician published in *Public Administration Review*. She is author of *Environmental Change: Federal Courts and the EPA* (1993) and a member of the board of editors of *Public Administration Review, Journal of Public Administration Research and Theory, Policy Studies Journal,* and *Natural Resources and Environment*.

*James L. Perry* is professor in the School of Public and Environmental Affairs, Indiana University, Bloomington. He received his Ph.D. degree (1974) in public administration from Syracuse University. His research focuses on public management and public personnel administration. He is author, coauthor, or editor of many books and articles and is the recipient of the Yoder-Heneman Award for innovative personnel research and the Charles H. Levine Memorial Award for Excellence in Public Administration.

# The Authors                          xxiii

*B. Guy Peters* is Maurice Falk professor of American government and chair of the Department of Political Science at the University of Pittsburgh. He received his Ph.D. degree (1970) in political science from Michigan State University. He has had Fulbright Fellowships at the University of Strathclyde (Scotland) and at the Hochschule St. Gallen (Switzerland) and has held visiting positions in Norway, Sweden, Mexico, and the Netherlands.

Peters's books include *The Politics of Bureaucracy* (3rd edition, 1989) and *American Public Policy* (1992). He has also edited *Organizing Governance, Government Organizations* (1988, with C. Campbell). He is past editor of *Governance* and current editor of the *International Library of Comparative Public Policy*.

*Hal G. Rainey* is professor of political science at the University of Georgia. He received his Ph.D. degree (1978) in public administration from Ohio State University. Rainey is author of *Understanding and Managing Public Organizations* (1990), as well as numerous articles on the comparison of public, private, and hybrid organizations and on incentives and work-related attitudes in organizations. He served as chair of the Public Sector Division of the Academy of Management and is chair-elect of the Public Administration Section of the American Political Science Association.

*David H. Rosenbloom* is distinguished professor of public administration in the School of Public Affairs at American University. He received his Ph.D. degree (1969) in political science from the University of Chicago. His published work focuses on the politics, personnel, and law of public bureaucracy, as well as on public administrative history. He became editor-in-chief of *Public Administration Review* in 1990. A member of the National Academy of Public Administration, he was appointed to the Clinton-Gore presidential transition team and has testified before the Governmental Affairs Committee of the U.S. Senate.

*Bernard H. Ross* is professor and chair of public administration at American University. He received his Ph.D. degree (1971) in government from New York University. Ross has had extensive experience in developing and administering executive training programs for major corporations, as well as for senior executives at the federal, state, and local levels. He also spent several years in sales and marketing positions with private sector corporations.

Ross's publications include articles and monographs on state and local government. He is also author of *Urban Management* (1979), *Business Regulation and Government Decision Making* (1980), *Urban Politics* (1985), and *How Washington Works* (1987).

*Ronald P. Sanders* is principal director of civilian personnel policy and equal opportunity for the U.S. Department of Defense and director of its Civilian Personnel Service. He received his Ph.D. degree (1989) in public administration from George Washington University and currently serves as adjunct professor at the Maxwell School of Citizenship and Public Affairs, Syracuse University. Responsible for human resource management policies and programs for one million civilian employees, he is a career member of the federal government's Senior Executive Service. He has also been elected to the board of directors of the Senior Executives Association.

*Lois Recascino Wise* is associate professor of public and environmental affairs at Indiana University, where she received her Ph.D. degree (1982) in public administration. Her research and teaching interests center on the broad area of employment policies and practices, with a special focus on the public sector. She has served as a consultant to public and private sector organizations in the United States and Europe.

Wise has published articles in *Public Administration Review, Public Administration Quarterly, British Journal of Industrial Relations, International Labour Review, Public Productivity and Management Review, Review of Public Personnel Administration, Public Personnel Management, Knowledge in Society,* and other publications. She is author of *Labor Market Policies and Employment Patterns in the United States* (1989).

# NEW PARADIGMS
# FOR GOVERNMENT

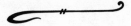

# Introduction

# Issues Raised by
# Current Reform Efforts

*Patricia W. Ingraham*
*Barbara S. Romzek*

As the United States moves into the twenty-first century, there is a profound dissatisfaction with many of the institutions of government. Indeed, in this country and in other industrialized nations, much of the past decade saw serious attacks on government itself. Ronald Reagan, Margaret Thatcher, and Brian Mulroney proclaimed that government was not the solution to societies' ills but a major part of the problem. The 1980s were a time of serious government-bashing that revealed how tenuous the link had become between citizens and the public institutions created to serve them.

At the center of this dissatisfaction, and often its target, was the public service. In the United States and elsewhere, civil service systems created to perform limited and relatively routine tasks struggled to adapt to new functions, more complex problems, and increasingly turbulent political and economic

1

environments. The bureaucratic structures that civil service systems reinforced were slow and sometimes unwilling to change; the employees within those structures faced a new set of rules and expectations regarding stability, performance, and productivity. At the federal level of government, the National Commission on the Public Service (1989) described a "quiet crisis" and advocated "rebuilding" the public service. Four years later, the National Commission on the State and Local Public Service (1993) called its report *Hard Truths/Tough Choices* and advocated sweeping reforms for those levels of government.

Just as the civil service systems themselves were initially products of policy diffusion from one national setting or one level of government to another, new but similar sets of proposals for reform are now beginning to circulate. Values from earlier in this century — economy and efficiency — are central to many of the reform ideas. The fountainhead for many of the components of the proposed reforms is again the private sector. Smaller, flatter, more innovative organizations are a common objective; pay for performance, performance management, and total quality are parts of most reform efforts.

To a considerable extent, the new efforts to change and reform public bureaucracies have exacerbated dissatisfaction with existing systems for personnel management. Virtually all the reforms have required new flexibility and discretion. The hallmarks of civil service — standardization, stability, and complex rules and regulations — were in conflict with many of the new initiatives. In addition, civil service systems had effectively removed many personnel responsibilities from managers, and reintegration of that function into ongoing management processes was difficult. Elected officials who wished to see results quickly were particularly unhappy with the realities of change in public organizations and in their management and personnel systems. The early months of the Clinton administration were spent emphasizing the need to "reinvent" government (Osborne and Gaebler, 1992). Vice President Gore was in charge of the National Performance Review, whose purpose was to examine every federal agency and recommend strategies for improvement. Reform and change are very much on the current agenda and are likely to be on the agenda in the future.

There are many questions, however, both about the reform activities and about their outcomes. Why are such efforts so consistent and so intense? Have any of the reform activities been successful? How do we know? Have we asked the right questions about how to change and what needs to change? What are appropriate models for change in public sector organizations? Does the private sector provide adequate guidance, or is looking there for solutions part of the problem? Are there uniquely public issues and potential public solutions that should be on the agenda but are not?

## Defining an Agenda for Effective Change: Do We Know the Right Questions?

Public management reforms in the United States have often been marked by three characteristics: they have been based on an inadequate or inaccurate view of what public organizations really do, they have failed to recognize the very fundamental constraints that civil service systems place on public managers and their activities, and they have been based almost exclusively on models borrowed from the private sector. Each of these characteristics has serious implications for effective reform. In combination, they have distorted many efforts to change public organizations and the public service. It will be useful to analyze each characteristic in more depth.

### Looking to the Private Sector for Models of Success

Since the inception of public administration and public management, both as an activity and as a field of study in the United States, the private sector model has served as a guide for effective public management. Woodrow Wilson (1887) observed that it was necessary to "render government activities more business-like"; theorists of scientific management argued that the separation of politics and administration in the public sector allowed the application of business principles to public management and permitted pursuit of the primary value, efficiency.

More recently, the Civil Service Reform Act of 1978 relied conspicuously on private sector techniques for solving public problems. The most obvious example is pay for performance, which was adopted governmentwide, without experimentation, because of its presumed success in private settings (Ingraham, 1993). Another example is the Reagan administration's reliance on the Grace Commission, headed by a private sector executive and composed entirely of other private sector executives. Another case in point is the Clinton administration's reliance, in the National Performance Review, on the private sector for models of high-performing organizations.

The assumptions underpinning these transfers from the private sector to the public sector are significant. First, it is necessary to assume that internal organizational systems and environments in both sectors are similar enough to permit effective transfer. Second, it is necessary to assume that resources and resource bases, both financial and human, are also similar enough for effective transfer. Third, and perhaps most significant, it is necessary to assume that the problems requiring remediation are similar and amenable to similar solutions. There is good evidence that all three of these assumptions are tenuous (Perry and Kraemer, 1983; Rainey, 1991; Milkovich and Wigdor, 1991). This is not to suggest that experience in the private sector has no relevance to public management or its reform; many creative and innovative management ideas have been spawned in smaller, more flexible, dynamic corporations. It does suggest, however, that the issue of transferability must be very carefully considered, and that elements of the public sector must be carefully excised (rarely the case) rather than transplanted whole.

### The Management Environment of Public Organizations

In the American federal government, as well as in state and local governments, civil service systems define how public organizations recruit, compensate, promote, and retain their employees. As these systems have evolved over the past century, they have increasingly moved the personnel function away from the managers responsible for organizational performance to a centralized and rigidly standardized set of personnel rules and specialists. The resulting diminution of managerial authority and flexibility has created a circumstance in which the underlying management systems must be repaired—or, more accurately, created—before other organizational changes can occur. There are several related issues to consider.

*Organizational Leadership.* Public organizations differ dramatically from private organizations in terms of leadership. Most public organizations have two kinds of leaders, who serve somewhat different but necessarily cooperative functions. Political executives—appointed by the president, the governor, the mayor, or other elected officials—serve as policy leaders and managers. They are change agents and managers in the most fundamental sense, attempting to direct the organization and its programs to reflect the mandates of elections and citizens' preference. Members of the career civil service who have attained executive status are also organizational leaders. They understand the organization and its program, the realities of constraints on managerial prerogatives, and the political environment of the organization. Many of these managers are also advocates for change and can be change agents according to their understanding of the need for and the potential levers of change initiatives.

The potential common ground is balanced and sometimes offset, however, by differences in the two kinds of leaders. Political leaders have relatively short tenure; eighteen months to two years is a common length of service in a given position. Career executives have substantially longer tenure. Political executives have a fairly small window of opportunity to effect change in the organization, whereas career executives can take a longer-term perspective. Political executives are not necessarily chosen for their management skills, particularly at the lower levels, but career managers have extensive education and development in management skills and abilities by the time they reach the executive level. These differences have important consequences. For one thing, political management strategies of the last twenty-five years have tended to devalue career expertise, and in some cases political appointees were introduced as a way to bypass career managers. The long-term potential for cooperation has diminished as a result (Ingraham, 1987).

Leadership in the public sector, in short, is bifurcated and has a shorter-term view of change than in the private sector. Cooperative management teams, fundamental to any effective organizational change or reform, must be created anew at every turnover in top elected officeholders, and sometimes more often. The vision necessary to effective long-term change is frequently in flux. The dynamic and turbulent nature of the public sector environment works against the crystallization of a clear vision for change and against the development of consensus on a shared agenda for public policies and organizations. This absence of clear vision becomes part of the leadership problem.

*Multiple Accountability Structures.* Although it is an oversimplification to say so, private organizations are commonly described as having a two-part accountability system: to the board of directors, and to the customers. Each component entails indicators of performance and accountability: profits and efficiency for the former, sales and satisfaction for the latter.

Public organizations and the managers who operate within them have a more complex set of expectations and accountability structures. They face a wider range of expectations from numerous public sector stakeholders: elected officials, organizational superiors, professional peers, co-workers, clientele groups, special-interest groups, and citizens. All of these have a role in the web of accountability within which public agencies and managers operate. As a result, the American public sector is characterized by numerous overlapping and sometimes contradictory accountability structures. An accountability mechanism frequently represents a trade-off of efficiency and flexibility for responsiveness and responsibility. One stakeholder sees a particular personnel policy (the employee's right to a hearing before dismissal, for example) as unnecessary and time-consuming; another sees the same policy as essential to accountability.

Civil service systems are characterized by top-down accountability for compliance with rules and regulations. Civil service systems and their impact on the quality of government are a central focus in any reconsideration of the role and responsibility of the public sector. Beyond the civil service, however, public agencies and employees face numerous other accountability structures. Chief elected officials and political appointees (for example, the president and his appointees) rely on hierarchical controls, policy direction, oversight, and persuasion. Congress and other legislative bodies utilize budgetary controls, rule-making authority, and oversight activity in their efforts to elicit accountability from public agencies and employees. The courts now also play a key role in holding public agencies accountable, both for performance and for adherence to law. Monitoring is the most common technique used by the courts, but it is not the only one; judicial mandates concerning organizational budgets and priorities are increasingly common.

Professional peers promulgate the standards of acceptable practice and the ethics by which professional performance is evaluated, and these create yet another level of accountability. Clientele groups have clear expectations for level and quality of service and often for policy content as well. Finally, public organizations and employees are accountable to those they serve, the citizens. Citizens' roles are somewhat less direct in the accountability relationship, but citizens represent the ultimate authority to which public agencies and employees must be accountable.

These webs of expectation and accountability both constrain and provide opportunities for public agencies and managers. Multiple stakeholders and structures provide different mechanisms for accountability, different views of what accountability means, and very different perspectives on what and to whom the permanent bureaucracy should be accountable. These conflicting perspectives are important to the determination of organizational effectiveness. Equally important, some reconciliation among them is critical to designing and implementing successful change.

*Lack of Managerial Discretion and Authority.* As noted earlier, one outcome of the many rules and regulations controlling personnel management in the public sector is a decrease in the authority and discretion of line managers and executives. It is possible to fire someone in the civil service, but it is very complicated. Multileveled grievance and appeals procedures further constrain managerial discretion. Collective bargaining has had the same effect. In many cases, the equity that these influences have sought to create has become instead a bland sameness that is not conducive to creativity or high performance. Hiring and retaining key employees is difficult in a civil service system. A seriously outdated classification system creates problems with keeping job descriptions current and with recruiting and hiring people on the cutting edge.

At the same time that public managers cope with the stultifying rules and regulations related to personnel, they must juggle the constraints and requirements of budgetary processes, financial management systems, and information management and reporting requirements, which have increased dramatically in recent years. Disjunction among these systems further attenuates the ability to operate from the foundation of a sound managerial base.

### What Do Public Organizations Really Do?

Two issues are most relevant here: variation among public organizations in terms of size, structure, and function; and the dramatically changing nature of what many organizations actually do.

The first issue is relatively straightforward: although it is common to refer to all government organizations collectively as "the bureaucracy," not all fit comfortably into that category. Some are already the smaller, flatter organizations that reforms seek to create. Others are very clearly bureaucratic: large, hierarchical, standardized, and rigid. For some, bureaucratic organization makes good sense. Routine tasks (such as ensuring that social security checks are mailed on time) benefit from the stability and predictability that bureaucracy provides. For other organizations, bureaucratic structure has been inappropriate and dysfunctional. The work of Romzek and Dubnick (1987) clearly demonstrates the problems that NASA, for example, has encountered in this regard. The point, of course, is that any reform will have a differential impact. Some problems are common to all or most government agencies; others are organization-specific.

Some government organizations exist specifically because the services they deliver could not be delivered equitably by other organizations or by the private sector, and some of the problems they face are created because they *are* public. They are not supposed to function like private sector organizations. They are responsible to standards — efficiency, effectiveness, responsiveness, equity — that require clear and sometimes counterproductive trade-offs. Reforms will not always have their anticipated impacts on organizations created to be essentially untidy.

The second issue, the dramatically changing nature of government work, is also very important for future research, reform, and change. Reinventing government necessarily implies very careful analysis, not only of what government actually does but also of what it should do. Throughout the 1980s, the federal government and many state and local governments privatized services and functions that had previously been delivered or performed by government organizations. Government employees became contract administrators, sometimes primarily so. (In the Department of Energy, for example, 20,000 permanent employees supervised 145,000 contract employees in 1991.) The contractors performed technical analyses and forecasts, provided policy advice and direction, and conducted evaluations of existing or proposed programs. They performed, in short, all the functions of full-time federal employees but were employed by private organizations; their expertise resided in the private sector and was available to the federal government only for a fee. No "institutional memory" was created in the permanent bureaucracy. Not only is accountability attenuated, but contract management has become so large a task that some departments have resorted to "bundling" contracts and hiring other contractors to manage them. Thus the link between traditional accountability mechanisms and the actual delivery of government services becomes more and more tenuous.

As more budgets and staffs are cut while service delivery is not, the situation will be exacerbated. The implications for government employees and for what they do are enormous. Kettl (1988) has called the emerging reality "government by proxy." Others refer to the "hollow state." According to Rainey (1991), the "irony" is that privatization was presented as a solution to the problems of government but has created new demands and problems for existing government agencies and employees. Government employees in general are not recruited or hired to be contract managers. They come because of program or professional expertise, and once inside the organization, they are rarely trained in contract management. Yet they are still accountable for the performance of contractors and their employees.

Where does it end? What must government retain, and what must it continue to know and do if it is to serve all citizens in the future? These are questions that have not been posed, much less answered, by advocates of privatization or reinventing government. They must be addressed, however, if government and its employees are to meet the challenges and demands of the future.

The chapters in this book do raise critical questions about these issues. The questions are fundamental to any consideration of shaping future organizations and the systems to support them. Obviously, this book does not raise all possible issues. As the chapters evolved, it became clear to us that some technical reforms (classification is the most obvious example) would require a level of analysis not possible in a book of this nature. This does not mean that such issues are insignificant, but only that the questions posed here focus on broader issues of change and governance. As a result, the book highlights fundamental problems in those reinvention strategies that fail to consider the political environment of public organizations and the critical role those organizations play in democratic governance. Our intent here is to focus on those issues and on the role of the public service in any new configurations that may emerge. The long-term vitality of the public sector requires that we take this special role seriously.

## Challenges of Public Sector Change:
## Issues for Research

The erosion of confidence in government's ability to solve society's problems has resulted in a steady stream of government-bashing and has fostered many proposals for government reform. Individuals both within and outside of government agree that change is needed. The Clinton administration's emphasis on government as problem solver and various state and local governments' embrace of reinvention strategies have heightened interest in government performance and change.

Old organizations, old systems, and old attitudes are all targets of change. At the same time, there is new recognition that only government can make the decisions and mold the policies that are increasingly central to several aims: maintaining an acceptable quality of life for all citizens, ensuring international competitiveness for both the nation and its products, and creating a future better than today. In the final analysis, a citizen is not the same as a customer. Public change and reform must be cognizant of democratic demands, as well as of the complex problems related to organizational change and changing.

This creates enormous challenges, which public organizations and employees and those who would change them must recognize. One challenge involves the dramatically expanded scope and complexity of the problem environment in which public organizations operate. Agencies such as the Department of Energy and the Environmental Protection Agency must make long-term environmental decisions for which there are no clear solutions. Organizations such as Housing and Urban Development operate in an arena where the problems are not even clear.

The recent collapse of the Soviet Union provides a different kind of challenge: when many of the new republics reverted to their traditional ethnic languages, the U.S. State Department found that it lacked the expertise to communicate directly with officials in many of the newly independent republics. This challenge demonstrates the need for learning organizations whose boundaries are permeable and flexible enough to predict and provide for new levels of complexity and uncertainty.

A different kind of challenge is provided by the move toward privatizing and contracting. Some of the services that have been privatized will probably never be returned to the public domain, and perhaps they should not be; that is not the issue.

The issue is how government will maintain a level of skills and expertise that permits government institutions—rather than those with whom they contract—to solve future problems. As Kettl (1988) and others have noted, most privatizing and contracting has occurred in a context of questions about what to get rid of, not what to keep. Yet what government must keep— not just in terms of a skilled, expert, and motivated work force but also in terms of processes for giving the work force flexibility and protection—is a central question of reinvention and reform.

Reinvention is not simple and cannot be approached in simplistic ways. Quite clearly, the public service of the future will be less centralized, with more opportunity for autonomy in structure and processes. That development cannot occur without consideration and reconciliation of the issues it will raise for accountability. A newly energized public service will not reward risk-averse behavior; it will find ways to cultivate and reward entrepreneurial activities. This must occur in the context of a shared vision for the organization and its programs, both among the branches of government and between elected officials and career civil servants. The future public service must recognize that public employment is a privilege but that some basic employee rights must also continue to be protected.

It is also clear that the traditional function of the central personnel office—organizational policing—will shift toward a function more closely identified with organizational facilitation and management. This challenges not only traditional norms of accountability but also past practices related to equity and fairness inside the organization. Equally important, it opens the door to reconsidering entrance requirements and the role of politics in the process. These tenuous balances must also be considered in reinvention.

The chapters that follow demonstrate that modern public organizations are caught in the interstices of the separation of powers. The executive, legislative, and judicial branches proceed as if each branch wielded unilateral and hierarchical authority over public organizations. In the view of each branch, accountability means responsiveness to its particular direction.

But, for many reasons (conflicting demands, limited resources, contracting, hollowed government), tidy public organizations no longer exist, and issues of accountability, authority, and legitimacy are not well understood.

The challenge of democratic governance in the future is formidable. Realizing the full potential for effective change and reform is critically important. The fundamental issues of what government does and how it does it, however, must be combined with the democratic issues of politics, responsiveness, and accountability if reinvention and reform are to succeed. This makes the job much harder, but failure to consider democratic issues in the reform process will result only in reinventing problems, not solving them.

## References

Ingraham, P. W. "Building Bridges or Burning Them? The President, the Appointees and the Bureaucracy." *Public Administration Review,* 1987, *47,* 425–435.

Ingraham, P. W. "Of Pigs in Pokes and Policy Diffusion: Another Look at Pay for Performance." *Public Administration Review,* 1993, *53,* 56.

Kettl, D. F. *Government by Proxy: (Mis)Managing Federal Programs.* Washington, D.C.: Congressional Quarterly Press, 1988.

Milkovich, T. G., and Wigdor, A. K. (eds.). *Pay for Performance: Evaluating Performance Appraisal and Merit Pay.* Washington, D.C.: National Academy Press, 1991.

National Commission on the Public Service (Volcker Commission). *Leadership for America: Rebuilding the Public Service.* Washington, D.C.: National Commission on the Public Service, 1989.

National Commission on the State and Local Public Service. *Hard Truths/Tough Choices: An Agenda for State and Local Reform.* Albany, N.Y.: Nelson A. Rockefeller Institute of Government, 1993.

Osborne, D., and Gaebler, T. *Reinventing Government: How the Entrepreneurial Spirit Is Transforming the Public Sector.* Reading, Mass.: Addison-Wesley, 1992.

14        New Paradigms for Government

Perry, J. L., and Kraemer, K. (eds.). *Public Management.* Mountain View, Calif.: Mayfield, 1983.

Rainey, H. *Understanding and Managing Public Organizations.* San Francisco: Jossey-Bass, 1991.

Romzek, B. S., and Dubnick, M. "Accountability in the Public Sector: Lessons from the *Challenger* Tragedy." *Public Administration Review,* 1987, *47*(3), 227–239.

Wilson, W. "The Study of Administration." *Political Science Quarterly,* 1887, *2*, 197–222.

# PART ONE

## *Understanding the Activities of Government Organizations and the Challenges of Change*

The many efforts at government reform of the past two decades have had important common themes: reducing a bloated and inefficient bureaucracy, creating flexibility and innovation, and delivering the same or better services at reduced cost. Besides being modeled most often on the private sector, the reforms had another and equally significant quality: they operated from an understanding of government that was seriously outdated. Government was viewed as a set of similar large bureaucratic organizations, operating with standardized procedures and rules. Government employees were also seen in the traditional bureaucratic way, as faceless bureaucrats delivering routine services. There was substantial evidence that these stereotypes were inaccurate in many respects, but they continued to inform efforts to change government and the public service.

This is not to suggest that rigid and standardized bureaucratic structures did not contribute to the problems of government. They did, and they still do. But to fully understand the
need for change, as well as the potential for effective change,
it is necessary to move beyond the bureaucratic paradigm to
a more accurate description of what government organizations
and employees really do and how they do it. The chapters in
this section begin that task.

In the first three chapters, the authors explore the contemporary reality of government work: the complexity of the
tasks and the problems addressed, the reality of contracting and
hollow government, and the critical mismatch between the demands placed on government and the ability of governmental
institutions and employees to respond.

In Chapter One, Kettl presents the learning organization,
one that faces essentially insoluble problems but must find acceptable solutions. Organizations such as the federal Department of Energy and the Environmental Protection Agency confront issues that take them to the edge of scientific knowledge.
The employees of such agencies are not performing routine tasks.
They are engaged in solving complex problems that have significant implications for generations to come. Information — its
quality, availability, and timeliness — is crucial.

Milward, in Chapter Two, approaches the new reality
of public organizations from another perspective, that of the "hollowing out" created by extensive privatizing and contracting.
In this context, organizations and the work performed within
them are dramatically changed. Managing contractors is not
the same as delivering services directly, and operating in a delivery network is very different from operating in a traditional bureaucratic organization. The implications for what government
really does or must be able to do are significant. Government
must be a "smart buyer." In addition, Milward argues, a core
task of government in such a system is to arrange networks,
not manage hierarchy.

Light, in Chapter Three, employs yet another lens to explore the changing nature of government work. Arguing that
the match between the demands on government and the capacity

of government is not a good one, he observes that public organizations find themselves in a worst-case scenario where conditions for producing high performance and innovation are concerned. He describes the need for "learning by doing" and for supportive leadership.

In Chapter Four, Cooper explores an often neglected area: the relationship of the organization, change efforts, and the rights of public employees. Noting both the difficulty and the importance of the issue, Cooper argues that public managers, instead of permitting uncertainty about employees' rights to create paralysis, should clearly include the courts as key participants in the normal "dialogue of government."

In Chapter Five, Rainey carefully analyzes the extent to which the existing literature and research can guide the emerging realities of public organizations and public management. He shows how the fact of multiple stakeholders exacerbates the public organization's problems, as does the debate about decentralization versus centralization in organizational and managerial redesign.

Together, the chapters in Part One clarify what government really does as we approach the twenty-first century. The diverse governmental organizations, tasks, and employees, as well as the increased difficulty of solving problems in an environment characterized by uncertainty and limited information, do not suggest a monolithic government amenable to simple reform. Public reform carries additional responsibilities as well: democratic governance, and government that is effective from a variety of perspectives. In this environment, simplistic reforms create good rhetoric. They do not address the reality of public change.

# 1

# Managing on the Frontiers of Knowledge: The Learning Organization

*Donald F. Kettl*

In April 1979, Dartmouth College president John G. Kemeny was startled by his appointment to the presidential commission to investigate the accident at the Three Mile Island nuclear power station near Harrisburg, Pennsylvania. He joked afterward (1980, p. 65) that "ten years of chairing faculty meetings must surely be ideal preparation" for stepping into the intense political and technical anarchy that surrounded the probe. Local citizens were terrified. Scientists were mystified. The nuclear industry was profoundly embarrassed, and government regulators were unsure about what had gone wrong. Everyone looked to the commission for clues to what had happened, why it happened, and how to prevent such a crisis from recurring.

*Note:* For suggestions on improving this chapter, I am indebted to the editors, as well as to comments by James Perry.

Two interrelated issues—the uncertainty surrounding the technology, and the difficulty that institutions had in dealing with it—became the focus of Kemeny's concerns. He concluded that the Nuclear Regulatory Commission (NRC) "had no systematic way—I mean that absolutely literally and I am repeating sworn testimony by senior NRC officials—they had *no* systematic way of learning from experience" (p. 69). The problem, Kemeny observed, was that the NRC had become convinced that "nothing bad could possibly happen" (p. 69) and therefore came to believe that it had done enough to guarantee safety. When problems developed early that March morning at Three Mile Island, the operators reacted badly. When federal and local government officials intervened, they first stumbled and then struggled to understand and control the situation. For days, thousands of local residents waited nervously with their bags packed and their gas tanks full, unsure about whether they would have to leave—and, if they left, whether they would ever see their homes again.

Reflecting on his service, Kemeny argued that it was no longer possible for American democracy to muddle through such problems: "I conclude that our democracy must grow up" (p. 74). And growing up would require the government to build a better base of expertise for learning how to manage the complexities of the programs for which it was responsible. Kemeny argued, in short, that government needed to learn or risk being captured and possibly overrun by the problems it was designed to solve.

## The Paradox of Public Authority

There was deep irony under the profound truth of Kemeny's conclusion. Government and its bureaucracy exist fundamentally to pursue the public interest, and to do so expertly. The Three Mile Island crisis uncovered grave doubts about the government's capacity to solve the problems it faced. These doubts continued to grow during the 1980s. At the outset of the Clinton administration the U.S. General Accounting Office starkly concluded, "The state of management in the federal government is not good. Too many principles, structures, and processes that may have worked well years ago no longer allow the government to respond quickly and effectively to a rapidly changing world" (1992, p. 4). The problem is that government bureaucracy, as conceived and developed through the last century, is not up to the challenges of the next. Its foundations do not fit new problems. The tasks that government faces, moreover, vary so widely that no single administrative approach can possibly deal with all of them. For instance, relatively new agencies must struggle with daunting problems (consider the Environmental Protection Agency's job of cleaning up toxic-waste dumps). Relatively old agencies are facing new tests (consider the Pentagon's task of adapting military power to a world without a single overarching threat). Agencies are on the cutting edge of scientific knowledge (consider the Department of Energy's efforts to neutralize and safely store the radioactive debris of the nation's nuclear-weapons program). Public agencies at all levels of government are finding that any attack on critical problems, such as health care or poverty, will require an integrated assault that involves multiple agencies, federal-state-local partnerships, and public-private alliances.

For government to surmount these challenges, it must discover how to learn effectively. It must learn how to design new ways of solving problems and do so far more quickly and cheaply. Organizational theorists have pointed out that individuals can learn, but organizations can, too. Organizational learning occurs when the individuals working in an organization observe the effects of their actions, when they recognize the problems that remain unsolved and the new problems that may be created, and when they adapt and change to solve these problems (Fiol and Lyles, 1985; Hedberg, 1981; March and Olsen, 1975). Thus organizations learn when their employees improve their understanding, on the basis of observed results, about what works, what does not, and why.

If learning is to occur, it must happen when and where "organizations interact with their environments" (Hedberg, 1981, p. 3). That, logically, is where organizations are most likely to detect what effects they are producing, what otherwise is happening that may affect them, and how it all matters. The primary locus for organizational learning is therefore at the organization's boundaries.

Learning requires effective communication. It is a process built on information. Communication within organizations is inevitably troublesome, however. Bias, distortion, and condensation of information can make it hard to detect and read signals accurately (Downs, 1966; Guetzkow, 1965; March and Simon, 1958; Porter and Roberts, 1983). Communication across organizational boundaries can be even more difficult, and therein lies the dilemma for organizational learning: "accurate information from external areas is vital to the innovation process yet relatively difficult to gather" (Tushman, 1977, p. 587).

Organizational boundaries are the crucial sites for learning, and learning depends on managing information, but it also hinges on organizations' ability to develop individuals who can operate effectively to span those boundaries (March and Simon, 1958; Thompson, 1967; Tushman, 1977). Effective learning—indeed, effective public management—requires organizations to look past their internal operations, to gauge what is happening in the broader environment, to estimate the implications of these events for the organization's mission, and to adapt to those new challenges. It also requires the recognition that the more complex and uncertain the environment is, the more difficult the job of learning will be *and* the more important it becomes. It requires the aggressive development of new ways of training public servants to solve the rapidly evolving problems they face. Environments are "changing, at an increasing rate, and towards increasing complexity" (Emery and Trist, 1965, p. 21).

Organizations must learn in order to survive. To learn, they must adapt their learning systems to fit the varying uncertainties and complexities in their environments. Four factors complicate the job of learning. First, the bureaucracy's presumed monopoly on information has declined: we can no longer assume that the government knows what it needs to know. Second, its dependence on outside sources of information has increased, and so the process of learning has become more complex. Third, citizens' confidence in knowledge of all kinds has declined, and so developing confidence in the learning process has become more difficult. Fourth, sources of knowledge are ever more decentralized, and conflicting interpretations vie to define what we know.

## Challenges to Learning

These four issues shape new problems for government and, just as surely, for those who work in government and must solve its problems. The result is a challenge of gigantic proportions for public servants, a challenge that creates staggering burdens as well as unprecedented opportunities.

### The End of Hierarchy

When we think of the characteristics of bureaucracy, we tend to retreat back to Max Weber's classic formulation of bureaucracy's "ideal type." This formulation has grown, in fact, into a "bureaucratic paradigm" characterized by rules, procedures, delegation of authority, a chain of command, and clear standards of responsibility (Barzelay and Armajani, 1992, p. 5). These features flow directly from the first pages of Weber's famous paper on bureaucracy (1946), but a closer reading of the paper reveals that Weber was not so much interested in enshrining rules and authority as he was in understanding how organizations could be made to work better. Rationality, not authority, was the underlying premise of his work, and technical expertise was the foundation of rationality. For Weber, bureaucracy makes sense because it promotes efficiency: "The decisive reason for the advance of bureaucratic organization has always been its purely technical superiority over any other form of organization" (p. 214). The presumed expertise and, hence, efficiency of bureaucracy lay at the core of Weber's thinking.

Early writers on administrative theory were acutely aware that the presumption of expertise had important political implications. For Woodrow Wilson and the other Progressives, government had the mission of controlling the growth of private power. To do so, it had to become "less unbusinesslike" (Wilson, 1887, p. 201). Weber was even more blunt: "The bureaucratic structure goes hand in hand with the concentration of the material means of management in the hands of the master" (1946, p. 221). Bureaucracy, Weber concluded, offers "above all the optimum possibility for carrying through the principle of specializing administrative functions" (p. 215).

Bureaucratic expertise and political power are inextricably linked. As Niskanen (1971, 1991) and others have pointed out, such concentration of government power in bureaucracy's hands can lead to monopolistic behavior. There is only one buyer for the services of most bureaus: the political officials who set their budgets. Moreover, for most of the services bureaus produce, there is only one seller. Even when there are actually or potentially other suppliers, competition rarely offers many real choices. The result, Niskanen argues, is a "bilateral monopoly" that introduces many inefficiencies into the behavior of bureaus and bureaucrats.

I want to put aside the implications of Niskanen's arguments—they have been hotly debated for years—and focus more narrowly on the fundamental assumptions he makes (see Blais and Dion, 1991). The expertise of bureaus and bureaucrats is their very reason for being. If they did not know how to do well what they do, then citizens would object to paying taxes to support them. This leads naturally, if not to a monopoly, then at least to a high concentration of expertise in the hands of bureaucrats. Here, Niskanen finds a surprising ally in Weber (1946). In fact, Weber argues, "Every bureaucracy seeks to increase the superiority of the professionally informed by keeping their knowledge and intentions secret" (p. 233).

The critical point is that information—based on expertise, not on authority and rules—is the foundation of bureaucracies. This is not to say that authority and rules are not bureaucratic characteristics; indeed, they are part of the "ideal type" that Weber identifies. They matter, however, because they promote the expertise on which the bureaucracy's power rests. Bureaucracies, after all, are instruments. They exist to perform tasks. Performing tasks well requires expertise, and authority and rules exist to maximize performance.

Over the last generation, the governmental bureaucracy's monopoly has eroded. With the rapid growth of contracting and other forms of "government by proxy" (Donahue, 1989; Kettl, 1988; Salamon, 1981), government now purchases goods and services from sources other than public agencies. Theories of pluralism, even if roundly attacked, at least demonstrate that the relationship between bureaus and elected officials is anything but monopolistic (Rourke, 1984). Moreover, in the market for the goods and services that government buys from private providers, imperfections are large and important (Kettl, 1993).

World War II brought new threats, which the nation met with new technologies, from radar to nuclear weapons. In developing these new technologies, the government developed new partnerships with private contractors. The political functions that individuals played increasingly came to be defined "not on the basis of the property they own[ed] but of what they [knew] and of the professional skills they command[ed]" (Price, 1965, p. 56).

The wartime program shaped policy innovation in post–World War II America. In space, natural resources, and defense policy, the government switched its role. No longer a passive recipient of technological changes developed and tested in the private sector, government became an active partner in stimulating new work (Danhof, 1968). In social programs, the government managed all major new programs—Model Cities, urban renewal, Medicare, Medicaid—through public-private partnerships. The same was true of the environmental initiatives launched in the 1970s and expanded through the 1980s. Joint public-private partnerships, in fact, became the dominant administrative pattern of post–World War II American government. Nearly 30 percent of the federal budget is spent through contractors, either directly (for military weapons) or indirectly (for Medicare and Medicaid). Most of the rest goes for transfer programs (like social security) and interest on the national debt. Government's presumed monopoly over the tools of government has ended, and that in turn has posed a serious dilemma for the Weberian-Wilsonian assumptions that established the foundations of government hierarchy.

Further disrupting the traditional view of hierarchy within organizational theory are two features identified by Perrow (1984). First, organizational systems are more tightly coupled. Fewer, public or private, are directly responsible for translating their inputs into outputs. The more complex problems become — and government tends to get only the toughest problems — the more interdependent (or coupled) organizations tend to be in trying to solve them. Second, organizational systems are developing more interactive complexity. Because the systems are more tightly coupled, failures in one part of a system can ripple throughout, causing serious and unpredictable problems. Indeed, Perrow cheerily argues, "given the system characteristics, multiple and unexpected interactions of failure are inevitable" (p. 5). The inevitability of major problems in today's systems puts an even higher priority on organizational learning. To become high-reliability organizations, some have sought to design novel patterns of redundancy and learning directly into the system (LaPorte and Consolini, 1991). Failing to do so invites failure. Avoiding failure requires designing the ability to learn into the very fabric of the bureaucracy.

## Governmental Reliance on External Expertise

As government's reliance on proxies increased, its monopoly on information diminished. There was a time when observers of government reassured citizens that their tax dollars bought the best expertise possible. Appleby, in a book dedicated to "John Citizen and Bill Bureaucrat," argued, "The public would be gratified and moved if it could know more" of the bureaucrats who serve them (1945, p. 2). Indeed, for generations, the argument was made that the federal bureaucracy was the home of the world's leading experts in virtually every field, from cartography to weapons analysis. The implication was that power over decision making in these areas would follow.

The presumption of government expertise eroded during World War II. Government, of course, had always relied on the private sector in producing goods and services. Now, with the new postwar challenges, it was relying more on the private sector for ideas as well. Gone were the days when the government decided which of all the commercially available goods or services it would buy. Instead, government came to depend more on the private sector for the concepts as well as the development and production of advanced new goods (Danhof, 1968). Since then, government's growing dependence on contractors for ideas and information has taken two forms.

*Policy Directions.* Government has shared its responsibility for shaping the direction of policy with its contractors. For example, a survey found that contractors had performed such work for agencies as developing the Department of Transportation's safety policy, preparing testimony for Department of Energy witnesses, and developing criteria for the Environmental Protection Agency to use in deciding what "inherently governmental functions" it should not contract out (U.S. General Accounting Office, 1991, pp. 5–6). The survey concluded, "The government does not have employees in sufficient numbers with all the skills to meet every requirement" (p. 6). Contracting out for key policy guidance was therefore inevitable. The government relied on contractors to tell it what to do, how to do it, what had been done, and how to present it all to others, including congressional committees. Personnel ceilings and the erosion of critical expertise within the government made heavy reliance on contractors inescapable (U.S. General Accounting Office, 1991).

*Auditing and Evaluation.* Where auditing and evaluation are concerned, the government increasingly knows only what contractors tell it. The government's own management information system, financial accounting, and program evaluation activities are in serious disrepair. Especially in programs managed through contracts including entitlement programs like Medicare and Medicaid, the emphasis has been on getting the money out the door: "Monitoring contractor performance and costs is not emphasized" (U.S. Office of Management and Budget, 1992, p. 12). The resources devoted to evaluation also declined during the 1980s; the government tended to conduct fewer studies, spend less money, take less time studying problems, and ask less probing questions (U.S. General Accounting Office, 1987).

Because of cuts in personnel throughout government,

agency managers have had little choice but to take the word of contractors that they are doing their jobs well. According to one report, lack of oversight cost the government $310 billion during the 1980s (House Committee on Government Operations, 1992, p. ix). Government's near-monopoly over information on the effects of its programs had disappeared, and government had little independent capacity to learn the results for itself.

## The Decline of Confidence in Science

American public bureaucracy matured, confident in its know-how. In the early years of the twentieth century, the nation built a strong central bank, established an income tax, created a large standing army backed by a sophisticated defense establishment, constructed a national network of first-class highways, dedicated itself to eliminating poverty, worked to clean up the environment, provided income support to retirees, and launched an aggressive health care program for the poor and elderly. It was, ironically, at the very height of this movement that public confidence in social engineering through a strong, centralized government began to ebb. In part, this was because of the growing costs of building such a government empire. In part, this was also because of declining public confidence that the programs worked, despite manifest evidence in everything from cleaner water to a dramatic decline in poverty among the elderly.

Ezrahi (1990, p. 241) notes that the growth of American public bureaucracies rested on the partnership of science and democracy; by the end of the twentieth century, however, "the diminishing political force of enlightenment visions of progress and political engineering in America" had disrupted this partnership. A new, "anti-instrumentalist mood" replaced Americans' earlier confidence in the potential of science, harnessed by government, to solve the nation's problems. Ezrahi contends that "irreducible uncertainties" weakened "the claims of knowledge and authority" of everyone involved; political authority was undermined by "the acknowledgment of shared ignorance" (p. 287). The problem was not just a failure of government, although problems in some areas were manifest. Rather, the public was less confident that any strong power, public or private, could understand or cope with the huge uncertainties surrounding public problems. At the same time, public pressures rose for decentralization — from the public to the private sector and, within the public sector, from the national to state and local governments. Forces supporting fragmentation increased as well. Americans' political values migrated from a sense of community to that of "a gigantic condominium, a hodge-podge of diverse industrial worlds" (Ezrahi, 1990, p. 284).

Price (1965, 1983) has charted how Americans' ideas about science have shaped their views toward government. The Progressive belief in government's capacity to understand and solve society's problems led to a stronger government. This support for a stronger government led naturally to a powerful, expert, Weberian bureaucracy. Increasing uncertainties about our ability to know how to solve problems undercut public support for the problem solvers, the bureaucrats.

This declining public support has three roots. First, citizens rely on experts to define problems. The experts tend to be organized by profession and tend to define problems in terms of their professional norms. From AIDS to substance abuse, professional blinders have limited the vision of problem definition and thus have limited the government's response. Second, since most governmental bureaucracies are built around professional definitions of problems, the limits in recognizing cross-professional elements of problems have also limited bureaucracies' ability to respond effectively. Too often, there is little recognition of the common ground on which different bureaus are working. Third, the first two problems have crippled government's ability to solve problems, and citizens have noticed. Results rarely match expectations. The decline of confidence in science has led to a decline of confidence in government's power to know, just as the risks associated with not knowing have grown even larger.

## Decentralization of Knowledge

Accompanying this uncertainty was an increase in the decentralized access to knowledge. Fundamental changes in budgetary politics provide one illustration. In the 1960s, the Bureau of the Budget had a near-monopoly over economic forecasting and over estimates of the budgetary implications of policy changes. By the late 1980s, however, the *Wall Street Journal* regularly ran a half-page collection of economic forecasts prepared by analysts around the country. Scores of players, each one equipped with a desktop computer, could do battle on any technical budgetary issue. The same pattern played itself out in environmental, poverty, housing, and economic growth issues.

Government lost its overwhelming technical advantage as technical uncertainties increased. The result was a significant leveling of political power. Government and its bureaucrats could no longer assume that others would defer to its superior technical knowledge. Well-armed combatants in the political process could fight with each other — and with government bureaucrats — on any issue. Meanwhile, a technological pluralism prevented closure on most issues. The nature of the problems themselves, the technological barriers to understanding and solving them, the growing ability of virtually any force to weigh in with an opinion supported by "facts" — all these factors combined to level the playing field just as the object of the game became less clear.

Gone are the days when the power of the bureaucracies rested on their ownership of information. Cleveland (1985) has argued forcefully that, as peculiar as it ever might have been even to think about an organization's "owning" an idea, emerging technologies make it ludicrous to believe that information can be husbanded or traded as a resource. Increasing access to information has led to increasing access to political power, and the result is a "twilight of hierarchy."

Together, these trends have undercut government's traditional hierarchy: its internal hierarchical structure and, in a more esoteric perspective, its place at the top of society's hierarchy as well. Smaller-scale, more decentralized, less concentrated technology has also helped level power, both power within government and power over government. These changes in turn raise critical questions for government. How can it learn effectively, so that it can govern well — and what challenges do these trends suggest for civil servants? How do these changes affect government's relationships with its citizens? How, in the end, can such a government be rendered more effective and accountable?

Hierarchy, at one time, answered all these questions. Expert civil servants with clearly assigned functions, operating within a clear chain of command, delivered goods and services. As taxpayers and service recipients, citizens interacted with government, but their role was hardly more challenging than that. Accountability was determined by the efficacy of government's production function. With the erosion of traditional patterns of hierarchy, an erosion accelerated by shifting patterns of information, these old answers have lost their relevance to government's operations and citizens' imaginations.

## A Learning Bureaucracy

Four propositions about organizational learning flow from the preceding analysis.

### Learning Is Essential

Government bureaucracies, like all organizations, have always needed to learn. Tuchman's reading of history led her to warn of "woodenheadedness," "the refusal to benefit from experience" (1984, p. 7). Now, though, the implications of those risks can often be far greater. The catastrophic explosion of the space shuttle *Challenger* did more than cost lives and destroy billions of dollars in equipment. It undermined Americans' faith in government and the technocracy it had built for a generation. The accident at Three Mile Island did the same for private industry. It also wrecked citizens' confidence in the ability of government to protect them from harm. The 1986 Chernobyl disaster illustrated all too harshly just how great the consequences of failing to construct a learning governmental bureaucracy could be. Learning is just as important for us today as it was for Caesar's legions. It is just that today the costs of failing to learn are potentially much greater and more immediate.

*Information Is the Key*

Organizational theory teaches that for a bureaucracy to learn, it has to perceive what is happening in the environment around it, know how to make sense of these perceptions, and then know what to do in response. In short, a learning bureaucracy must be an open bureaucracy, permeable at its boundaries. It also has to be peopled by employees smart enough to make sense of the overwhelming flood of signals the environment generates. The traditional Weberian views of bureaucracy focused on form and function, but generations of critiques of the Weberian approach have demonstrated just how lacking this vision is (see, for example, Katz and Kahn, 1966; Thompson, 1967).

Generations of reformers, however, have underlined just how enduring is the belief that government can be made more effective by our tinkering with its structure and processes in just the right way. In the 1960s, this belief led to the creation of many new programs. In the 1970s, reformers struggled to move the boxes around the organizational chart and create a more rational structure. In the 1980s, critics claimed that government was inherently inefficient and that only resorting to market mechanisms, through privatization, could solve the problem. There was merit in each of these movements, and yet each shared a common flaw. Each one resorted to a mechanistic view of governmental organizations, a view that ignored the imperative to create learning bureaucracies. Each one sought structural or process solutions to problems that were increasingly information-based. Only by building reform on a foundation that recognizes the primacy of the information problem can government's performance be improved.

*Information Flows from the Bottom Up
and from the Outside In*

A parallel element of the failed bureaucratic reforms of the last generations has been the folly that government's problems could be solved from the top down, if only highly placed policy makers could find the right cure. The Weberian approach to bureaucracy, reinforced by "lessons" learned from the private sector, supported this approach. Sometimes this meant that bureaucrats were the problem, a problem that had to be solved by changes in their inefficient incentives. Sometimes it meant that bureaucrats, along with policy makers and citizens, were victims of a structural framework that frustrated effective public programs. In either case, the approach tended to be the same: the fix for government's ills had to come from top-down authority.

The failure of this prescription to work is readily explained by two enduring truths. The first is that the power of top-level officials, regardless of what they try to do, is inevitably dictated by the behavior of rank-and-file bureaucrats. Barnard ([1938] 1968), writing about "the fiction of superior authority," pointed out long ago that an organization's effectiveness depends on the ability of its leaders to obtain the cooperation of its employees, on the acceptance of a common purpose, and on a system of communication to tie it all together. The authority of top officials depends on the willingness of lower-level officials to accept direction. This notion led to March and Simon's contention (1958) that obtaining workers' willingness to participate in the organization's goals is the foundation of all other transactions the organization conducts.

Barnard's innovation was to argue for the fundamental role that information plays within organizations: "Fundamentally, communication is necessary to translate purpose into terms of the concrete action required to effect it—what to do and when and where to do it" (pp. 106–107). The first job of the leader is to fashion the communication system so that it serves the organization's purpose (p. 226). Authority within the organization, moreover, is derived from the communication system. It "arises from the technological and social limitations of cooperative systems, on the one hand, and of individuals, on the other" (p. 184). For the organization to achieve its purposes, it must process information. Information about directives tends to come from the top down. The information on which those directives are based, however, comes from the bottom up. The folly of top-down reforms lies in their ignorance of the critical information channels—in their failure to recognize the importance of building learning bureaucracies, and in their propensity to undermine the bottom-up channels of communication on which learning rests.

Likewise, reformers have often persisted in the conceit that they could solve the problems of bureaucratic performance by increasing control over the bureaucracy. It is tempting to view a governmental bureaucracy as a closed system, subject it to the rigorous methods of business efficiency, and rid it of impediments to its effectiveness. The leveling of access to information in society, however, casts the problem of bureaucratic reform in a very different light. If government is to be more effective, it must learn better. If it is to learn better, it must develop better ways of collecting and digesting information. The collection and analysis of information, moreover, depends on focusing the bureaucracy on the sources of information: from the bottom up, the sources of bureaucratic expertise and effectiveness that Barnard identified; and, from the outside in, the sources of information that changing technology has made inescapable. It also requires transforming the entire bureaucracy into a learning organization. According to Senge, if an organization is to learn, a learning culture must permeate the organization: "Team learning is vital because teams, not individuals, are the fundamental learning unit in modern organizations" (1990, p. 10). Effective learning rests on a sense of the organization as an indivisible whole.

### Knowledge Is Power

The observation that knowledge is power is scarcely profound, but in the context of modern learning bureaucracies it has profound implications. Regardless of the formal structure of a bureaucracy, real power follows the flow of information. Information flows from the bottom up and from the outside in, and so does bureaucratic power. There are two important implications for bureaucratic power.

First, within a bureaucracy, managers must move away from authority-based systems to management styles that are more consensual. The approaches range from flattening and decentralizing hierarchies to empowering public employees (Osborne and Gaebler, 1992). The faddishness surrounding these approaches has sometimes obscured their underlying logic. These reform strategies reflect an enduring and, indeed, a growing truth: "Decision making proceeds not by 'recommendations up, orders down' but by development of a shared sense of direction among those who must form a parade if there is going to be a parade" (Cleveland, 1985, p. 188). This is an observation born not of the search for self-actualization of government employees but of the realities that the flow of information creates.

Second, sources of information outside governmental bureaucracies give outsiders political power. Research by industry on pollution abatement gives industry a strong voice in how antipollution policy is shaped. Moreover, as government has come to rely on outside information to generate its own expertise, it inevitably has come to share its power with industry. As information has moved from being a private good to being a public good, political power has followed. Collegial decision making has replaced decision by hierarchy. Networks have replaced structures of authority, and organizational structures themselves — informally, if not formally — have come to reflect the flow of information. As information has become less hierarchical, so too has political power.

## Implications for the Public Service

A rich irony has informed the struggles over reforming government since World War II. Governmental bureaucracies, like other organizations throughout society, have undergone fundamental changes fueled by shifts in patterns of information. Many of the reform efforts have actually worsened underlying problems by undermining the ability of bureaucracies to learn. For example, the Office of Management and Budget admitted that with the zeal to increase privatization through contracting during the 1980s, hardly anyone in government was paying attention to what the government was buying. The result was a pattern of waste and fraud whose full dimensions are unknown because the government has systematically underinvested in its

ability to learn (U.S. Office of Management and Budget, 1992;
House Committee on Government Operations, 1992).

In the process, government's responsibilities have changed.
In the past, analysts and managers tended to conceive of the government's role in terms of a production function. Government
took in resources (taxes), processed them according to its own expertise (presumed to be unmatched), and then delivered goods
and services to citizens. The first part of the function remains;
but, because of the growth of government by proxy, the government is now as much an arranger as a direct provider of services.
The higher the level of government, the more this is the case.

That fact fundamentally alters the role of bureaucrats,
as well as what their leaders must expect of them. When government did operate principally through the production function,
the closed-system focus derived from the Weberian vision made
more sense. The enlargement of the government's toolbox demands that the government's bureaucrats become far more effective learners—just as learning has become much more difficult.
Government employees must learn not just on behalf of the programs they are trying to run but also on behalf of the broader
public interest. They pursue, even define, this public interest
through complex relationships with proxies outside government.
These proxies in turn both determine the results of government
programs and produce the information from which government
must learn if the programs are to be made more effective. Therefore, bureaucratic learning must be seen as a broader and more
important task than making government programs work. It must
be seen as the job of constructing active networks closely attuned to three things: the complexity of society's problems, the
information available for solving them, and the public-private
networks through which they will be solved.

These networks are far more complex, more unstable, and
less predictable than orderly bureaucracies, and this fact presents
far greater risks to government workers. They are told to be
more innovative and entrepreneurial at a time when penalties
for mistakes have increased. They are called upon to promote
the public interest at a time when their dependence on private
information has increased. The challenge lies in creating incen-

tives for entrepreneurship. These have to include ways of punishing mistakes without making public employees risk-averse. That, indeed, is the central challenge of personnel policy as America enters the next century.

Government must create learning systems to develop and support learning bureaucrats. The development — indeed, the redefinition — of human resources management lies at the core. For bureaucracies to learn, bureaucrats must themselves learn. They need to learn where the most useful information is most likely to be, how to sift through it to discover what really matters, how to interpret it in a way that gives shape to the bureaucracy's goals, and how to pass key information along without excessive fear of retribution. As Barnard would recognize, this is the job of leadership at the highest levels of the bureaucracy. Top leaders are responsible for making bottom-up, outside-in learning work. They must foster the professional training, structural flexibility, flatter bureaucracies, and decentralized power required to make it happen. They must be tolerant of mistakes. They must even encourage bureaucrats to take prudent risks. We have learned, painfully, from the public policy fiascoes of the last decade that the passion for avoiding errors allows small problems to become huge disasters.

If government does not encourage learning behavior, government's effectiveness will suffer. Its power will erode as competing sources of information sweep in from elsewhere. Sharing of power has become inevitable, since the government's monopoly over information has disappeared. More than anything else, however, government and government alone can ensure that the public interest triumphs over competing individual interests. Bureaucratic learning will determine not only how effectively government can manage its programs but also how well it can govern in the end.

## References

Appleby, P. H. *Big Democracy*. New York: Knopf, 1945.
Barnard, C. I. *The Functions of the Executive*. Cambridge, Mass.: Harvard University Press, 1968. (Originally published 1938.)

Barzelay, M., and Armajani, B. J. *Breaking Through Bureaucracy: A New Vision for Managing Government.* Berkeley: University of California Press, 1992.

Blais, A., and Dion, S. (eds.). *The Budget-Maximizing Bureaucrat: Appraisals and Evidence.* Pittsburgh, Pa.: University of Pittsburgh Press, 1991.

Cleveland, H. "The Twilight of Hierarchy: Speculations on the Global Information Society." *Public Administration Review,* 1985, *45,* 185–195.

Danhof, C. H. *Government Contracting and Technological Change.* Washington, D.C.: Brookings Institution, 1968.

Donahue, J. D. *The Privatization Decision: Public Ends, Private Means.* New York: Basic Books, 1989.

Downs, A. *Inside Bureaucracy.* Boston: Little, Brown, 1966.

Emery, F. E., and Trist, E. L. "The Causal Texture of Organizational Environments." *Human Relations,* 1965, *18*(1), 21–32.

Ezrahi, Y. *The Descent of Icarus: Science and the Transformation of Contemporary Democracy.* Cambridge, Mass.: Harvard University Press, 1990.

Fiol, C. M., and Lyles, M. A. "Organizational Learning." *Academy of Management Review,* 1985, *10,* 803–813.

Guetzkow, H. "Communications in Organizations." In J. G. March (ed.), *Handbook of Organizations.* Skokie, Ill.: Rand McNally, 1965.

Hedberg, B. "How Organizations Learn and Unlearn." In P. C. Nystrom and W. H. Starbuck (eds.), *Handbook of Organizational Design.* New York: Oxford University Press, 1981.

House Committee on Government Operations. "Managing the Federal Government: A Decade of Decline." Unpublished report by the majority staff, 1992.

Katz, D., and Kahn, R. L. *The Social Psychology of Organizations.* New York: Wiley, 1966.

Kemeny, J. G. "Saving American Democracy: The Lessons of Three Mile Island." *Technology Review,* 1980, *83,* 65–75.

Kettl, D. F. *Government by Proxy: (Mis?)Managing Federal Programs.* Washington, D.C.: Congressional Quarterly Press, 1988.

Kettl, D. F. *Sharing Power: Public Governance and Private Markets.* Washington, D.C.: Brookings Institution, 1993.

LaPorte, T. R., and Consolini, P. M. "Working in Practice but Not in Theory: Theoretical Challenges of 'High-Reliability Organizations.'" *Journal of Public Administration Research and Theory*, 1991, *1*, 19–47.

March, J. G., and Olsen, J. P. "The Uncertainty of the Past: Organizational Learning Under Ambiguity." *European Journal of Political Research*, 1975, *3*, 147–171.

March, J. G., and Simon, H. *Organizations*. New York: Wiley, 1958.

Niskanen, W. A. *Bureaucracy and Representative Government*. Hawthorne, N.Y.: Aldine, 1971.

Niskanen, W. A. "A Reflection on *Bureaucracy and Representative Government*." In A. Blais and S. Dion (eds.), *The Budget-Maximizing Bureaucrat: Appraisals and Evidence*. Pittsburgh, Pa.: University of Pittsburgh Press, 1991.

Osborne, D., and Gaebler, T. *Reinventing Government: How the Entrepreneurial Spirit Is Transforming the Public Sector*. Reading, Mass.: Addison-Wesley, 1992.

Perrow, C. *Normal Accidents: Living with High-Risk Technologies*. New York: Basic Books, 1984.

Porter, J. W., and Roberts, K. H. "Communication in Organizations." In M. D. Dunnette (ed.), *Handbook of Industrial and Organizational Psychology*. New York: Wiley, 1983.

Price, D. K. *The Scientific Estate*. Cambridge: Harvard University Press, 1965.

Price, D. K. *America's Unwritten Constitution: Science, Religion, and Political Responsibility*. Baton Rouge: Louisiana State University Press, 1983.

Rourke, F. E. *Bureaucracy, Politics, and Public Policy*. (3rd ed.) Boston: Little, Brown, 1984.

Salamon, L. M. "Rethinking Public Management: Third-Party Government and the Changing Forms of Government Action." *Public Policy*, 1981, *29*(3), 255–275.

Senge, P. M. *The Fifth Discipline: The Art and Practice of the Learning Organization*. New York: Doubleday, 1990.

Thompson, J. D. *Organizations in Action: Social Science Bases of Administrative Theory*. New York: McGraw-Hill, 1967.

Tuchman, B. W. *The March of Folly*. New York: Ballantine, 1984.

Tushman, M. L. "Special Boundary Roles in the Innovation Process." *Administrative Science Quarterly*, 1977, *22*, 587–605.

U.S. General Accounting Office. *Federal Evaluation: Fewer Units, Reduced Resources, Different Studies from 1980.* PEMD-87-9. Washington, D.C.: U.S. Government Printing Office, 1987.

U.S. General Accounting Office. *Government Contractors: Are Service Contractors Performing Inherently Governmental Functions?* GAO/GGD-92-11. Washington, D.C.: U.S. Government Printing Office, 1991.

U.S. General Accounting Office. *Government Management Issues.* OCG-93-3TR. Washington, D.C.: U.S. Government Printing Office, 1992.

U.S. Office of Management and Budget. *Summary Report of the SWAT Team on Civilian Agency Contracting: Improving Contracting Practices and Management Controls on Cost-Type Federal Contracts.* Washington, D.C.: U.S. Government Printing Office, 1992.

Weber, M. "Bureaucracy." In H. H. Gerth and C. W. Mills (trans. and eds.), *From Max Weber: Essays in Sociology.* New York: Oxford University Press, 1946.

Wilson, W. "The Study of Administration." *Political Science Quarterly,* 1887, *2*, 197–222.

# 2

# Implications of Contracting Out: New Roles for the Hollow State

## H. Brinton Milward

Several years ago, *Business Week* ran a cover story on the "hollow corporation." The editors believed that a new organizational form had emerged and that Nike, the athletic-shoe company, was the template for a new type of organization. The hollow corporation consisted of a lean headquarters operation that had only four departments—research and development, design, marketing, and financial control. What was unique about Nike was that it had no production capability of its own. Nike shoes were made all over the world, under contract with various manufacturing firms (see "Special Report: The Hollow Corporation," 1986).

An even more extreme type of hollow corporation is cited by Peters (1990). In a recent article, he advocates subcontracting for anything and everything: "Subcontracting is hardly new. What's new is that major firms [MCI, Apple, and Boeing] are

41

looking at subcontracting as a way of life" (p. 13). Such a corporation conceives of itself as a "systems integration unit," sitting at the center of a web of subcontractors. (Incidentally, the management literature on network organizations has begun to generate its first critical assessments of the "hollow corporation"; see Miles and Snow, 1992. *Business Week* is now advocating a "sadder but wiser" version of the hollow corporation, called the "virtual corporation"; see "Special Report: The Virtual Corporation," 1993.)

In recent years, organization scholars have attempted to describe, operationalize, and model the resulting new organizational forms — often called *network organizations* or *service implementation networks* — in the public, nonprofit, and private sectors (Chisholm, 1989; Landau, 1991; Lawless and Moore, 1989; Miles and Snow, 1986; Wise, 1990).

## The Hollow State

The hollow state is the analogue of the hollow corporation. The hollow state is a metaphor for the intense effort the Reagan and Bush administrations made to privatize public services. This privatization has consisted of contracting with private firms and nonprofit groups to implement government programs. Advocates of privatization (Savas, 1987) often make the point that government can provide or arrange for citizens to receive a service without government's actually producing it. A government intent on privatization would decide what it wanted done and then contract with the private sector to provide it.

Government officials are assumed to be self-interested parties who seek their own interests at taxpayers' expense. The implication that flows from this assumption is that citizens are no different from consumers. Efficiency, effectiveness, and consumer satisfaction are the relevant criteria to use in selecting the mode of provision, as well as the standards of performance for public service delivery. However, "citizens are not [just] the customers. They are [also] the owners. Customers choose between products presented in the market; citizens decide what is so important that the government will do it at public expense"

(Frederickson, 1992, p. 13). The hollow state is neither better nor worse than a strong state that implements its own programs; it is, however, fundamentally different. "Hollow" and "strong" are literary rather than empirical categories; what is needed are studies that compare different systems of public service provision, since hollowness is a matter of degree and hinges on the degree of separation of government from its output (Milward, Provan, and Smith, forthcoming).

"The government has taken on many functions . . . precisely because the private sector either will not or would not do them in a way that respects competing values such as equality, for instance, over efficiency" (Kettl, 1988, p. 12). A strong state would hold its performance accountable to an array of standards—efficiency, effectiveness, accountability, responsiveness, and equity—that conflict and require explicit trade-offs. The extent to which "econocrat" thinking blurs these explicit trade-offs can be seen in the complaints of Charles A. Bowsher, head of the U.S. General Accounting Office (GAO). Bowsher cites the Farmers Home Administration as a flagrant example of bad management, since it has a high delinquency rate on loans to farmers but farmers who have defaulted in the past can still qualify for new loans: "Federal officials seem to believe that keeping farmers on the land is more important than making prudent lending decisions," Bowsher has said ("Federal Audit . . . ," 1993, p. A1). Bowsher, inadvertently, makes the point precisely: the wisdom of a policy of keeping farmers on the land can be questioned, but government exists to make the kinds of trade-offs that a prudent manager of a business would not. These values, and the trade-offs they imply, are much more difficult when services are largely delivered by third parties: "Instead of a chain of authority from policy to product, there is a negotiated document that separates policy maker from policy output" (Kettl, 1992a, p. 1).

The hollow state is virtually indistinguishable from a set of similar and related concepts. Wolch (1990) uses the term "shadow state" in referring to the role that nonprofits increasingly play in the delivery of human services to clients. Kettl (1988) and Smith (1990) describe government contracting to third parties as, respectively, "government by proxy" and "the contracting regime." Salamon (1981) and Mosher (1980) have called our attention to the growing phenomenon of "third-party government." In his syndicated column, David Broder uses the term "hollow government" to describe what has happened to domestic public services. On February 21, 1993, ABC aired a special report on "shadow government," which described how hiring freezes and cutbacks of direct government services had led to the hiring of contractors to do the work of government that must, by law, be done. One example involved the Department of Energy (DOE), whose 20,000 employees are responsible for supervising 145,000 employees under contract to them.

## Dimensions of the Hollow State

The hollow state is the result of several trends. The federal government has always relied on state and local government to deliver services for which the federal government paid. Government funding of nonprofit agencies increased during the grant-in-aid explosion of the 1960s and 1970s and continued during the Reagan and Bush administrations under the banners of privatization, limited budgets, and getting government off the backs of those it regulates. In addition, contracting for such services as public works and defense has been with us for a very long time.

Control of agents in a federal system like the United States is always difficult, which is one of the virtues of Madison's "compound republic." Different levels of government share authority for the implementation of health, welfare, education, and many other policies. The traditional problem of control in a federal system is how to implement policy effectively when the relation between levels of government is based on bargaining rather than hierarchy (Ingram, 1977).

A different type of implementation problem is the implementation of public policy by nonpublic entities. Whether nonprofit or for-profit organizations are involved, the problem is how to control the behavior of people who are not public servants and whose primary loyalty is to their own firms or nonprofit agencies.

In a story on a U.S. Office of Management and Budget (OMB) study of contracting, the *New York Times* reported that the federal government spent $210 billion in fiscal 1992 on contracting for goods and services — roughly one-sixth of all government spending ("U.S. Says . . . ," 1992). (It should be noted, however, that this figure is not confirmed in the OMB study itself.) OMB reported that at the Environmental Protection Agency (EPA), at DOE, and at the National Aeronautics and Space Administration (NASA), contractors were doing virtually all the work. If this work were being performed well, there would be no problem. But, according to the same OMB report, contractors are squandering vast sums because federal agencies fail to supervise how hundreds of billions of dollars are spent each year. This failure, according to the report, is not rooted in bureaucratic ineptitude but rather in the severe cutbacks that federal audit staffs have suffered during a period when the number and value of contracts were increasing. The Defense Contract Audit Agency, which audits 99 percent of the government's contracts, has cut 1,200 employees since 1989, leaving 5,900 employees, and this has led to a five-year backlog in audits, with 12,000 contracts worth nearly $160 billion unaudited (U.S. Office of Management and Budget, 1992). The report, issued by Richard Darman, director of OMB in the Bush administration, is "among the most incisive critiques ever published by the Government of a central philosophical tenet of the Reagan-Bush era: the idea that private companies can do the Federal Government's work better and for less money" ("U.S. Says . . . ," 1992, p. A1).

The hollow state is not simply the federal government as it contracts with the private sector for goods and services. State and city governments are also in the business of creating hollow service systems as they turn over hospitals and mental health centers, parks, water-treatment plants, prisons, and transportation facilities to nonprofit or for-profit entities.

Since the taxpayer revolt of the late 1970s, there have been major limitations on governmental spending at all levels. In addition, an antigovernment zeitgeist, reflected in the Carter, Reagan, and Bush administrations, has significantly changed the way in which policy can be implemented. In regard to privati-

zation, most policy analysts would recommend that government
rationally weigh the costs and benefits of direct provision of a
service by government versus provision of the same service by
firms under contract with the government. Given the resource
and capacity limitations faced by many governments today, the
choice often has little to do with the merits of the case for or
against privatization. It is simply a question of finding some
scheme for doing the job without direct costs to taxpayers. Barriers to revenue increases and capacity constraints are so strin-
gent, and the privatization ethos is so strong, that government
is turning over not only the delivery of services to private or
nonprofit concerns but also the functions of financial control and
eligibility determination to nongovernmental entities, for the
simple reason that there are few other options.

In the case of EPA's Superfund program, contractors are
actually performing the basic work of the agency. Because of
severe manpower and technical constraints, contractors "were
involved in literally every phase of the program, for virtually
no important task within EPA was not contracted out. Contractors researched Freedom of Information Act requests received by the agency. They drafted memos for top EPA officials.
They prepared congressional testimony. They wrote regulations
and drafted international agreements on behalf of EPA. They
trained and wrote statements of work for other contractors and
then evaluated their performance. They even wrote the Superfund program's annual report to Congress" (Kettl, 1991, p. 12).
What the effect of the nongovernmental provision of public services will be in the long run, we do not yet know.

## Dimensions of Contracting

"As a percentage of federal budget outlays, the government employees' payroll dipped from a . . . high of 17.7 percent in 1951,
to 12.5 percent in 1975, to about 9.5 percent at the end of fiscal
year 1981" (Hanrahan, 1983, p. 23). Furthermore, in fiscal year
1982, the entire federal civilian payroll was estimated to be only
40 percent of the $160 billion paid to government contractors:
"the increase in 'big government' in recent decades has not been

due to any expansion of the civil bureaucracy, but rather linked to the ascendancy of the contractors' bureaucracy" (Hanrahan, 1983, p. 23).

Much recent discussion and controversy concerning contractors deals with consulting firms that provide regulatory and economic support for the government. The amount that the federal government paid for these professional support services increased, in current dollars, from $3.6 billion in fiscal year 1980 to $9.4 billion in fiscal year 1990 (U.S. Office of Federal Procurement Policy, 1992).

Figure 2.1 illustrates increases in amounts spent for all executive branch service contracts, from $23 billion in 1979 to $48 billion in 1989. A GAO report on contracting notes that limits on the number of authorized federal positions may have contributed to this increase in contracting (U.S. General Accounting Office, 1991). EPA has experienced a remarkable increase in the amount spent on service contracts, including consulting. In fiscal year 1979, EPA spent $130.8 million; by fiscal year 1989, EPA had contracted for $737.5 million in services, as illustrated in Figure 2.2. In fiscal year 1991 alone, EPA awarded contracts worth $1.15 billion. The Superfund program is commonly mentioned in discussions of federal contractors. In its study of contractors, GAO discovered that the limitation on administrative costs is one of the reasons why the Superfund program contracts for services. GAO also stated that ceilings on personnel, imposed by Congress, often required EPA to hire contractors and consultants rather than conduct Superfund-related work in-house. Overall, though, the number of EPA personnel has expanded recently. In fiscal year 1991, EPA was authorized to create about 900 new positions. Figures 2.3 and 2.4 illustrate changes in amounts spent on service contracts by DOE and the Department of Transportation (DOT), respectively. DOE increased its spending on contractors steadily, from $5.7 billion in fiscal year 1979 to $15.3 billion in fiscal year 1989. Starting at $381.5 million in fiscal year 1979, DOT increased spending on service contractors to $566.6 million in fiscal year 1985, then decreased spending to $386.8 million in fiscal year 1989. Employment at both DOE and DOT declined during

Figure 2.1. Total Contract Actions for Services
in the Executive Branch, Fiscal Years 1979 to 1989.

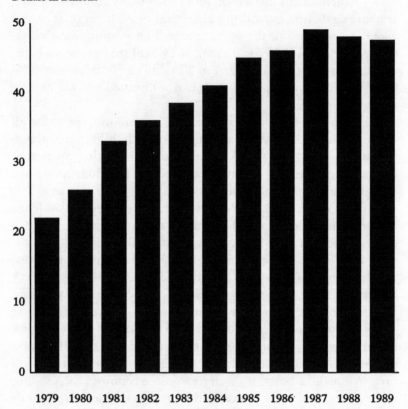

Dollars in Billions

1979  1980  1981  1982  1983  1984  1985  1986  1987  1988  1989

Source: U.S. General Accounting Office, 1992, p. 48.

the same period, which may account for some of the increase in contracting. At DOE, employment declined from 19,600 in fiscal year 1980 to 16,500 in fiscal year 1989; at DOT, from 68,800 in fiscal year 1980 to 63,200 in fiscal year 1989. Another reason for the increase in contracting in federal agencies is lack of staff with the required expertise. With the enactment of the Federal Employees Pay Comparability Act of 1990, Congress took steps to improve pay for some federal jobs, making them

Figure 2.2. Total Contract Actions for Services at EPA,
Fiscal Years 1979 to 1989.

**Dollars in Millions**

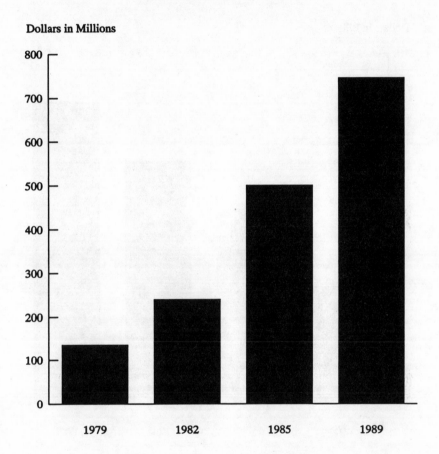

*Source:* U.S. General Accounting Office, 1992, p. 50.

comparable to jobs in the private sector. But the GAO report notes
that the problem of noncompetitive salaries still contributes to
the federal government's inability to attract and retain employees.

## Voices of Vendors

If personnel who do the work of government increasingly work
in private firms, what do we know about them? In my review

Figure 2.3. Total Contract Actions for Services at DOE,
Fiscal Years 1979 to 1989.

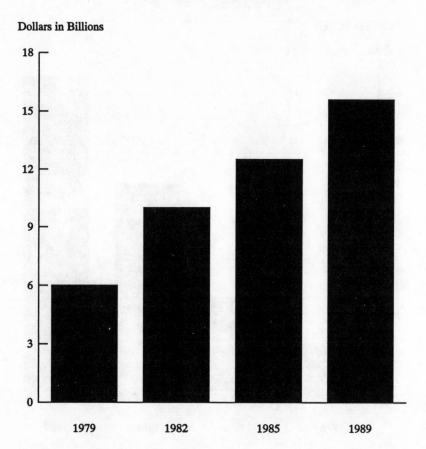

Source: U.S. General Accounting Office, 1992. p. 49.

of the literature on contracting, I did not find any studies of
whether consultants who work on government contracts differ
in any way from government employees. In January 1993, interviews with senior consultants in two large firms were conducted, to discuss the personnel aspects of government consulting. This section is based on those interviews. The consultants
interviewed work primarily for EPA.

The personnel in both firms have a wide variety of educational and professional backgrounds. Many employees hold

Figure 2.4. Total Contract Actions for Services at DOT,
Fiscal Years 1979 to 1989.

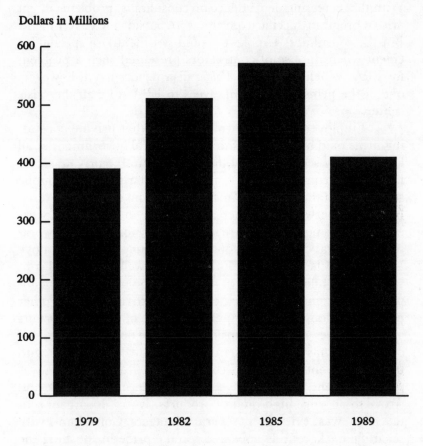

*Source:* U.S. General Accounting Office, 1992, p. 50.

doctoral degrees in such areas as economics, the sciences, and
law. Degrees are important elements of proposals when a firm
wants to prove that its employees are qualified. At the entry
level, however, the firms had a preference for hiring undergradu-
ates from prestigious liberal arts colleges, with no professional
training. The ability to write well, work hard, and think clearly
were valued at the entry level.

Several high-level managers were formerly employed by
EPA. Often, expertise gained at EPA makes individuals better

qualified to work as consultants, since they understand both the government agency and the people who will award the contracts. With the increasing dependence on consultants, problems might arise if program-specific expertise were outside the government. But the consultants I spoke to could not identify a specific incident when the use of contractors presented such a problem for EPA. When the Exxon *Valdez* disaster occurred, however, one of the firms sent its employees to EPA, to staff the crisis center.

Employees in these firms assumed that private consulting firms paid higher wages than the federal government at all levels. Many seemed to feel that working in the private sector for an EPA contractor was generally similar to being a public servant, with the benefits of higher wages, no civil service tests, reduced paperwork, and increased variety in work. This variety in work is possible because larger contractors are often working on several contracts at once, and so employees can move among projects, as needed. Furthermore, well-established consulting firms offer employees a degree of job security: if the company fails to renew a contract, employees are reassigned to other projects, as long as the company's volume of business permits and employees' skills are transferable. Since our interviews, one of the firms has laid off several employees as its business with the government declined. A concern with professionalism was quite apparent. The employees took pride in their work and strove to produce high-quality products. Every document sent to a client was reviewed by several managers. Consultants with scientific backgrounds appeared to take pride in "pushing the envelope," to present the most sophisticated analyses using the most accurate data possible. Many employees seemed committed to improving the environment and were drawn to federal consulting in the first place as a way to work for a cause they believed in. At higher levels, employees seemed more committed to their professions than to the environmental cause. The commitment of lawyers, economists, and scientists to their professions and professional standards seemed to serve as a control on the quality of the analytical work they produced.

The goal of personal advancement also seemed to contribute to the work ethic. An employee's rate of promotion was linked to the quality and quantity of her work. Employees at all levels often worked long hours, which contributed to a corporate culture that further encouraged this type of behavior.

One consultant I spoke with felt that consulting for the federal government provided him with unique opportunities unavailable to others in his field. The traditional practice of law is retrospective, applying existing laws to past events; government consulting allows him to present prospective analysis on the implementation of the law.

The fact that private consultants are dependent on the government and beholden to shareholders is quite evident. These private organizations respond to environmental pressures and concerns different from those of their federal clients. Pressure to win new contracts and renew existing ones is intense. When a contract proposal is due, employees are often expected to work and bill forty hours each week and then work as many additional hours as necessary to prepare the proposal. A manager who leads a team in preparing a successful proposal is sometimes rewarded with a substantial bonus. One consultant stated that the hours are often "extraordinary"; she felt that government employees have more control over their hours than consultants, who are constantly concerned with winning the next contract.

Many employees felt that a significant difference between public and private organizations is the degree of flexibility in assignments. They believed that the typical federal employee works for one department or office for his or her entire career. At a large firm with several government contracts, a consultant can work in different policy and regulatory areas on a regular basis, depending on where expertise is needed. For many consultants, this variety is a significant advantage over federal government employment.

While some elements of consulting firms clearly distinguish them from public organizations, many consultants seemed to think that they were simply extensions of the federal government. When goals and priorities of clients changed, the consultants adjusted their work to reflect those changes. The consultants did not believe that they had any ability to advance personal agendas through their work.

One consultant discussed the idea of divided loyalties. Her first loyalty was to her client, but she acknowledged that her loyalties (and those of her co-workers) were divided, since the company is publicly owned. She mentioned her company's shareholders and the need for a respectable rate of return on investment.

The consultants felt that they were extremely responsive to the desires of their government clients. They seemed very aware that if their work was not of high quality, their contracts could easily go to other firms instead of being renewed. These companies' objectives — completing their projects with the highest quality possible, and in a timely manner — advance both their own goals and the goals of their government clients. One consultant remarked that working as a consultant combined the best of both worlds — work on important public policy problems with all the benefits of the private sector.

## Contracting Problems

One outstanding problem related to federal government contracting is the economic inefficiency of the process for bids and proposals. In this process, the consumption of public and private resources reduces the resources available for more productive pursuits. Federal agencies spend time and other resources preparing requests for proposals. Likewise, private contractors and consultants commit significant resources to preparing their proposals. Regulations to promote fair competition add to the complexity of the process. In order to survive, contractors must recoup these resources through the contracts they receive. Resources used in the process are considered transaction costs and reduce the economic efficiency of the contracting process in the short run. In the long run, the assumption is that frequent bidding should make the market, if not the firm, work more efficiently.

Contract management is an increasingly important area for the government but is generally not considered central to the mission of an agency. Federal government organizational cultures may not reward contract managers. A recent EPA document on contract management noted that EPA "has operated under the paradigm that the Agency's environmental mission is so important that contract management is secondary to accomplishing it" (U.S. Environmental Protection Agency, 1992, p. 9). Reports from GAO, EPA, and other federal agencies and departments indicate that the system of contract management needs improvement. In order for improvements to occur, the culture and the reward system in the federal government must be revised to encourage and reward effective contract managers.

### A Research Agenda for the Hollow State

This chapter closes with two sets of questions that need exploration if the hollow state is to be more than a metaphor. The concept has significance for public policy, public management, and governance. The contracting questions flow from this very limited study; the governance questions flow from a long-term research project on the hollow state. They are focused on community-level services, often funded by federal dollars that are passed through the states, but the qustions have significant implications for how the federal government performs its work.

*Contracting Questions*

1. *Are we contracting out inherently governmental functions?*
   The U.S. General Accounting Office (1991) examined this question in detail but was unable to reach any conclusion. There was no consensus on what constituted an inherently governmental function.
2. *Is there adequate monitoring and auditing of contractors?*
   The answer to this question, even from the limited data presented here, is that neither monitoring nor auditing is adequate, given the volume of contracting. If there is a five-year delay in auditing of contracts, and if there are few penalties other than reimbursement of disputed sums, firms stand a good chance of having the government accept whatever bills are submitted. It is only when particularly outrageous contracts are exposed, through the media or whistleblowers, that auditing becomes an issue. The

most recent case involved the Resolution Trust Corporation's contract with a major accounting firm to make copies of millions of bank documents at $.67 per page. What was particularly galling was that the accounting firm subcontracted with a copying firm to have the job done at $.04 per page. As privatization increases, governments faced with hiring freezes and cutbacks will find it increasingly difficult to monitor and audit effectively.

3.  *Do we have adequate data to determine the extent of contracting?*
        Data exist at the federal level but are inconsistent. Different definitions of contracting give different totals, and the categories for contracts often are not illuminating. There is no fine-grained detail to help us understand the nature of contracting at the federal level. All government reports on contracting have called for better data. No central data sources exist at the state and local levels. The Advisory Commission on Intergovernmental Relations has conducted studies of municipal contracting, but much local contracting is done by nonprofit agencies that are funded by the state, sometimes with federal block-grant money, to deliver social services. Here, there is no central source of data.

4.  *Are personnel who work for nonprofit agencies and for-profit firms different from their counterparts who work for government?*
        We know of no data that could shed light on this question. Do educational qualifications differ? Does level of professionalization differ? Is the government's work force more diverse than the contractor's work force? Do pay and benefit levels differ? In contracting with nonprofits at the local level, some observers believe, nonprofits are chosen over government agencies to deliver services because their pay and benefit levels make them cheaper, not because they are more effective (Smith and Lipsky, 1993).

## Governance Questions

1.  *What does privatization do to the legitimacy of the state?*
        In the 1970s, jails were often used in public finance classes as an example of a public service that could not be

privatized. The reason given was that since the state monopolized the legitimate power of coercion in society, the power to take away a person's liberty was viewed as a function that, if delegated to a private firm, would lead to the state's becoming illegitimate in the eyes of its citizens. Today the courts have not been privatized, but some prisons are run by private companies. An attorney under contract to the courts may recommend which petitions requesting that individuals be institutionalized in mental hospitals be granted. What are the long-run effects when agencies and individuals who are not agents of the state, and are not publicly accountable, make decisions that deprive citizens of their liberty? In many community mental health systems, a nonprofit mental health authority, which serves as the conduit for tax dollars to provide treatment, also determines who is eligible to receive services from the system. Should nonpublic organizations be determining who should receive public services?

2. *What impact does the hollowing out of the state have on policy design, control of the implementation process, and evaluation of the quality of the contracted services?*

Privatization often occurs because severe capacity limitations force the government to contract for services it does not have the ability to provide. Policy design, control of the implementation process, and evaluation of the quality of the contracted services can and often do remain the jobs of public agencies. Nevertheless, the capacity limitations that led to contracting out in the first place may extend to the guidance and evaluation functions of government. In a recent study of a community mental health system, policy design and control of the implementation process were performed by the nonprofit mental health authority and the providers. Evaluation was not performed by the state because its administrative resources were stretched thin by a lawsuit that, among other things, requested systematic evaluation of the treatment services provided by the nonprofits (Milward, Provan, and Else, 1993).

3.  *What impact does the hollow state have on our theories of bureaucracy?*
    Theories of bureaucracy begin with the assumption
    that public organizations are boundary-maintaining enti-
    ties. Red tape, rigidity, and rule-mindedness are all by-
    products of the attempt by leaders to control the behavior
    of subordinates in the organization. That they often fail in
    their purpose, or elicit behavior that is unintended, does
    not negate the fact that much of bureaucratic theory is
    intraorganizational. When bureaus interact, the assump-
    tion of boundary maintenance still exists. Bureaus conflict
    over turf and money. Even when scholars speak of policy
    subsystems, bureaus, together with special-interest groups
    and congressional committees, are the actors. The hollow
    state calls theories of bureaucracy into question in two ways.
    First, some community-based systems have very few govern-
    mental bureaucrats in them. This is certainly the case in
    mental health. In a study comparing four community men-
    tal health systems in four different states, there were few
    if any bureaucrats, and state officials were few and far be-
    tween (Milward, Provan, and Smith, forthcoming). This
    question should be explored in other privatized systems.
    Second, in the hollow state, interpenetration of public and
    private is a fact of life. The central task of government in
    a privatized system is to arrange networks, not manage
    hierarchy.

4.  *What impact does lobbying by contractors have on legislators who
    exercise oversight of government agencies that monitor the performance
    of the contractors?*
    One virtue of privatization is that it transfers services
    from politicized settings to professional and business set-
    tings. In the latter, decisions are supposedly made on the
    basis of best professional practice or management efficiency.
    Whether or not privatization removes service provision from
    the realm of politics is an empirical question. There is a
    great deal of anecdotal evidence — in mental health, health
    care, and welfare — that professional associations of non-
    profit contractors are relatively powerful political actors who
    use campaign contributions and the other tools of lobby-
    ing to influence the legislators who oversee the agencies they

contract with. In other privatized settings, the same thing occurs with business associations and industries that government contracts with, from the highway lobby to waste haulers. Therefore, it is not clear that privatizing services avoids the problem of the providers' politics. If Superfund consulting firms, nonprofit substance-abuse treatment providers, and such government employees as teachers and postal workers all attempt to influence Congress, state legislatures, and city councils, where is the benefit of removing politics by privatizing public services?

5. *Is the hollow state permanent or an epiphenomenon?*

This question will be answered by time. Is privatization an end state, or is it an epiphenomenon that contains within itself the seeds of its own demise? Will the inherent contradictions of governmental contracting for services lead to demands for a "republicization" of the state?

Making progress on these two sets of research questions will take a major effort on the part of public policy and public management scholars. The hollow state encompasses aspects of both citizenship and policy design. One key design issue is what Hal Rainey has called the irony of privatization: privatization is portrayed as a solution to government mismanagement and efficiency, but privatization is not self-implementing; the contractor must be highly competent and effective for a privatized system not to become a nongovernmental monopoly. Privatization takes very good public management to make it work, and the government must be a very smart buyer (Kettl, 1992b). Is this possible without significantly enhancing the capacity of government?

One of the reasons given for private firms' being more efficient than government is that they can ignore external influences, to a degree that government cannot. For citizenship, a privatized system raises the question of how third parties can balance the multiple and conflicting ends of government — efficiency, effectiveness, responsiveness, accountability, and equity — while enhancing citizens' responsibility and efficacy. How is this possible when the citizens are removed from the process of policy implementation?

# 60                    New Paradigms for Government

## References

Chisholm, D. *Coordination Without Hierarchy: Informal Structures in Multiorganizational Systems.* Berkeley: University of California Press, 1989.

"Federal Audit for Clinton Finds That Billions Are Being Wasted." *New York Times,* Jan. 8, 1993, pp. A1, A7.

Frederickson, H. G. "Painting Bull's-Eyes Around Bullet Holes." *Governing,* 1992, *6*(1).

Hanrahan, J. D. *Government by Contract.* New York: Norton, 1983.

Ingram, H. "Policy Implementation Through Bargaining: The Case of Federal Grants in Aid." *Public Policy,* 1977, *25*(4), 499–526.

Kettl, D. F. *Government by Proxy: (Mis?)Managing Federal Programs.* Washington, D.C.: Congressional Quarterly Press, 1988.

Kettl, D. F. "Who's Minding the Store? The Decline of Competence in American Administration." Paper presented at the annual meeting of the American Political Science Association, Washington, D.C., Aug. 29–Sept. 1, 1991.

Kettl, D. F. "Beyond Hierarchy: Public Management Through Private Markets." Paper presented at the annual research conference of the Association for Public Policy Analysis and Management, Denver, Oct. 29–31, 1992a.

Kettl, D. F. "The Smart Buyer Problem: Public Oversight of Private Markets." Paper presented at the Midwest Political Science Association meeting, Chicago, Apr. 8–11, 1992b.

Landau, M. "On Multiorganizational Systems in Public Administration." *Journal of Public Administration Research and Theory,* 1991, *1*(1), p. 18.

Lawless, M. W., and Moore, R. A. "Interorganizational Systems in Public Service Delivery." *Human Relations,* 1989, *42*(12), 1167–1184.

Miles, R. E., and Snow, C. C. "Organizations: New Concepts for New Forms." *California Management Review,* 1986, *28*(3), 62–73.

Miles, R. E., and Snow, C. C. "Causes of Failure in Network Organizations." *California Management Review,* 1992, *34*(4), 53–72.

Milward, H. B., Provan, K. G., and Else, B. "What Does the Hollow State Look Like?" In B. Bozeman (ed.), *Public Management: The State of the Art.* San Francisco: Jossey-Bass, 1993.

Milward, H. B., Provan, K. G., and Smith, L. J. "Human Services Contracting and Coordination: The Market for Mental Health Services." In J. Perry (ed.), *Research in Public Administration.* Vol. 3. Greenwood, Conn.: JAI Press, forthcoming.

Mosher, F. C. "The Changing Responsibilities and Tactics of the Federal Government." *Public Administration Review,* 1980, *40*(4), 541–552.

Peters, T. "Get Innovative or Get Dead." *California Management Review,* 1990, *33*(1), 9–26.

Salamon, L. M. "Rethinking Public Management: Third Party Government and the Changing Forms of Government Action." *Public Policy,* 1981, *29*(3), 255–275.

Savas, E. S. *Privatization: The Key to Better Government.* Chatham, N.J.: Chatham House, 1987.

Smith, S. R. "Managing the Community: Privatization, Government and the Nonprofit Sector." Paper presented at the annual meeting of the American Political Science Association, San Francisco, 1990.

Smith, S. R., and Lipsky, M. *Nonprofits for Hire: The Welfare State in the Age of Contracting.* Cambridge, Mass.: Harvard University Press, 1993.

"Special Report: The Hollow Corporation." *Business Week,* March 3, 1986, pp. 56–85.

"Special Report: The Virtual Corporation." *Business Week,* Feb. 8, 1993, pp. 98–103.

U.S. Environmental Protection Agency. *Contract Management at EPA: Managing Our Mission.* Washington, D.C.: U.S. Government Printing Office, 1992.

U.S. General Accounting Office. *Government Contractors: Are Service Contractors Performing Inherently Governmental Functions?* GAO/GGD-92-11. Washington, D.C.: U.S. Government Printing Office, 1991.

U.S. Office of Management and Budget. *Summary Report of the SWAT Team on Civilian Agency Contracting: Improving Contracting Practices and Management Controls on Cost-Type Federal Contracts.* Washington, D.C.: U.S. Government Printing Office, 1992.

"U.S. Says Lack of Supervision Encouraged Waste in Con-
  tracts." *New York Times,* Dec. 2, 1992, pp. A1, A14.
Wise, C. R. "Public Service Configurations and Public Organi-
  zations: Public Organization Design in the Post-Privatization
  Era." *Public Administration Review,* 1990, *50*(2), 141–155.
Wolch, J. R. *The Shadow State: Government and Voluntary Sector in
  Transition.* New York: The Foundation Center, 1990.

# 3

# Creating Government
# That Encourages Innovation

## *Paul C. Light*

Government has never been under greater pressure to innovate. Call it *reinventing, reengineering, paradigm shifting,* or plain old *change,* the bottom line remains the same: government must produce more with less and satisfy the customer while doing it.

Yet imagine for a moment the worst possible circumstances for creating high-performance, innovative government. Start at the top of government, where we would make being a champion of change as difficult as possible. We would create huge pay gaps between the public and private sectors, so as to

*Note:* This work is part of the Innovations and Organizations project at the Hubert Humphrey Institute of Public Affairs. I appreciate the helpful input of many colleagues on this work, particularly John Brandl, who has forced my thinking on the interaction of structure and innovation, and my dean, G. Edward Schuh, for his efforts to educate me on the new institutional economics. This is my work, alas, and so I cannot blame either one for any errors.

discourage outside champions who might want to join the reinventing movement. We would limit executives' orientation
and training, so as to undermine our champions' ability to
move quickly in leading the change effort. We would encourage
high turnover at the top of our agencies, so as to limit the sur-
vivability of whatever ideas our champions might actually champion. And we would foster impenetrable boundaries within and
between our agencies at all levels of government, so as to frustrate the kind of boundary-spanning initiatives that often produce
innovation.

　　Next, we would weaken the very organizations our champions seek to lead. We would add layer upon layer of needless
management to our already towering organizations, so as to push
the front line so far down that ideas have no chance to bubble
up. We would aid and abet the steady fragmentation of our federal, state, and local government, so as to increase the number
of roadblocks, vetoes, and opponents to successful collaboration. We would slow the decision process through mind-numbing
regulations on everything from filling key personnel vacancies
to purchasing needed supplies to providing just-in-time training, all so as to frustrate the implementation of change. And
we would create such a highly stratified and complex personnel
system, such a short-term budget process, and such a distrust-
ful procurement mechanism that most good ideas would die
aborning.

　　Finally, we would make sure that the eighteen million
public employees who work in those agencies, and who ultimately hold most of the ideas and energy we need for change,
were utterly demoralized and underprepared to heed the call
for involvement. Even if a champion were to sneak into government, even if an agency managed to shake free of the rules, even
if we could get our chief executives and legislators to ask for
help, we would erode the human capital of government to the
point where risk taking and initiative were not only difficult but
often the farthest thing from daily experience. We would make
halfhearted commitments to diversity and advancement, so as
to deny our agencies access to the alternative perspectives and
ideas that come from a "not like us" work force. We would

tolerate cut after cut in our training budgets, all the while defining training in such narrow, parochial, and specialized terms that the cuts would hardly matter anyway. We would undermine employee morale and teamwork by creating a pay system that pitted one worker against another in a competition for a pitifully small reward yet would often fail to provide that reward anyway, so as to further weaken employees' cooperation and risk taking. Finally, our central staff agencies — personnel, administration, purchasing, and so on — would see their role in innovation not as one of facilitation and support, not as one of serving internal customers at all, but as one of monitoring an endless list of prohibitions against the very innovation we sought.

In short, we would create a government that would place one obstacle after another in the path of champions. In a process fraught with difficulties already — not the least of which is merely coming up with the spark of a new idea in the first place — we would create enormous odds against success.

The problem, of course, is that this imaginary "worst case" is not imaginary at all. It is the most familiar case. Despite a number of exceptions to the rule — governments and agencies that are moving away from the command-and-control complexity that frustrates many innovators — the sad truth is that most governments would find many parallels between the worst case and their own systems.

### In Search of the Best Case

The rest of this chapter, and the research from which it is drawn, is based on a simple assumption: governments can increase the probability that innovation will both occur and endure. Even if we are reluctant to talk with great confidence about designing *the* innovative public organization, we can still detect central tendencies in organizations that either favor or impede innovation and change (see Galbraith, 1982).

This is not to argue that studies of innovation and organization have agreed on either a basic definition of innovation or the characteristics of particularly innovative organizations.

The number of articles on innovation increased exponentially over the 1980s, and even such stick-to-your-knitting authors as Peters (1990) have been converted to the innovation bandwagon. Peters now recommends that corporations "get innovative or get dead."

If only the literature told us where to begin in building innovative governments! Should we start by recruiting more champions, as Roberts (forthcoming) recommends? by flattening our hierarchies, as Lawler (1988) argues? by developing employee involvement programs, as Nickel (1990) advises? by designing "phantom" stock ownership plans for the public sector, as Rosen and Quarrey (1987) might propose, with Blinder (1989) and Smith, Lazarus, and Kalkstein (1990) in agreement? Or should we start by fostering a participative management structure, as Levine and Tyson (1989) might suggest? by learning how to "grope along," as Golden (1990) counsels? by adopting an employee suggestion program, as Ballard and Trent (1989) suggest? The list of possible reforms appears endless. Of the independent variables that Damanpour (1991) examines in his meta-analysis of the literature, ten show significant relationships with innovativeness:

1.  Specialization, which provides a broader knowledge base for idea generation
2.  Differentiation among units, which provides some limited autonomy for innovators and champions
3.  Professionalism, which increases the commitment to change
4.  Decentralization, which also provides limited freedom
5.  A favorable management attitude toward change
6.  Technical knowledge
7.  A higher proportion of managers, who provide needed resources and coordination
8.  Slack resources, in the form of dollars or staff
9.  External communication, which exposes the organization to new ideas
10. Internal communication, which fosters dispersal of the best practices

Alas, Damapour's list yields hundreds and even thousands of possible combinations in the search for a best case. It is no wonder that we so often curl up with the familiar command-and-control systems. We simply do not know where to begin the reform effort. Indeed, my reading of the growing literature on innovation suggests at least twenty-one categories of potential reforms in the campaign for innovation and change. My own list (drawn in part from Kimberly and Evanisko, 1981) is presented in Exhibit 3.1. At least for now, there is no way to reorder these factors into a recipe for innovative government. That task must be left for future research. Instead, Exhibit 3.1 should be taken as merely a first attempt at compiling a best-case portrait of government. Ultimately, however, our challenge is to winnow through the categories, if not in search of a single silver bullet then perhaps in search of guideposts for would-be champions and funders.

Let me start this winnowing process with an admittedly incomplete inventory of obstacles to innovation, drawn from eighteen case histories conducted over the last two years. This work suggests that the obstacles to innovation are both numerous and varied, falling into every category already mentioned and, to a certain extent, thereby validating the broad typology of factors. The list of obstacles is presented in Exhibit 3.2.

## Dakota County, Minnesota

One way to test the impact of the assorted obstacles is to find governments in which innovation has flourished. It may be true, for example, that all innovations involve strong leadership and that all governments have turbulent environments. Since leaders come and go, however, and since the environment may be immutable, perhaps governments would do best to invest in strong systems for idea generation and learning, to match those environments and structures while reducing hierarchy. (See Garvin, 1991, for similar research on the Malcolm Baldrige Quality Award in the private sector.)

There may be no better place to start this search than in

Exhibit 3.1. Literature Review of Factors Affecting Change.

---

*External Context* (Haveman, 1992; Hannan and Freeman, 1984; Pfeffer and Salancik, 1978; Ruttan and Hayami, 1984)

Turbulence: the uncertainty that buffets organizations

Shocks: the crises and opportunities that may focus a given organization on innovating

Culture: the political and social context surrounding the change effort

Boundaries: the level of cooperation or conflict among external agencies

Slack: the external resources that can be leveraged for change

*Internal Structure* (Acs and Audretch, 1988; Gooding and Wagner, 1985; Tushman and Nadler, 1986)

Organizational shape: the height and width of a given agency, including both the number of layers between top and bottom and the number of units across the span of control

Demographics: the age and diversity of the work force, as well as the age of the organization

Turbulence: the degree of internal uncertainty

Boundaries: the level of cooperation and conflict among internal units

Slack: the internal resources for change, particularly time and money

*Internal and External Leadership* (Kanter, 1988; Van de Ven, 1986; Howell and Higgins, 1990)

Clarity: the articulation and communication of a vision supporting innovation

Durability: the ability to deal with the physical and emotional pressures associated with change

Caliber/temperament: knowledge, experience, personal values, and skills

Choices/strategies: general management style and overall leadership approach

Innovation management: specific approaches to the nurturing and implementing of innovation

*Linkage Systems (Internal)*

Pay and personnel: systems of recruitment, retention, and reward (Blinder, 1989; Ingraham, 1991; Kanter, 1987; Perry, 1986)

Learning: systems of training and information technology that encourage exposure to new ideas (Senge, 1990)

Idea generation: systems for both finding and developing innovations (Cotton and others, 1988)

Exhibit 3.1. Literature Review of Factors Affecting Change, Cont'd.

---

Budget: systems for allocating and reserving funds for new ideas

Accountability: systems for tracking and ensuring the relationship between what the organization wants and what its work force actually does (Kellman, 1990; Light, 1993)

Organizational culture: the general patchwork of norms, expectations, and behavior that constitutes the unwritten organizational charter (Schein, 1985)

---

Dakota County, Minnesota, where county government came of age during the 1980s. Over the past ten years, the county increased its work force by one-third, built a new mixed-use government center, reorganized its patchwork of thirty-five departments into two integrated divisions, and hired a new management team (see Krueger, 1992). At the same time, it adopted a host of new administrative systems — personnel, accounting, data processing — and earned a reputation as one of the most innovative governments in the state, captured a number of awards, and launched a large number of grant-supported projects, including two that formed the basis for further field research (Doying, Dudrow, Hartzell, and Hole, 1992; Bennett, Carter, Figueiredo, and Swenson, 1992). This chapter draws on the works just cited, as well as on a dozen in-person and telephone interviews that my colleagues, students, and I conducted with Dakota County officials and external observers in July and August of 1992.

The first project we examined was Project Fast Forward (FF). Launched in March 1988, this welfare reform melds state-of-the-art information technology to a collaboration between the county and nine nonprofit social service agencies. The hope is that clients will be given greater access to a panoply of public and nonprofit services through aggressive case management and an integrated data base. The second project was the Developmental Disabilities Account Management Project, originally misnamed the Vouchers Project. Launched in October 1989, this social service initiative involves a full cashout of disability assistance. The aim is to give parents of disabled children

Exhibit 3.2. Incomplete Inventory of Obstacles to Change.

---

*Context (External)*

Turbulence
   Pace of political, social, and economic change
   Growing number of unfunded mandates
   High number of small crises

Opportunities/shocks
   No competition, pressure for change
   Highly severe shocks
   Growing budget "uncontrollables"

Culture
   Short-term politics
   "Clientelization" of communities
   Disinvestment in public infrastructures
   Declining trust in government

Boundaries
   Historical labor-management tension
   Turf battles among external groups
   Few collaborations across sectors

Slack
   No alternative sources of funding
   Limited political patience during setbacks
   Limited applied knowledge about how to succeed

*Structure (Internal)*

Shape
   Overlayered between top and bottom
   Fragmentation within and across units
   High administrative overhead
   Large size

Demographics
   Old organizations
   Limited number of new employees
   Lack of diversity
   Declining work commitment among employees

Turbulence
   Frequent reorganizations
   Innovation for innovation's sake
   High turnover within key units, teams

Boundaries
   Internal fiefdoms
   Strong loyalties to subunits, professions
   Inflexible personnel classifications
   High labor-management conflict

Exhibit 3.2. Incomplete Inventory of Obstacles to Change, Cont'd.

Slack
  No time to think
  No resources for experiments
  No planning, information, analytical backup
  No work-load reductions possible for key staff

*Leadership (Internal and External)*

Clarity
  Uncertain signals about tolerance of risk
  Uncertain championship of change
  Inability to articulate clear vision, goals
  Poor communication

Durability
  High turnover
  Physical and emotional exhaustion, family conflicts
  Difficulties running old and new systems at the same time
  Isolation from peers

Caliber/temperament
  Lack of knowledge, experience
  Lack of people, management skills
  Lack of courage, faith
  Lack of trust in employees
  Narrow thinking, business as usual

Choices/strategies
  Failure to share power, information
  Focus on individual glory, credit taking
  Failure to recognize, involve key stakeholders
  Failure to make tough choices

Innovation management
  Failure to react to transitions and stages
  Low tolerance for "groping along"
  Failure to match management to situation

*Systems (Internal)*

Pay and personnel
  Pay and promotion compression
  No funding for merit or performance pay
  Overemphasis on individual performance
  No employee stake in outcomes

Learning
  No money for training
  Not enough talk in the hallways
  Antiquated information technologies
  Little flexibility in assigning, reassigning staff

Exhibit 3.2. Incomplete Inventory of Obstacles to Change, Cont'd.

---

Idea generation
   Reluctance among employees to voice ideas
   No contact between top and bottom
   Unwillingness to collaborate with labor
   Little organizational contact with customers

Budget
   No flexible money for investment
   Budget categories that restrict options
   Budget cycle that crowds out creative thinking
   Spend-it-or-lose-it budget system

Accountability
   Overemphasis on rules, regulations
   Little discretion to act
   No performance measures, trend lines, benchmarks
   Too much time on needless paperwork

Organizational culture
   Fear of making mistakes
   Lack of hope, confidence, faith in the possible
   Cynicism, low morale, overemphasis on surviving

---

complete freedom to purchase whatever services they deem necessary, from whomever they deem fit.

Once again, the problem comes in untangling the organizational sources of innovation. Exhibit 3.3 lists the best guesses about what has gone right: either Dakota County has worked hard to lower the barriers to innovation, or Dakota County had lower barriers from the beginning. Obviously, this list is impressionistic and builds on Exhibit 3.2. Since I spent a limited amount of time in the county, the list should be understood as highly speculative.

## Context

There is no question, for starters, that the county has a turbulent environment — state mandates are up, along with citizens' demands. One of seven counties in the Twin Cities metropolitan area, Dakota County is among the fastest-growing counties in the Midwest, jumping from 78,000 residents in 1960 to

Exhibit 3.3. Incomplete Inventory
of What Dakota County Does Right.

---

*Context (External)*

Turbulence
  Growing economy
  Growing mid- and high-income population base
  Growing tax base

Opportunities/shocks
  Relatively few crises
  Low tax rates
  Willingness to invest in high technology

Culture
  "Don't tread on me" history
  Moderate to high trust in government
  Willingness to invest in public infrastructure
  Wide geographical spread

Boundaries
  Little history of public-private tension
  Declining turf battles among external groups
  Growing collaboration across sectors

Slack
  Growing potential for external funding

*Structure (Internal)*

Shape
  Flat organization
  Integration in general
  Low administrative overhead
  Relative smallness

Demographics
  Young organization; few rules, procedures
  Large number of new jobs
  New public infrastructure

Turbulence
  Infrequent reorganization
  Low turnover within key units, teams

Boundaries
  Fewer internal fiefdoms
  High integration through technology

Slack
  Some resources for experiments
  Strong planning, information, analytical backup

Exhibit 3.3. Incomplete Inventory
of What Dakota County Does Right, Cont'd.

---

*Leadership (Internal and External)*

Clarity
Clear signals about tolerance of risk
Strong championship of change
Clear vision, goals

Durability
Low turnover
Strong physical, emotional endurance

Caliber/temperament
High reservoir of knowledge, experience
Strong management skills
Faith in future
High trust in employees, particularly among part-time board members

Choices/strategies
Willingness to share power, information
Limited focus on individual glory, credit taking
Involvement of key stakeholders
Priority setting

Innovation management
High tolerance for "groping along"
Projects built for success

*Systems (Internal)*

Pay and personnel
Competitive pay with metropolitan counties
No automatic seniority-based pay increases

Learning
Reasonable support for training
Talk in the hallways
State-of-the-art information technologies

Idea generation
Willingness among employees to voice ideas
Considerable contact between top and bottom
Moderate willingness to collaborate with labor
Significant contact with customers

Budget
Some flexible money for investment
Less budget categorization

Accountability
Low emphasis on rules, regulations

Exhibit 3.3. Incomplete Inventory
of What Dakota County Does Right, Cont'd.

---

Discretion to act, little micromanagement by internal or external leaders
Limited performance measures, benchmarks
Organizational culture
Lower fear of making mistakes
Hope, confidence, faith in the possible
High commitment among managers

---

275,000 three decades later. This growth has created enormous pressure on the county's social and physical infrastructure, yet it is the kind of growth that creates an opportunity to write on a clean slate of sorts — new agencies, new buildings, new systems. As our student case-study team observed, "Government is constantly being invented in Dakota County."

This growth also creates the occasional shocks and opportunities that may spur innovation. In the Developmental Disabilities Account Management Project, complaints by parents about their better ability to determine their children's needs certainly played a role in generating the cashout plan. One such complaint eventually led to a conciliation conference with the county, which may have triggered actual adoption of the cashout. This innovation involved more than parental exasperation, however. The county had been working toward greater parental involvement for several years before the complaints, in part under pressure from the suburban Association for Retarded Citizens, and in part because the first director of Community Services had a long-standing interest in reform. Further, as our student team noted, the mid-1980s were years when empowerment of individuals with developmental disabilities and their families was a focal point.

Similarly, no shock was involved in creating Project Fast Forward. The project was driven in part by ongoing conversations between the county and the nonprofit sector. These discussions preceded, by some months, efforts of the McKnight Foundation to create new funding, but they were clearly accelerated by the prospect of a large external grant. In sum, Dakota

County appears to have been ripe for this kind of innovation, driven less by any specific shock than by a general opportunity to try new solutions.

Within a statewide culture that already supports progressive government and experimentation, Dakota County has forged a particular reputation for nontraditional thinking. The county became something of a haven in the 1970s and 1980s for metropolitan citizens who wanted a taste of rural freedom, and it has maintained the lowest tax rate in the region. It is also the last of the metropolitan counties to be governed by a five-member part-time board. Yet the county also prides itself on its new public facilities, pays highly competitive public wages, and—who says unionization is an obstacle to innovation?—has a work force that is 60 percent unionized. Nevertheless, as the county manager said, "There is a culture of independence here, individual merit-based progress, a pioneer mentality. The revolutionary flag, 'Don't Tread on Me,' could fly here."

We cannot move all our public organizations into fast-growing, progressive regions with historical traditions of experimentation, but Dakota County teaches us to lower the boundaries among external agencies. In both of the innovations we studied, collaboration across external nonprofits was the key to sustaining lower boundaries within the county government and to discovering new approaches to existing problems. In the case of Project Fast Forward, a state Department of Human Services analysis of replicability noted that "much of FF's success comes about because a group of individually autonomous agencies chose to cooperate. Absent a complete change in how helping agencies are established and funded (haphazardly, if I may say so,) FF replication will depend on the degree to which this type of *profound voluntary cooperation* can occur. The state can do things to encourage this, but cannot force it."

There are several reasons why boundaries among public agencies may be lower in Dakota County. The county, although it is increasingly dense at its northern interface with the Twin Cities, has enormous geographical spread. It retains much of the prairie flavor that attracted many of its residents. Dakota County has a population density of 483 per square mile, nearly four times lower than in the two counties to the north. No single nonprofit can hope to provide services across this vast territory.

This geographical reality may have affected Dakota County's government as well. Even before the McKnight Foundation had signaled its interest in funding collaborative projects, the county was working to lower the barriers among its outside agencies and between those agencies and itself, partly through simple ongoing conversations around client problems and partly through collaborative efforts to develop grant proposals aimed at local foundations.

Dakota County has also used its unyielding search for external slack, particularly in the form of foundation and state or federal grants, to create incentives for internal and external collaboration. This strategy has had some costs, not the least of which was innovation for innovation's sake (see Exhibit 3.2), but both of our student teams noted the value of the proposal process for forging common goals and trust.

*Structure*

Besides luck in its location and growth — some of the growth accidental, some planned — Dakota County has fewer obstacles in its internal structure. First, the county government is relatively flat, compared to others of similar size. By happenstance, the deputy director of Community Services also occupies the post of social services director, thereby flattening the organization even further, while Project Fast Forward case managers are co-located in off-site nonprofit agencies. This flatness and the grants of organizational trust that go with it have created corridors for more effective collaboration across units.

Second, the government is much smaller than its metropolitan counterparts, both in terms of overall size and in terms of ratio to county residents. With just 1,250 employees, the county has maintained a sense of community that may foster a somewhat greater willingness to trust both employees and clients. Further, at a little over 500 employees, Community Services has been small enough to be housed in the same building. This in turn has allowed ease of access between top and bottom.

As one manager said about the benefits of smallness, "You know almost everybody, and it's real easy to interchange. When I first got here, we didn't have any rules or regulations. Now we're moving in those directions, which is both good and bad. Being small, having no rules, gives people a lot of energy. It gives them a feeling of power." With so much innovation occurring "in the hallways," as this manager described it, the challenge will be to continue talking once the hallways are in separate buildings.

Third, both in bureaucratic and in demographic terms, Dakota County has a relatively young government: 300 of the county's employees are in positions created over the last five years, and 54 percent have worked for the county five years or less. Almost all employees work in new or remodeled buildings, most of them equipped with state-of-the-art technologies. Whether commitment will wane as buildings, equipment, and workers age is an open question.

Together, these three structural factors may create an internal turbulence that drives Dakota County's innovation. Simply put, the government is too small for its mission, creating pressure on its workers to be flexible. As one senior manager said, "Because it's not so big, you're drawn into doing different kinds of things. Roles are not as defined as in a stable organization with close to adequate staffing levels. I'm convinced that it's not good to have totally adequate staffing. It's not as much fun. You're never needed beyond your own area. There aren't new opportunities."

Using turbulence to leverage innovation creates obvious risks, not the least of which is stress on individual employees. This has been particularly true in the economic assistance branch of Community Services, where labor conflicts threatened to produce a strike: "When everybody is busy serving clients, and clients are backed up six weeks to get in for basic services, that hurts innovation somewhere. You need a waiting list and pressure, but I don't think you need to be overwhelmed," another manager said.

Yet the fact that this kind of turbulence could be perceived as positive suggests the value of the lower internal boundaries that characterize the Dakota County government. It is a strength well worth replicating in other public agencies. The 1984 decision to consolidate once-separate social service agencies — public health, employment, economic security, developmental disabilities, even veterans' affairs — into a single division and the 1990 decision to add community corrections and extension have allowed the county to avoid the fragmentation that other county and state systems struggle to repair through co-location and assorted service-integration strategies. This integration was critical in developing Project Fast Forward, where the county has but one vote out of ten on the council of collaborating agencies.

None of this is to say that Community Services is free of conflicts. Budgets still come in categories, as do most clients, which divides subunits against one another. Economic assistance is still handled through the welfare office, although this is part of a larger establishment and is thereby shielded somewhat against the isolation that similar units experience in other jurisdictions. Still, the potential for internal cooperation exists, and the director of Community Services still has a chance to think holistically about the people whom the county serves. Moreover, this integrated structure has allowed the county to deploy its limited internal slack more effectively. Slack can take many forms; in the two Dakota County innovations we studied, the four-person Community Services planning staff became, in effect, a form of living slack. "Planners are usually a buffer between the political and administrative functions," one of our respondents said. "They keep change from occurring by planning new ideas to death. The planning section in Dakota County is left free until an innovative idea comes along. Once it does, planners are given the resources and told to make it happen."

In both innovations we studied, a customer-driven planning unit was necessary but not sufficient for the final launch. In a highly turbulent and overworked internal environment, a single social worker or team of line supervisors simply could not have freed the time to draft a formal proposal. According to one of the social workers, "I didn't even know the county could apply for grants from the governor's council. A line worker just wouldn't have been able to do it — write the grant proposal, do the quarterly reports, the financing." Ultimately, of course, the planners did not make it happen at all. They were catalysts for harnessing energy and ideas that already existed, ideas that public employees have wherever they work.

*Leadership*

That the county told the planners — indeed, all its employees — to
"make it happen" is very much a function of leadership. Here,
it is tempting to attribute all of Dakota County's success to entrepreneurial leadership. Lyle Wray, who moved up from his
Community Services directorship in 1988 to become county administrator, deserves considerable credit for sending clear signals of support, as do his key lieutenants. But what attracted
Wray to Community Services in the first place was the potential for change. Dakota County was ripe for innovation. More
to the point, the county board and its chair of human services
had made it clear that they were searching for an innovator when
they recruited Wray to become Community Services director.
Thus context, structure, and, to a certain extent, lack of systems made Dakota County a good bet for success. By 1988, there
was so much activity already under way, and there were so many
ideas percolating upward in Community Services, that a morato-
rium was imposed on new projects.

Acknowledging the positive energy that already existed
in 1985, Dakota County's elected and appointed leaders gave
very clear signals that innovation would be valued and protected.
For its part, the county board had a "hands off" policy with
respect to county management, leaving internal operations to
the county administrator. This reluctance to meddle in day-to-
day decision making was a consequence of the part-time board
members' all having other jobs and interests. Moreover, as members of the last five-member part-time board in a Minnesota
metropolitan area, the commissioners had clear incentives to
trust their county executive. Not the least of these was the geographical demand of representing such a dispersed polity. Part-
time commissioners already had more than enough to do without micromanaging the county administrator.

As for the Community Services leaders, there is no doubt
about their support for innovation, their tolerance of risk, and
their durability. Their motto, according to one of our student
teams, was "Do first, apologize later." That commitment was
tested when the county attorney warned of potential liability

costs in the Developmental Disabilities Account Management Project. Using public funds to purchase private services, no matter whether the county or an individual parent made the final choice, created clear risks. Wray and his associates decided to move ahead anyway, as did the county board when informed of the liability question. According to our team, one of the key managers said he had been sued before, and "that's what lawyers are for." The county did begin lobbying the legislature immediately for a change in the law but proceeded undaunted with the project.

There is also little doubt that Wray and the others knew what they were doing, in terms of both sheer smarts and good choices. Wray had a long résumé of technical experience in human services, as did his subordinates. "Lyle did tremendous things," one of the Community Services staff members said of Wray, "in having ideas, taking initiative. He showed quality leadership. There was a creative sense of freedom, a time to influence the state, go outside the boundaries of the county." As one of Wray's greatest admirers admitted, "He was kind of a grouch, crabby, short with you in the first few minutes. In spite of that, his interest in quality and commitment to clients was there. He saw the broader picture."

Something of a science-fiction buff, Wray had long been intrigued by the potential payoffs of information technology, and he clearly left his mark on the county in a host of systems, from laptop computers for social service workers to electronic mail. "Under the last director, I couldn't get a calculator," one worker said. "He came, and within a few months I had a personal computer and a mainframe terminal. Next, the personal computer was networked with the mainframe, and I no longer needed two terminals on my desk." By the time Wray left, in 1992, the county had three hundred personal computers, four hundred mainframe terminals, and a growing inventory of laptops. Wray surely knew that the county board would fund almost any initiative involving new technology: "Anything to save a position," one county manager explained. "If they could see that laptops would save half a dozen intake workers, they'd fund it, no matter how much it cost. They seemed to be fixated on keeping the number of employees low, even if everyone had the top of the line."

In the area of innovation management, Wray and the others appeared to follow five general principles for adopting new projects. The first was to build for success. In launching the Developmental Disabilities Account Management Project, for example, the first twelve families were selected to demonstrate the validity of the basic theory that parents could manage the choice of care as well as or better than the county. Much as this principle undermines quasi-experimental design and possibly weakens replication, it does increase momentum and minimize political risks.

The second principle was to select projects with low start-up costs. Even with the board's commitment to high technology, Wray started virtually every project on a small scale. This strategy had both positives and negatives. Obviously, small-scale projects take less energy and political protection and, once established, can be expanded. Yet small-scale projects often stay that way. Created at the periphery of the organization, they may never receive the attention or commitment that create success and may never reach the critical mass to deserve replication. Thus, with just twelve families in the first year and twenty-five in the second, the cashout concept still has not been tested, even if it has been an apparent success for the families involved.

The third principle was to fine-tune along the way — what Golden (1990) defines as "groping along." In both cases we studied, the final shape of the innovation is still evolving. Project Fast Forward was still adjusting itself even in its third year. In the collaboration formed between the county and the nonprofits, only recently has it been decided to eject one member, a nonprofit that was less committed to the endeavor. Clients seem to be doing well in both programs, but we still do not know what the final outcomes will be. Moreover, as the McKnight Foundation money starts to run out, Project Fast Forward now begins the struggle for institutionalization that characterizes so many innovations.

The fourth principle was to avoid the big mistake. Although Wray and his staff all recognized the need for fine-tuning, they also understood the devastating impact of a highly visible failure. Thus their staffs report using something called the "I-team test," so named in honor of a local television station's investigative unit. This is, in part, why the Developmental Disabilities Account Management Project started with twelve families who had the skills to use the cashout, and why those families took some interest in making sure that the next families picked for the initiative would be equally able.

Despite these worries, the fifth principle was to trust employees to do the right thing. For example, the county has let the social workers on the Developmental Disabilities Account Management Project have their head, loosening the normal accounting rules about what constitutes a valid receipt to prove that services were rendered. The fact that the county has repeatedly elected to trust its front-line employees (albeit in projects designed for success, with low start-up costs) suggests the overall tolerance for mistakes that seems an essential part of an innovative culture.

Ultimately, what comes through in these unwritten principles is a basic faith in the future, a belief in what can happen. Indeed, almost all the staff members we interviewed seemed to have a basic hope in their ability to create change. This is not to say that they are not sometimes angry, or frustrated by the slow pace of change or by the growing manifest of county rules. But they do appear to share the belief that their work will make a difference.

*Linkage Systems*

Despite the lack, until 1987, of a unified personnel system, Dakota County's linkage systems reinforced or at least did not hamper the general drive for innovation. On pay and personnel, for example, the county has been one of the state's leaders, offering relatively high wages at the middle and upper levels of management. Of equal importance for line employees is the lack of a seniority- and step-based pay system. It may not matter much whether the recently adopted pay-for-performance system works (indeed, the senior managers we interviewed reported a general lack of confidence in the new system); employees no longer see individual increases as automatic. And, for line workers and management, working on a special project has come to be known as the best and perhaps only way to get a top score in the pay-for-performance system.

Beyond these pay-linked strategies, Wray and the others clearly signaled their interest in innovation through nontangible rewards. Managers knew they would get Wray's attention, and perhaps a bit of slack, for coming up with innovative ideas. "In the past four years, we have relocated or remodeled facilities for everyone," a senior manager said. "Employees have good space, good pay, benefits, flexibility, with sick and vacation time. What's left? Involvement in decision making and recognition."

As for learning systems, such as new technology, Dakota County has long been willing to invest in its employees. Equally important investments have been made in training. According to the staff members involved in the Developmental Disabilities Account Management Project, thinking began to crystallize around a cashout option after a conference sponsored by the Association for Retarded Citizens. The fact that employees had the time and resources to attend such training activities is one example of the county's commitment. Investment in employees' knowledge in turn feeds idea generation, which includes the kind of talk in the hallways that may ignite cross-unit collaboration, and which is supported in part by somewhat lesser categorization in the Developmental Disabilities budget and by greater willingness to trust employees.

Dakota County bases its accountability system more on the development of employees' capacity to do their jobs effectively than on highly detailed rules and regulations. In contrast to the federal government, which has invested in compliance-based accountability, Dakota County continues to trust its employees to do what is right and has given them enough information and technology to do so. (See Light, 1993, for a discussion of how accountability systems may distort management at the federal level of government.) This does not mean that Dakota County has no compliance systems; rather, the county still appears to value at least some level of rule breaking. To impose a tight compliance system might smother the culture of innovation that has taken hold, while carrying its own budgetary costs.

Substantial numbers of employees, perhaps 40 percent by one estimate, may still be outside the innovation culture, more interested in putting in time than in inventing projects or finding new ways of working better. "Projectitis" may also be alienating substantial numbers of line workers, whose lives simply are not affected by the long list of innovations. Nevertheless, Dakota County has established a dominant culture in support of invention. Our Fast Forward Project student team concluded that this culture exists beyond the borders of the county government and extends into the broader community of public concern: "The entire conceptualization, development, and implementation (to date) of Fast Forward took place within the nurturing, sheltering embrace of the county. The project is known as a product of the county. This allows all the members [of the collaboration] to enjoy the project as a shared success, not as an individual achievement for any of the agencies. Even with the best of intentions, a different arrangement might have produced significantly different results and certainly would have required additional effort to persevere."

### An Overview of the Dakota County Case

We already know that Project Fast Forward cannot survive in its current form. The county recognizes that it cannot afford the kind of labor-intensive case management funded by the McKnight Foundation and is now struggling with the question of how to institutionalize the less costly portions of the program. We do not know whether the developmental disabilities initiative will survive, either, or in what form. Both cases may be examples of good ideas that cannot survive, even in the best of organizational settings.

Yet we also know that Dakota County has created incentives for learning, whatever the outcome. The technologies purchased for Project Fast Forward will have effects elsewhere (reduced income-verification times, for example), and the collaboration has already created the basis for other initiatives, including an integrated after-hours, first-call-for-help phone line. The county has also created a vision of its social service population as whole individuals and is now developing a plan for unified case management across public and nonprofit organizations. The hope is for a system that, through technology and collaboration, will allow any individual in need of help to reach any provider in the county and have immediate access to all resources. Lessons drawn from Project Fast Forward will certainly help.

Beyond helping validate the assortment of organizational sources of innovation identified in Exhibit 3.1, the experience in Dakota County may also narrow the search for a "best case." Given the importance of being in a fast-growing county with low tax rates and a broad tax base, there appear to be four organizational factors that may work to spur innovation in other settings.

First is the shape of the organization. The Dakota County case suggests that relatively flat agencies are essential in moving ideas upward from the front line, encouraging departmental integration, and reducing the need for rule-laden accountability systems. If this is true, we must rethink the impact of attrition-based approaches for reducing the size of government. However politically palatable it may be to "thin" government through retirement, this approach may contribute to the "thickening" of government, which may reduce the potential for lasting change.

Second is the role of elected leaders in letting innovation prosper. Although part-time governing bodies are hardly the only way to reduce micromanagement, senior managers repeatedly mentioned the value of amateurs (well-informed ones, to be sure) as a source of "running room." The Dakota County board has ample reason to work with the county government — to see it as a source of advice and counsel, not as an adversary to be browbeaten every two or four years.

Third is the need for public agencies to create slack for their middle- and lower-level managers. One government may choose to create a standing unit, modeled on the Community

Services planning staff; another may establish special grant or subbatical programs, or an innovation investment fund, perhaps with external support. Regardless, what is clear from Dakota County is that front-line workers, particularly in social service units, cannot maintain crushing volumes of work and develop project proposals at the same time; they must have relief.

Fourth is the impact of faith in innovation. Faith in the future seems to make mistakes tolerable, since one must believe in eventual redemption in order to persevere in the face of one's own failures. Faith may also provide a reservoir of endurance for those who make the commitment to change and may permit the broad grants of freedom that make new ideas possible. This factor is more speculative, of course. But the question may be how to reengender faith in those who have lost it and sustain faith in those about to lose it. This, too, may be the leader's work.

## References

Acs, Z. J., and Audretch, D. "Innovation in Large and Small Firms." *American Economic Review,* 1988, *78*(4), 678–690.

Ballard, J., and Trent, D. "Idea Generation and Productivity: The Promise of CSM." *Public Productivity Review,* 1989, *12*(4), 373–386.

Bennett, C., Carter, S., Figueiredo, C., and Swenson, D. "Dakota County Project Fast Forward." Unpublished paper, 1992.

Blinder, A. (ed.). *Paying for Productivity: A Look at the Evidence.* Washington, D.C.: Brookings Institution, 1989.

Cotton, J. L., and others. "Employee Participation: Diverse Forms and Different Outcomes." *Academy of Management Review,* 1988, *12*(1), 8–22.

Damanpour, F. "Organizational Innovation: A Meta-Analysis of Effects of Determinants and Moderators." *Academy of Management Journal,* 1991, *34*(3), 555–590.

Doying, R., Dudrow, J., Hartzell, B., and Hole, D. "Dakota County Account Management Program." Unpublished paper, 1992.

Galbraith, J. R. "Designing the Innovating Organization." *Organizational Dynamics,* 1982, *11*(1), 5–25.

Garvin, D. "How the Baldrige Award Really Works." *Harvard Business Review,* 1991, *69*(6), 67–89.

Golden, O. "Innovation in Public Sector Human Services Programs: The Implications of Innovation by Groping Along." *Journal of Policy Analysis and Management,* 1990, *9*, 219–248.

Gooding, R., and Wagner, J., III. "A Meta-Analytic Review of the Relationship Between Size and Performance: The Productivity and Efficiency of Organizations and Their Subunits." *Administrative Science Quarterly,* 1985, *30*, 462–481.

Hannan, M., and Freeman, J. "Structural Inertia and Organizational Change." *American Sociological Review,* 1984, *49*, 149–164.

Haveman, H. "Between a Rock and a Hard Place: Organizational Change and Performance Under Conditions of Fundamental Environmental Transformation." *Administrative Science Quarterly,* 1992, *37*(1), 48–75.

Howell, J., and Higgins, C. "Champions of Change: Identifying, Understanding, and Supporting Champions of Technological Innovations." *Organizational Dynamics,* 1990, *19*, 40–55.

Ingraham, P. *A Summary of the Experience with Pay for Performance in the United States.* Paris: Organization for Economic Cooperation and Development, 1991.

Kanter, R. M. "The Attack on Pay." *Harvard Business Review,* 1987, *20*(2), 60–67.

Kanter, R. M. "When a Thousand Flowers Bloom: Structural, Collective, and Social Conditions for Innovation in Organization." *Research in Organizational Behavior,* 1988, *10*, 169–211.

Kellman, S. *Procurement and Public Management: The Fear of Discretion and the Quality of Government Performance.* Washington, D.C.: American Enterprise Institute, 1990.

Kimberly, J., and Evanisko, M. "Organizational Innovation: The Influence of Individual, Organizational, and Contextual Factors on Hospital Adoption of Technological and Administrative Innovation." *Academy of Management Journal,* 1981, *24*(4), 689–713.

Krueger, R. "Discovering the Rhetorical Culture of a County Government." Unpublished paper, 1992.

Lawler, E. E. III. "Substitutes for Hierarchy." *Organizational Dynamics,* 1988, *17,* 5–15.

Levine, D., and Tyson, L. D. "Participation, Productivity, and the Firm's Environment." In A. Blinder (ed.), *Paying for Productivity: A Look at the Evidence.* Washington, D.C.: Brookings Institution, 1989.

Light, P. *Monitoring Government: Inspectors General and the Search for Accountability.* Washington, D.C.: Brookings Institution, 1993.

Nickel, J. "Can Your Organization Achieve Better Results by Sharing Gains With Employees?" *Employment Relations Today,* 1990, *10,* 173–184.

Perry, J. L. "Merit Pay in the Public Sector: The Case for a Failure of Theory." *Review of Public Personnel Administration,* 1986, *7*(1), 261–278.

Peters, T. "Get Innovative or Get Dead." *California Management Review,* 1990, *33,* 9–26.

Pfeffer, J., and Salancik, G. *The External Control of Organizations: A Resource-Dependence Perspective.* New York: HarperCollins, 1978.

Roberts, N. C. "Public Entrepreneurship and Innovation." *Policy Studies Review,* forthcoming.

Rosen, C., and Quarrey, M. "How Well Is Employee Ownership Working?" *Harvard Business Review,* 1987, *65*(5), 126–129.

Ruttan, V., and Hayami, K. "Toward a Theory of Induced Institutional Innovation." *Journal of Development Studies,* 1984, *20,* 203–223.

Schein, E. *Organizational Culture and Leadership.* San Francisco: Jossey-Bass, 1985.

Senge, P. *The Fifth Discipline: The Art and Practice of the Learning Organization.* New York: Doubleday, 1990.

Smith, W., Lazarus, H., and Kalkstein, H. "Employee Stock Ownership Plans: Motivation and Morale Issues." *Compensation and Benefits Review,* 1990, *5,* 37–46.

Tushman, M., and Nadler, D. "Organizing for Innovation." *California Management Review,* 1986, *28*(3), 74–92.

Van de Ven, A. "Central Problems in the Management of Innovation." *Management Science,* 1986, *32*(5), 590–607.

# 4

# Reinvention and Employee Rights: The Role of the Courts

## Phillip J. Cooper

The authors who have contemplated a reinvented civil service in these pages have anchored their evaluations in the changes in the economy, the electorate, state and local governments, and the White House. But there is another arena to examine: the courts. Consider some of the important developments in the law governing public employment, the significance of those changes for civil servants and their managers, and the lessons that can be learned about how to incorporate these issues into efforts to reinvent public personnel administration.

Writing of a police officer fired by the mayor of New Bedford, Massachusetts, Justice Holmes said, "The petitioner may have a constitutional right to talk politics, but he has no constitutional right to be a policeman. There are few employments for hire in which the servant does not agree to suspend his constitutional rights of free speech as well as of idleness by the implied terms of his contract. The servant cannot complain, as he takes the employment on the terms which are offered him. On the same principle the city may impose any reasonable condition upon holding office within its control" (*McAuliffe* v. *Mayor of New Bedford*, 1892, p. 517).

That ruling came a century ago, but things changed dramatically during the middle of this century. As the Supreme Court warned government employers, "For at least a quarter-century, this Court has made clear that even though a person has no 'right' to a valuable government benefit and even though the government may deny him the benefit for any number of reasons, there are some reasons upon which the government may not rely. It may not deny a benefit to a person on a basis that infringes his constitutionally protected interests—especially, his interest in freedom of speech. . . . We have applied the principle regardless of the public employee's contractual or other claim to a job" (*Perry* v. *Sindermann*, 1972, pp. 597–598).

By 1990, however, things appeared not to be all that clear. As Justice Scalia wrote in a dissent, "I am not sure . . . that the right-privilege distinction has been as unequivocally rejected as Justice Stevens supposes. . . . [T]hat the government need not confer a certain benefit does not mean that it can attach any conditions whatever to the conferral of that benefit. But it remains true that certain conditions can be attached to benefits that cannot be imposed as prescriptions upon the public at large. If Justice Stevens chooses to call this something other than a right-privilege distinction, that is fine and good—but it is in any case what explains the nonpatronage restrictions upon federal employees that the Court continues to approve" (*Rutan* v. *Republican Party of Illinois*, 1990, p. 80).

If Justice Scalia is not sure what the status of the so-called right-privilege dichotomy is, then public employees and their supervisors must also be permitted at least as much uncertainty. If it has been so clear for so long that public employment is not simply a privilege to which any conditions an employer chooses may be attached, and if it is equally clear that government may not force someone to surrender his or her constitutional rights and liberties in order to obtain a government job or benefit, then why is there so much confusion? The answer to that question is the subject of this chapter.

The problem is that the Supreme Court (along with the lower courts that have followed its lead) has largely reimposed the right-privilege dichotomy on public employment, permitting significant restrictions on the constitutional rights and liberties of public servants while denying that it has done so. The vehicle for this estimable piece of sleight of hand is the application of a wide-ranging set of balancing tests that, applied to most situations, result in the common conclusion that the asserted interests of the individual employee do not outweigh the broader concerns of the public and its government. Nevertheless, precisely because these decisions are based on balancing tests to be applied case by case to individual disputes between employers and their employees, managers can never be truly certain of their decisions and have met some surprising defeats.

## The Move Back and the Questions Ahead

There are a variety of legal arenas in which to evaluate experience to date, including claims associated with the First Amendment, privacy issues associated with the Fourth Amendment, due-process disputes raised under the Fifth and Fourteenth Amendments, and life-style questions that arise under several legal categories. Each of these addresses differences of public employees from their private sector counterparts and imposes restrictions on them that government would not be able to impose on other citizens.

### *Speech and Other "First Freedoms"*

Many of the important battles involving public employees' rights over the years have arisen in connection with First Amendment issues. Until the 1950s, the Supreme Court followed the right-privilege approach employed by Holmes in 1892, upholding a range of restrictions on public employees' speech, associations, and political participation (*Adler* v. *Board of Education,* 1952; *Garner* v. *Board of Public Works,* 1951; *United Public Workers* v. *Mitchell,*

1947). However, in a series of decisions in the 1950s and 1960s, growing out of the Communist witch-hunt and other abuses, the Court moved away from the right-privilege approach (see, for example, *Wieman* v. *Updegraff,* 1952; *Shelton* v. *Tucker,* 1960). By 1963, the Court was well into the development of its doctrine of unconstitutional conditions, under which it found that it was unacceptable for government to require a person to surrender his or her constitutional rights as a condition for the receipt of a public job or benefit (*Sherbert* v. *Verner,* 1963). In 1967, the Court stated flatly: "The theory that public employment which may be denied altogether may be subjected to any conditions, regardless of how unreasonable, has been uniformly rejected" (*Keyishian* v. *Board of Regents,* 1967, pp. 605–606). Government need not create a position or hire any particular person to fill one; but, having chosen to employ someone, the Court said, it cannot impose unconstitutional conditions on the job. Any government employer who tries to impose such conditions, said the Court, "proceeds on a premise that has been unequivocally rejected in numerous prior decisions of this Court" (*Pickering* v. *Board of Education,* 1968, pp. 568). A few years later, the Court would announce that this principle had been firmly established for a "quarter-century" (*Perry* v. *Sindermann,* 1972).

The Court did not prohibit employers from taking action when employees' speech had actually been disruptive and had an adverse impact on the ability of the agency to perform efficiently. If that occurred, the Court said, it would apply a balancing test to determine whether the interests of the employer outweighed the employee's free-speech interests (*Pickering* v. *Board of Education,* 1968; *Perry* v. *Sindermann,* 1972). Even when an employee's statements were found to be inaccurate, they were protected if they were "neither shown nor [could] be presumed to have in any way either impeded the [employee's] proper performance of his daily duties in the classroom or to have interfered with the regular operation of the [organization] generally" (*Pickering* v. *Board of Education,* 1968, pp. 572–573).

In the years that followed, however, things changed. First, the Court shifted the burden and level of proof necessary for an employee to win reinstatement where it had been alleged that his or her speech was the reason for dismissal (see *Mt. Healthy Board of Education* v. *Doyle,* 1977, p. 287; *Givhan* v. *Western Line Consolidated School District,* 1979, p. 417). Second, the Court dramatically altered the standard for First Amendment evaluation of employees' free-speech claims.

The Court changed the entire discussion by reinterpreting the cases back to *Pickering* in a 1983 opinion written by Justice White, *Connick* v. *Myers.* The *Connick* Court claimed to be breaking no new ground, but in fact it made dramatic changes that departed from the mode of analysis that had been used for more than a decade. First, the Court required a clear showing that the employee's speech was about "a matter of public concern." Second, the Court concluded that the balance should weigh in the government's favor, even though there had admittedly been no evidence of disruption of the organization. In the process, Justice White told the lower courts to stay out, even if the action taken was "mistaken or unreasonable."

But before managers applaud this idea too loudly, it is important to consider the uncertainties that emerged from *Connick.* What is speech "of public concern"? The lower courts have found this a terribly difficult concept to apply (see Allred, 1988; Smith, 1990). *Connick* rejected the idea that the management practices of a public organization constitute a matter of public concern. It is also unclear, under *Connick,* when it is that an employer reaches the point where he or she can justify removing an employee on the grounds that the employee's conduct "hinders efficient operations." Finally, the Court left a very broad balancing test to be employed in the ultimate resolution of cases. Since *Connick,* the employer has reason to believe that the Supreme Court is inclined toward his or her position, but it is not possible to be sure how the balance will weigh until a case is actually litigated, and then it will depend on the assessment of one of the many lower-court judges around the country, whose understanding of the balancing process may be quite different from Justice White's.

Just how unpredictable the legacy of *Connick* is became clear later. *Rankin* v. *McPherson* (1987) was a case that stemmed from the termination of a nineteen-year-old probationary employee, a data-entry clerk, in Harris County, Texas. Upon hearing of the attempted assassination of President Reagan, she told a co-worker, "If they go for him again, I hope they get him" (*Rankin* v. *McPherson,* 1987, p. 381). Four members of the Court concluded that her comment was speech on a matter of public concern and that, given her position and the limited nature of her duties, her employer could not carry the weight in the balancing test.

Still, advocates of public employees' rights would not be justified in jumping to the conclusion that *Rankin* provides solid support for their views. Similarly, reactions suggesting that the ruling would "handcuff public employers" (*"Rankin* v. *McPherson:* The Court Handcuffs Public Employers," 1988) were premature. Three of those voting to support the employee — Justices Brennan, Marshall, and Powell — are no longer members of the Court. Four other members spoke strongly through the pen of Justice Scalia, who completely rejected the notion that the employee's speech fit the "public concern" requirement; even if it had, he said, it should not be permitted to survive a properly applied balancing test. The lower courts that have ruled since then have been anything but clear about how to distinguish public from private concerns, much less about what to do in situations where the two are mixed (see *Crain* v. *Board of Police Commissioners,* 1990; *Barkoo* v. *Melby,* 1990; *Dodds* v. *Childers,* 1991).

The Court's willingness to control speech has not been limited to contexts in which managers were attempting to maintain efficient operations or group morale. In a 1990 case, *Rust* v. *Sullivan* (cited in Cooper, 1992), the Court upheld the so-called gag rule issued by the U.S. Department of Health and Human Services, which prohibited federally funded family-planning clinics from providing information on abortions to their clients, even if a client asked a direct question about that option. In rejecting free-speech claims, the majority of the Court concluded that the family-planning counselors could go outside the federally funded clinics and say anything they chose. That, however, is precisely what is meant by the right-privilege dichotomy, and it is specifically what the doctrine of unconstitutional conditions was designed to prevent.

The Supreme Court has added another set of variables to the calculus of public employees' disputes over freedom of expression, under the so-called public forum doctrine. In one case, it upheld a prohibition on distribution of information by a rival union to teachers through their school mailboxes, even though the school permitted the use of the mailboxes for private communications and for distribution by community groups of information on their activities (*Perry Education Association* v. *Perry Local Educators' Association*, 1983).

In the area of freedom of the press, the Court issued a sweeping ruling, with wide-ranging implications for public employees, concerning prepublication review requirements for former employees. Without so much as accepting briefs on the merits of the case, the Court found in favor of the CIA and imposed an unprecedented remedy against a former employee (*Snepp* v. *United States*, 1980).

There is also confusion, as well as signals of declining protection, in cases concerning political participation by public employees. The Hatch Act was upheld during the period before the Court struck down the right-privilege dichotomy (*United Public Workers* v. *Mitchell*, 1947). Later challenges to regulations under the Hatch Act, based on the regulations' vagueness and overbreadth (see *Shelton* v. *Tucker*, 1960), also failed (*National Association of Letter Carriers* v. *Civil Service Commission*, 1973; *Broadrick* v. *Oklahoma*, 1973), but the Court ignored the obvious problems with those regulations. The Court struck down termination, transfers, and promotion limits based on partisan patronage in three cases (*Elrod* v. *Burns*, 1976; *Branti* v. *Finkel*, 1980; *Rutan* v. *Republican Party of Illinois*, 1990), but the last of these was decided by a 5-4 majority made up in part of members who are no longer on the Court. Justice Scalia wrote for a four-person bloc of dissenters, arguing specifically against the idea that the right-privilege dichotomy had been completely rejected by the Court in *Rutan* v. *Republican Party of Illinois* and calling for other rulings against patronage to be overturned.

Despite its denials, then, the Supreme Court moved very far, during the 1970s and 1980s and into the 1990s, from its development of the doctrine of unconstitutional conditions and back toward the right-privilege dichotomy, at least with respect to First Amendment freedoms in public employment. The same is true with respect to the Fourth Amendment.

## The Fourth Amendment: From Desk Searches to Drug Testing

The Court moved a considerable distance from 1959, when it concluded that administrative searches were not governed by the Fourth Amendment's prohibition against unreasonable searches and seizures (*Frank* v. *Maryland*, 1959), to 1967, when it overturned that ruling and concluded that the right to be secure in one's person, papers, and so on, would have little meaning if it applied only in criminal situations (*Camara* v. *Municipal Court*, 1967). Administrative searches would be covered. Reasonable searches within the meaning of the Fourth Amendment would require search warrants based on reasonable cause and some degree of specificity about the reasons and targets of the search, although administrative warrants would not require the kind of probable cause needed in a criminal investigation (*Marshall* v. *Barlow's Inc.*, 1978).

In a 1987 ruling, however, the Court opened the door to wide-ranging warrantless searches of public employees' offices and files (*O'Connor* v. *Ortega*, 1987) and laid the foundation for a ruling that would uphold employee drug testing (*National Treasury Employees* v. *Von Raab*, 1989; see also Kaplan and Williams, 1988; Wald and Kahn, 1990). After noting that "individuals do not lose Fourth Amendment rights merely because they work for the government instead of a private employer" (*O'Connor* v. *Ortega*, 1987, p. 717), the Court avoided stating any principle by which to assess such cases and threw the whole question wide open, declaring that "the question of whether an employee has a reasonable expectation of privacy must be addressed on a case-by-case basis" in a process that would "balance the invasion of the employees' legitimate expectations of privacy against the government's need for supervision, control and the efficient operation of the work place" (pp. 719–720). These special needs would be considered case by case. Justice Scalia concurred, but he blasted the Court's opinion, noting the problems caused by "an ad hoc, case-by-case definition of the Fourth Amendment standards to be applied in differing factual circumstances" and objecting to "the formulation of a standard so devoid of content that it produces rather than eliminates uncertainty in this field" (p. 730).

That ruling was cited in a variety of important opinions in the lower courts (see Wald and Kahn, 1990) and was significant in the Court's ruling in *National Treasury Employees* v. *Von Raab* (1989). In the latter case, the Court employed the same kind of "special needs" approach to reduce employees' reasonable expectation of privacy and called for each drug-testing program to be subjected to a balancing test. The Court itself was uncertain of how the balancing test would work with respect to all the employees in the Customs Service and sent portions of the case back for further consideration. Several lower courts later upheld drug-testing programs for police and other public safety employees, persons with top-secret security clearances, and others (*Harmon* v. *Thornburgh*, 1989), whether they had access to classified documents or not (*Hartness* v. *Bush*, 1990).

Apart from the relatively easy cases of security clearances and public safety workers, however, the case-by-case balancing approach resolves little. The bias of any such balance is clearly in favor of the employer against the employee, but the manager cannot be sure. The employee is utterly adrift, and it seems that the most reasonable approach would be to assume lack of protection. If that is the result, then the right-privilege dichotomy is alive and well, as Scalia suggests, and the doctrine of unconstitutional conditions is dead.

### The Due-Process Quagmire

The same kinds of factors that shape the other constitutional fields have come to govern the availability of due-process protections for public employees. The same abuses during the 1950s that initially brought expanded First Amendment protection also caused the Court to issue a wide range of rulings through the 1960s and into the early 1970s ensuring that when the government turned its power on an individual and threatened him or her with a "grievous loss," the rudiments of due process would be provided (see, for example, *Goldberg* v. *Kelly,* 1970). Specifically, the Court rejected the idea that the right to due process could be balanced away in the interests of administrative efficiency (*Stanley* v. *Illinois,* 1972). Moreover, those kinds of protections were retained by public employees, as well as by recipients of public benefits (*Board of Regents* v. *Roth,* 1972). The task was to ensure fundamental fairness and prevent arbitrariness.

By the time of the Court's ruling in *Mathews* v. *Eldridge* (1976), however, the Court had changed its view. Now the requirement for a prompt hearing principally had to do with ensuring accuracy in fact finding rather than with fundamental fairness. Any call for a hearing of any kind—a more timely hearing, or a more adequate hearing—would be assessed according to a balancing test that specifically addressed the cost and administrative burdens imposed by the procedures demanded. Few cases brought to the Court after *Eldridge,* except those involving incarceration in mental health facilities or certain prison disputes, were able to meet the *Eldridge* balancing test.

With respect to cases involving public employees, it quickly became clear that the Court was moving to reimpose a right-privilege approach on due process. In *Arnett* v. *Kennedy* (1974), the Court rejected the call for a more adequate pretermination process that would accord due process in the sense of fundamental fairness, given that waiting a lengthy period for a posttermination hearing would work a serious hardship on the employee. The Court insisted that due process protected only liberty or property interests, and that insofar as government employees had a property interest in their jobs, the nature and scope of the due-process rights to that job were defined by the statute that conferred the property right.

As late as 1985, Chief Justice Rehnquist reiterated the position he had taken in *Arnett:* that "one who avails himself of government entitlements accepts the grant of tenure along with its inherent [procedural] limitations" (*Cleveland Board of Education* v. *Loudermill,* 1985, p. 536). Justice Powell concurred in *Arnett* but insisted on the use of a balancing test. Rehnquist's view was as clear a restatement of the right-privilege dichotomy as one is likely to find. That position had also been reiterated in a previous case (*Bishop* v. *Wood,* 1976). Even so, the balancing approach eventually carried the day in *Cleveland Board of Education* v. *Loudermill.* But even if employees' claims survived the balancing test, the Court concluded, public employees were not entitled to any particular level of due process beyond the minimum:

> Here, the pretermination hearing need not definitively resolve the propriety of the discharge. It should be an initial check against mistaken decisions — essentially, a determination of whether there are reasonable grounds to believe that the charges against the employee are true and support the proposed action. . . . The essential requirement of due process, and all that respondents seek or the Court of Appeals required, are notice and an opportunity to respond. The opportunity to present reasons, either in person or in writing, why proposed action should not be taken is a fundamental due-process requirement. . . . The tenured public employee is entitled to oral or written notice of the charges against him, an explanation of the employer's evidence, and an opportunity to present his side of the story. . . . To require more than this prior to termination would intrude to an unwarranted extent on the government's interest in quickly removing an unsatisfactory employee" [pp. 545–546].

Rehnquist issued a stinging dissent, in which he emphasized that he would stand on his position in *Arnett.* While his conclusion about what to do was constitutionally unsound, Rehnquist rightly saw that "the lack of any principled standards in this area means that these procedural due-process cases will recur time and again. Every different set of facts will present a new issue on what process was due and when" (pp. 562–563). His solution was simply to reimpose the right-privilege dichotomy.

Activity in the lower courts after the *Loudermill* case has indeed presented the kinds of inconsistencies to be expected from the balancing approach advanced by the Supreme Court (see "Bias and the Loudermill Hearing," 1989; "Procedural Due Process . . . ," 1989; see also *Garraghty* v. *Jordon,* 1987; *Schaper* v. *City of Huntsville,* 1987; *Duchesne* v. *Williams,* 1988; *AFSCME Local 2477* v. *Billington,* 1990; *D'Acquisto* v. *Washington,* 1990; *Brown* v. *Houston Independent School District,* 1991; *Cobb* v. *Village of Oakwood,* 1991).

### Life-Style and Related Considerations

The Court has taken the same kind of right-privilege approach, either directly or de facto, through the use of loose balancing tests in a number of cases dealing with what might be called life-style considerations. For example, the Court decided by way of an opinion involving six members — without even bothering to note probable jurisdiction and hear the case — that a sixteen-year veteran of the Philadelphia Fire Department could be terminated because he moved outside the city. That case has been used to support clearly unreasonable and unfair conclusions in the lower courts (see *Clinton Police Department Bargaining Unit* v. *City of Clinton,* 1991).

In *Kelley* v. *Johnson* (1976), the Court upheld a regulation governing the length of a police officer's hair. Justice Rehnquist wrote, for the Court, that if the government could justify intrusion into protected First Amendment freedoms, then surely it could justify interference with such life-style considerations. Rehnquist placed the burden on the employee to show that "there is no rational connection between the regulation, based as it is on the county's method of organizing the police force, and the promotion of safety of persons and property" (p. 247). Justice Marshall, in dissent, expressed frustration with the Court's lack of care in addressing the question and dismissing the interests of public employees on the assumption that they should be governed by the right-privilege dichotomy. He wrote, "To hold that citizens somehow automatically give up constitutional rights by becoming public employees would mean that almost 15 million American citizens are currently affected by having 'executed' such 'automatic waivers'" (p. 254).

Rehnquist gave similarly offhand treatment to an Air Force officer, a rabbi, who had challenged regulations prohibiting his wearing of a yarmulke in the hospital where he worked (*Goldman* v. *Weinberger*, 1986). Justice Brennan was correct in his dissenting observation that there was not even a serious attempt to provide a "credible explanation" of the problem created by the yarmulke under the conditions at issue in the case, or under any other conditions, for that matter. As he suggested of Rehnquist's opinion, "Unabashed *ipse dixit* cannot outweigh a constitutional right" (p. 516).

As is true of the other rulings discussed up to this point, these decisions have been taken to heart by the lower courts, and the character of the explanations in these opinions is as important as the rulings themselves (see *Grusendorf* v. *City of Oklahoma City*, 1987, upholding a ban on off-duty smoking). As one commentator has pointed out, the idea of cutting down on the negative consequences of smoking, on or off duty, may be attractive, but there is still the question of how far the government may "control private activity with such minimum standards of justification" ("Constitutional Law," 1988, p. 763).

## Wrong Directions and Troublesome Assumptions

In his dissent in the *Rutan* case, Justice Scalia correctly recited a laundry list of restrictions that can be applied to civil servants but not to private citizens (*Rutan* v. *Republican Party of Illinois*, 1990, p. 80). In the face of all that, he demanded, how could the Court continue to insist that there is no right-privilege dichotomy? He asked a question the Court could not in good conscience answer without revealing the inconsistencies in its own logic and decisions. While Scalia and Rehnquist would openly recognize the right-privilege dichotomy, other members of the Court, by virtue of their use of loosely defined and patently biased balancing tests, reached the same outcome, as Scalia says, whether they admitted it or not. There are those who regard this move as useful, particularly from a manager's point of view, but they should exercise great caution.

During the 1980s and into the 1990s, the courts have indeed been moving to reassert the importance of administrative discretion in the management of public employees. From the civil servant's point of view, courts and managers appear to want to treat public employees as individuals with special situations that allow constraints to be placed on them, but not as special in terms of their need for protection. That justification of their public status and asserted need for accountability have been used to undermine the protections that the courts historically have said should be provided. It seems that the only reason a government employee is told how special his or her status is these days is to justify deprivation of a right.

One of the great problems is that the Court's rhetoric often does not match its actions. It frequently uses rhetoric that suggests protection of the employee, on the one hand, but it rules in favor of the employer, on the other, and vice versa. Partly, this is the kind of unwillingness to recognize the incommensurability of precedents that Scalia and Rehnquist have pointed out. From the manager's perspective, the difficulty is that the Supreme Court and the lower federal courts have moved to recognize the need for administrative discretion but their rulings have usually employed balancing tests that ultimately depend on evaluation by a court of the particular facts of individual cases. That approach can make it extremely difficult for a manager to understand and predict the consequences of a given managerial decision in a particular set of circumstances. Cases in the lower courts indicate that this uncertainty among managers is well founded.

Ultimately, this attempt at justifying the invasion of civil servants' rights and liberties, on the grounds that their situation is special and that the normal rules constraining government behavior do not apply, faces a fundamental contradiction: many of the same arguments that claim to justify the special need for concern about public employees' positions can also be interpreted to support a special need for protection of public employees. The Court does badly not to recognize that its rulings

represent a two-edged sword, a weapon that too often has been
used to damage the public service and too rarely has been wielded
in its defense.

## Lessons for Reinventing
## Public Personnel Administration

In the end, then, there have been changes in the courts that
have been just as important as those that have occurred in other
arenas. If there is to be an attempt to reinvent public personnel
administration to meet new realities, then the role of the courts
must be included in that process. In particular, there are concerns about the recent developments described earlier, but there
are also larger issues about how to integrate thoughts about
courts, law, and legal process into personnel management.

### Dangers of the Elusive Balance and
### the Reemerging Right-Privilege Dichotomy

The reaction of many managers to the change in direction taken
by the U.S. Supreme Court and by many lower courts has been
resounding if nervous applause. Even with a host of caveats attached, there is an occasional and almost audible sigh of relief
from some managers, who are tempted to say that at last the
judges seem to be catching on to the problems faced by administrators. The reality, though, is that the move back toward the
right-privilege dichotomy, and the Supreme Court's use of loose
balancing formulas to define the outer boundaries of the rights
of civil servants, pose difficulties not only for traditional managers but also for those contemplating the reinvention of personnel administration. First, these rulings have increased rather
than eliminated uncertainty, which complicates the management
task. Second, they reinforce an outmoded Theory X approach
to management at a time when the challenge of reinventing
government requires precisely the opposite kind of relationship
between employees and their managers. Third, the changes are
likely to undermine recruitment and retention of precisely the
kinds of people needed to meet the new challenges of the public

service. Finally, the so-called doctrine of special needs threatens to break down whatever useful protections still exist between the most volatile political forces and the professional civil service.

The Supreme Court, as Justice Scalia has pointed out, has had great difficulty admitting its reimposition of the right-privilege dichotomy. Like other judges who have been either unable or unwilling to clearly articulate firm principles, the Court has reached for a balancing test to use in civil service cases. The result is less predictability for managers and employees alike. The likelihood also diminishes that there will be uniform definitions of employees' rights and employers' authority because the Supreme Court's approach quite literally invites the lower courts to act individually, without standards, and on a case-by-case basis.

What are the consequences of this enhanced uncertainty for the premises inherent in the discussion about reinventing government? It discourages risk taking, complicates risk management, does not relieve anxieties about tort liability, and increases disruption in the workplace. Just when lack of benchmarks and clear principles reduces predictability, and just when the mechanism for resolving open questions has become less standardized and more complex, managers face clear pressure to behave in a manner as risk-averse as possible. The kind of experimental approach to management that lies at the core of reinventing government cannot succeed without a dramatic increase in risk taking.

The overall trend is clearly in favor of management, as against the claims for employees' rights, but there is relatively little gain in terms of risk management. Not only is there no reduction in insurance or legal costs, there is every reason to believe that the current balancing formulas will increase both kinds of expense. The level of uncertainty and the lack of uniformity discourage risk sharing. After all, one dimension of personnel disputes is the question of who prevails, but another is the exposure to tort liability, since the employer may suffer substantial liability judgments, in addition to the possibility of having its management decisions reversed.

To the degree that managers attempt to reduce their risks

by practicing defensive management, they not only cannot use their creative energies to reinvent their workplaces but also may actually undermine morale and damage career development programs. The difficulty is not simply the uncertainty of the balancing test. The larger concern is the return to the right-privilege dichotomy itself. If one starts from Theory X management, then presumably a return to the right-privilege dichotomy is an appropriate and useful way to get control and ensure efficiency, by making prompt disciplinary action readily available. But if one chooses a management style based on a more positive framework, then instability, unpredictability, and the ever-present potential for threat undermine morale and effective informal work patterns. There is no reason to believe that forcing public employees simply to accept the sacrifice of their rights — rights otherwise enjoyed by citizens against government's power — will improve their creativity or productivity. In fact, *protection* of these rights can buffer potential demands for negative action. Wise supervisors know what their colleagues in the private sector have realized for some time: the person who should become a top executive at forty-five may very well be the same one who would be fired at thirty-five for insubordination or some other charge.

The implications of reducing public employees' rights extend beyond the question of what employers can expect their people to produce. The issue raises serious questions about the ability of governmental units to recruit and retain the kinds of people needed to meet the challenge of reinvention. From the employee's point of view, why should a manager voluntarily waive so many freedoms in exchange for lower pay and vulnerability to lawsuits? Why should managers stay in a context of growing pressure and increasing uncertainty? At some point, commitment to public service is simply not enough to justify the costs. One answer to these questions involves the idea that more of what government will do in a reinvented public administration will be accomplished by contracting with outside providers. Rather than solving some of these problems, however, increased use of contracting and other alternative modes of service delivery may complicate the situation. This is true even if we assume that the many uncertainties that now exist regarding the precise status of government contractors' employees will soon be eliminated. The problem is still far from resolution. Reinvention may result in a smaller public work force, but the challenges of recruitment, retention, and management will increase because government must build administrative capacity it does not now possess to handle contracting.

A number of factors suggest that, to the degree that reinventing government depends on increased contracting, personnel management will be extremely complex, even if the scale of tasks is smaller. Consider just three of the more obvious issues. First, government contracts are not simply agreements for the purchase of goods or services. They represent something closer to a kind of treaty, by which government forms an ongoing working relationship, a kind of merger, with service providers and product vendors. In many respects, government becomes as dependent on one or a few providers as those contractors are on the government. The idea that government can somehow just hire and fire by granting or terminating contracts is a vast oversimplification. Besides, those who think it is easier to terminate a contract and obtain sanctions against a contractor than it is to discipline a civil servant under existing law will learn how seriously wrong they are.

Second, government contracts have long carried what has been called "social overhead"—the set of ongoing policy commitments pursued by government, ranging from affirmative action to environmental responsibility. Contract managers face not only the task of ensuring delivery of goods and services but also the compliance-monitoring for these other aspects of the contracting commitment.

Third, there is reason to believe that public and political demands for accountability in contract administration will, if anything, be greater than in contemporary civil service management, precisely because of the fear that contractors are not motivated by a public service commitment and are not subject to the range of accountability mechanisms applicable to public employees.

All three of these factors mean that the people needed to conduct contract-based operations will be more difficult to recruit, retain, and manage than their predecessors. They and their managers will face new vulnerabilities under contracting laws and liability claims. They must operate within a negotiation culture that is exceedingly complex (Burton, 1990). They carry much more to the negotiating table than their counterparts do in the private sector.

These obvious aspects of the complexity of managing contract administration highlight a problem that has been exacerbated by the Court's rulings in recent years. The Supreme Court has used the argument that public employers have special needs, but the Court has not been particularly helpful in explaining the nature of the special needs or the reasons that support those claims, beyond the simple assertion that they are public. If it is true that public employment is special, then it must follow that the rights and obligations of civil servants are also special. The simplistic — and, frankly, arbitrary — approach of the Supreme Court in many civil service cases has not helped employees and employers understand either what is special or how to manage the special dimensions of public employment in a manner that both protects government employees from abuse and facilitates employers in moving toward a reinvented government.

*Lessons for Public Personnel Administration*

Despite the problems just mentioned, there are some lessons that can be helpful as managers think about reinventing personnel management to meet the needs of a reinvented government. We can change the way we think about the law and the courts as part of the management task, consider ways to work with the problems of uncertainty, and ensure that we take public employees seriously in the process of reinventing the civil service.

Managers have had a tendency to use the courts as an excuse not to act, to see the law as a barrier, and to confuse law and ethics in ways that seem to make change and progress impossible. Too often, the claims "The courts won't let us" and "We'll be sued" have been used as ways to end discussion of new initiatives. In some cases, the concern is real and the doubts are serious; in others, the use of the courts as a foil is tactical. Many a career manager has used the courts to discourage political superiors from moving in new directions. It is true that the law does sometimes stand as a barrier to action, and in many of those cases it should. But it is not particularly helpful for managers to allow legal paralysis to govern their operations. In most cases, it simply is not useful to wait for the courts or to use the law as an excuse.

Law is a tool of management. It empowers as well as constrains. The courts are a normal part of the dialogue of government (Fisher, 1989), in the same way that legislatures involved in the appropriations process are involved in management: on some occasions, they constrain; on others, they support action.

Quite apart from wins and losses, managers can learn important lessons about fairness, reasoned decision making, and the issues at the heart of broad debates (like the argument over special needs; see Rohr, 1989). As is often true of lessons learned from the legislative and executive branches, lessons learned from the courts can sometimes be learned from the courts' mistakes as much as from the stirring opinions that attract broad support as statements of important principles of democratic government. But the courts cannot be expected to answer all our questions, not even in some of the areas where they are expected to do so. For example, law and ethics are not the same thing. The courts can provide useful commentaries and rulings on matters of law, but it is not a good idea to expect them to give us answers to ethical dilemmas. There are some things managers can do to facilitate things, even in such a complex environment. If we begin from the assumption that the courts are participants in the normal dialogue of government, then we should pay more attention to them and be less surprised by some of what they say. There are too many occasions on which judicial rulings are treated as shocking, when they simply should have been anticipated.

One of the best examples in recent memory of an unwarranted surprise is the Supreme Court's overturning of *National League of Cities* v. *Usery* (1976). In overturning the earlier ruling, the Supreme Court in 1985 applied the Fair Labor Standards Act to local government employees in *Garcia* v. *San Antonio*

*Metropolitan Transit Authority.* The *Usery* ruling, which had pur-
ported to insulate local governments against such federal regulation, was itself a dramatic departure from existing constitutional doctrine (compare *Maryland* v. *Wirtz,* 1968). It had been
decided by a one-vote majority, and that one vote was a very
limited agreement, as explained in a concurring opinion. Almost
immediately, a string of cases followed, raising the federalism
issues presented by *Usery.* At least by 1981 it had become apparent, that the fifth vote in *Usery* had moved in the other direction (*Hodel* v. *Virginia Surface Mining Association,* 1981). Over the
next several years, a series of rulings emerging from the Court
made it absolutely clear that the *Usery* ruling would not stand.
In fact, two years before the *Garcia* ruling that ultimately dis-
posed of *Usery,* Justice Stevens wrote a concurring opinion that
specifically called for overturning *Usery,* recognizing that the
Court had all but killed it already (*EEOC* v. *Wyoming,* 1983).
The point is that anyone paying the least attention to what the
Court had been doing in the important area of federalism would
have known that local governments should have been preparing to implement Fair Labor Standards Act requirements at least
two (and perhaps as many as four) years before the actual mandate ultimately emerged from the Supreme Court. Yet the *Garcia* ruling was treated as shocking and contrary to the history
of constitutional law. Both claims were empirically untrue, and
no one should have been surprised.

   Apart from general trends, it is clearly possible to antici-
pate problems and opportunities in many areas. Thus very few
jurisdictions that operate correctional facilities or mental health
institutions should be surprised by litigation or its consequences.
Knowing this, rather than simply hoping that a governmental
unit will not face a loss in court, permits a community to do
two things: first, it can begin to take action to prepare for what
is probably inevitable; and, second, a governmental unit can
make a careful decision about when and how hard to fight in
a legal contest, and when and how to resolve disputes by some
other means. Communities can also attempt to understand the
perspective of the judge and to develop their own responses with

an understanding of the task the judge must accomplish. For example, the judge often faces what is called the *deference paradox:* if a judge writes a ruling in a moderate tone, hoping to gain the cooperation of government officials, but is met by recalcitrance, an appeals court may overturn the ruling because the findings are not sufficiently severe; but if the judge delivers a sharply worded rebuke to a governmental unit in a punitive ruling, conflict between the court and the community increases. Officials who seek to work with judges, to the degree that it is possible to do so, may make their own lives easier and accomplish more.

It is important for managers in the federal government to understand the dialogue with the judiciary in intergovernmental terms. In reinventing government, if the performance of many federal agencies is to be measured by outcomes, then it is critical to recognize that those outcomes often depend on action by state or local governments. The legal issues that affect local governments and states also influence their ability to carry out federal mandates.

Managers who seek to reinvent the civil service need to be careful to take public employees seriously. If we as managers expect our employees to give up a degree of their freedom, then we must also be prepared to commit ourselves to them. Preservation of the essential rights of citizenship—freedom from abuse by government in such areas as traditional First Amendment rights, the right to privacy, and due process—is good law and good management. In these areas, it is possible to provide greater protection for employees than the Supreme Court has mandated, and it is a good idea to do so, not only to reduce the likelihood of losing lawsuits but also to enhance the values likely to engender creativity and effectiveness, the driving assumptions behind the movement to reinvent government.

In the end, the Supreme Court has been right about one thing: public employees *are* special. In our effort to find new ways for them to use their talents effectively and creatively in the public interest, we managers must take care not to underestimate public employees' special character, mission, and needs.

## Cases Cited

*Adler* v. *Board of Education,* 342 U.S. 485 (1952).

*AFSCME Local 2477* v. *Billington,* 740 F.Supp. 1 (D.D.C. 1990).

*Arnett* v. *Kennedy,* 416 U.S. 134 (1974).

*Barkoo* v. *Melby,* 901 F.2d 613 (7th Cir. 1990).

*Bishop* v. *Wood,* 426 U.S. 341 (1976).

*Board of Regents* v. *Roth,* 408 U.S. 564 (1972).

*Branti* v. *Finkel,* 445 U.S. 507 (1980).

*Broadrick* v. *Oklahoma,* 413 U.S. 601 (1973).

*Brown* v. *Houston Independent School District,* 763 F.Supp. 905 (S.D.Tex 1991).

*Camara* v. *Municipal Court,* 387 U.S. 523 (1967).

*Cleveland Board of Education* v. *Loudermill,* 470 U.S. 532 (1985).

*Clinton Police Department Bargaining Unit* v. *City of Clinton,* 464 N.W.2d 875 (Iowa 1991).

*Cobb* v. *Village of Oakwood,* 789 F.Supp. 237 (N.D.Ohio 1991).

*Connick* v. *Myers,* 461 U.S. 138 (1983).

*Cornelius* v. *NAACP Legal Defense and Education Fund,* 473 U.S. 788 (1985).

*Crain* v. *Board of Police Commissioners,* 920 F.2d 1402 (8th Cir. 1990).

*D'Acquisto* v. *Washington,* 750 F.Supp. 342 (N.D.Ill. 1990).

*Dodds* v. *Childers,* 933 F.2d 271 (5th Cir. 1991).

*Duchesne* v. *Williams,* 849 F.2d 1004 (6th Cir. 1988).

*EEOC* v. *Wyoming,* 460 U.S. 226 (1983).

*Elrod* v. *Burns,* 424 U.S. 347 (1976).

*Frank* v. *Maryland,* 359 U.S. 360 (1959).

*Garcia* v. *San Antonio Metropolitan Transit Authority,* 469 U.S. 528 (1985).

*Garner* v. *Board of Public Works,* 341 U.S. 716 (1951).

*Garraghty* v. *Jordon,* 830 F.2d 1295 (4th Cir. 1987).

*Givhan* v. *Western Line Consolidated School District,* 439 U.S. 410 (1979).

*Goldberg* v. *Kelly,* 397 U.S. 254 (1970).

*Goldman* v. *Weinberger,* 475 U.S. 503 (1986).

*Grusendorf* v. *City of Oklahoma City,* 816 F.2d 539 (1987).

*Harmon* v. *Thornburgh,* 878 F.2d 484 (D.C. Cir. 1989).

*Hartness* v. *Bush,* 919 F.2d 170 (D.C. Cir. 1990).
*Hodel* v. *Virginia Surface Mining Association,* 452 U.S. 264 (1981).
*Kelley* v. *Johnson,* 425 U.S. 238 (1976).
*Keyishian* v. *Board of Regents,* 385 U.S. 589 (1967).
*McAuliffe* v. *Mayor of New Bedford,* 29 N.E. 517 (Mass. 1892).
*Marshall* v. *Barlow's Inc.,* 436 U.S. 307 (1978).
*Maryland* v. *Wirtz,* 392 U.S. 183 (1968).
*Mathews* v. *Eldridge,* 424 U.S. 319 (1976).
*Mt. Healthy Board of Education* v. *Doyle,* 429 U.S. 274 (1977).
*National Association of Letter Carriers* v. *Civil Service Commission,* 413
  U.S. 548 (1973).
*National League of Cities* v. *Usery,* 426 U.S. 833 (1976).
*National Treasury Employees* v. *Von Raab,* 489 U.S. 532 (1989).
*O'Connor* v. *Ortega,* 480 U.S. 709 (1987).
*Perry* v. *Sindermann,* 408 U.S. 593 (1972).
*Perry Education Association* v. *Perry Local Educators' Association,* 460
  U.S. 37 (1983).
*Pickering* v. *Board of Education,* 391 U.S. 563 (1968).
*Rankin* v. *McPherson,* 483 U.S. 378 (1987).
*Rutan* v. *Republican Party of Illinois,* 111 L.Ed.2d 52 (1990).
*Schaper* v. *City of Huntsville,* 813 F.2d 709 (5th Cir. 1987).
*Shelton* v. *Tucker,* 364 U.S. 479 (1960).
*Sherbert* v. *Verner,* 374 U.S. 398 (1963).
*Snepp* v. *United States,* 444 U.S. 507 (1980).
*Stanley* v. *Illinois,* 405 U.S. 645 (1972).
*United Public Workers* v. *Mitchell,* 330 U.S. 75 (1947).
*Wieman* v. *Updegraff,* 344 U.S. 183 (1952).

## References

Allred, S. "From Connick to Confusion: The Struggle to Define
  Speech on Matters of Public Concern." *Indiana Law Journal,*
  1988, *64,* 43–81.
"Bias and the Loudermill Hearing: Due Process or Lip Service
  to Federal Law?" *Fordham Law Review,* 1989, *57,* 1093–1105.
Burton, L. "Ethical Discontinuities in Public–Private Sector
  Negotiations." *Journal of Policy Analysis and Management,* 1990,
  *9,* 23–40.

"Constitutional Law: *Grusendorf* v. *City of Oklahoma City* [816 F.2d 539]. Is Big Brother Watching?: How Far Can Government Go in Regulating Off-Duty Conduct?" *University of Missouri at Kansas City Law Review,* 1988, *56,* 757–763.

Cooper, P. J. "Rusty Pipes: The *Rust* Decision and the Supreme Court's Free-Flow Theory of the First Amendment." *Notre Dame Journal of Law, Ethics, & Policy,* 1992, *6,* 359–392.

Fisher, L. *Constitutional Dialogues.* Princeton, N.J.: Princeton University Press, 1989.

Kaplan, E., and Williams, L. G. "Will Employees' Rights Be the First Casualty of the War on Drugs?" *University of Kansas Law Review,* 1988, *36,* 755–785.

"Procedural Due Process and the 'Mere Right of Reply'— *Duchesne* v. *Williams.*" *Toledo Law Review,* 1989, *20,* 765–796.

"*Rankin* v. *McPherson:* The Court Handcuffs Public Employers." *Pacific Law Journal,* 1988, *19,* 1543–1563.

Rohr, J. A. *Ethics for Bureaucrats.* New York: Marcel Dekker, 1989.

Smith, D. G. "Beyond 'Public Concern': New Free Speech Standards for Public Employees." *University of Chicago Law Review,* 1990, *57,* 249–277.

Wald, M., and Kahn, J. D. "Privacy Rights of Public Employees." *The Labor Lawyer,* 1990, *6,* 301–318.

# 5

# Rethinking Public
# Personnel Administration

## *Hal G. Rainey*

Performance is a fundamental topic in administration, probably the most fundamental. Personnel administration seeks to
contribute to administrative performance, especially if we define
performance properly, to include such objectives as equity, fairness, and responsiveness. Critics contend, however, that public personnel administration plays a very weak role in influencing the performance of government agencies and therefore does
not perform well itself. This chapter seeks to contribute to rethinking public personnel administration, especially in relation
to the performance issue, from the perspective of an organization theorist. From that viewpoint, the chapter discusses problems with the conception and assessment of performance as these
apply to such complex systems or institutions as public personnel systems or the administrative branch of government. Having noted these problems and the difficulties they raise for ap-

plying the concept of performance and assessing it, the chapter then covers important developments in organization theory, including the topics of organizational effectiveness, strategy, culture, leadership, and individual motivation.

This discussion underscores some ways in which current literature and practice in public personnel administration conflict with the performance implications of the literature on organization theory. Public personnel administrative systems have sought to standardize personnel practices in the agencies they cover, emphasizing relatively centralized control over personnel procedures. Public personnel administration agencies and officials have also tended to concentrate on regulating the personnel practices of agencies, with inattention to integrating human resource management into comprehensive approaches to agency missions and strategies, or with inability to achieve such comprehensiveness.

In contrast, contemporary organization theory contends that organizations must respond to complexity and uncertainty by relaxing centralization and standardization. Organization theorists have developed contingency theories that emphasize the need for organizations to vary, rather than standardize, their structures and procedures in response to such contingencies as uncertainty in tasks and operating environments. Furthermore, many writers on organizations and management also stress the importance of comprehensiveness in achieving successful management, strategy, and change in organizations (for example, Tichy, 1983). Private sector personnel administrators face similar challenges, but public sector personnel administrators and systems appear to confront particular difficulties in integrating human resource management into more comprehensive managerial strategies. From the perspective of contemporary organization theory and management thought, then, a key challenge in rethinking public personnel administration is developing the capacity of public personnel systems to recognize and encourage variations among administrative entities under their jurisdiction without becoming further enfeebled as contributors to organizational performance. How can such efforts to relax centralization and standardization be balanced with the need for public personnel administration to play a strong role in comprehensive, as opposed to piecemeal or fragmented, approaches to organization and management in the public sector?

## Public Personnel Administration and Administrative Performance

Numerous observers have criticized the performance of public personnel administration and its allegedly weak contribution to the general performance of the administrative branch of government (Sampson, 1993; Lee, 1987). The fairly typical critique holds that public personnel administration plays at best a minor role in important administrative decisions and actions and has actually been distinct from agency management. Line agency executives tend to restrict personnel administration to maintenance and service functions, such as providing basic procedures for employee selection and counseling, as opposed to setting policy or advising executives about personnel matters or other major topics.

Critics further contend that agency executives do not assign personnel administrators important roles in major strategic decision-making and policy-making initiatives. According to some of the critics, executives tend to regard personnel administrators and personnel agencies as obstructionists and rulekeepers. Consequently, line executives typically view personnel administration as a cost rather than a resource. Some observers argue that many personnel officials deserve this reputation because they have become isolated in central personnel agencies, with a focus on defending the merit system against potential abuses and with an "us against them" mentality (Lee, 1987).

Personnel experts have called for more attention to strategic human resource management, for more incorporation of personnel specialists into strategic planning and decisions, and for the adoption among personnel specialists of a more supportive, consultative role in relations with agency executives and managers. Very recent survey research, however, indicates that line executives still express little enthusiasm for summoning personnel administrators to the executive suite for strategy sessions.

Instead, line executives still perceive personnelists as primarily and properly restricted to maintenance and service roles (Sampson, 1993). At the federal level, the U.S. Office of Personnel Management has made some efforts to decentralize authority over personnel matters and to adopt a more supportive and consultative role (Ingraham and Rosenbloom, 1989). Yet there appear to be no convincing indications that these developments have strengthened the role of personnel administration in important decisions and actions (U.S. Merit Systems Protection Board, 1992), and in certain ways these developments may well weaken it. Therefore, the performance of public personnel administration, including its contribution to the performance of government and its administrative branch, remains dubious and controversial. This situation raises the questions of how we can conceive of this performance problem and what we can draw from organization theory in considering our responses to it.

## How Are We Doing, and How Do We Know?

As we take up the issue of performance, we immediately encounter problems concerning its meaning and measurement. It is important to confront these problems, since they illustrate why organization theorists have emphasized ambiguities in performance assessment of complex organizations and why organization theorists have responded with an emphasis on decentralization, flexibility, and comprehensive approaches. Exhibit 5.1 summarizes common interrelated problems in assessing the performance of large complex systems. The list of problems includes at least the ones discussed in the following sections.

### The "Who Knows?" Problem

Complex administrative systems pursue goals and values that are multiple, conflicting, controversial, and ambiguous or hard to assess. Performance assessment therefore remains debatable and indeterminant in any ultimate or conclusive sense. As an example of the debatable nature of such questions, Kennedy (1987) claims that the United States is declining as a world economic and political power, whereas Nau (1980) claims that

Exhibit 5.1. Problems with Conception and
Assessment of Complex Administrative Systems.

---

*The "Who knows?" problem*
Multiple, conflicting, hard-to-assess goals and values
Ultimately disputable, inconclusive

*The "How do we know?" problem*
Measurement problems
Research-design problems in determining causation

*The "Who cares?" problem*
Multiple and conflicting interests and stakeholders
Apathy and inattention from officials and the general public

*The "It's their fault" problem*
Blaming games
Bureaucracy-bashing
Hypercritical context

*The "It's not their (or our) fault" problem*
Employees, clientele, and other beneficiaries as defenders, even where
    shortcomings are apparent

*The self-promotion problem*
Employees, clientele, and other beneficiaries as sources of favorably biased
    information

*The politics problem*
Political responsiveness as a performance criterion that conflicts with
    other criteria, such as efficiency
Inherently conflictual nature of politics—ideology and partisanship

*The parts-and-pieces problem*
"Piecemealization" of research and practice
Fragmentation, reductionism, and specialization in administrative structure
    and process, and in research and theory
(Example: personnel system as only one part of the performance puzzle)

---

it is not. A large army of critics, in academia and elsewhere,
says that the administrative agencies of government perform
poorly; other authors—enough to make up almost a platoon—
disagree (Goodsell, 1985; Milward and Rainey, 1983; Wamsley and others, 1990).

## The "How Do We Know?" Problem

Inevitably, even when we can agree on goals, there are measurement and assessment problems. For example, one of the

most vaunted performance indicators in all the administrative literature is profit, or the "bottom line." Even when industrial organizations have profit indicators, however, profit statements often convey ambiguous information. One analyst claims that IBM thought it was making money on its personal computers but was actually losing money; accounting procedures obfuscated the losses (Carroll, 1993). Profit has its problems. Obviously, the problem of precise definition and measurement becomes more severe for less quantifiable criteria.

There are also research design and logic-of-inquiry problems, such as the difficulty of eliminating alternative explanations. For example, does the U.S. educational system perform poorly, or does it only seem to because of family deterioration, drugs, movies, television, and other external factors beyond the control of the educational system?

### The "Who Cares?" Problem

Performance evaluation may depend on who cares about it in at least two senses. First, diverse interests and stakeholders promote conflicting values, thus precluding conclusive performance assessment, since evaluation depends on whose point of view one accepts. Advocates of economic development think a state Department of Natural Resources has performed very well when it builds a golf course where a forest used to be; environmentalists disagree. Second, this kind of problem also concerns apathy. Inattentiveness or apathy on the part of certain groups can complicate evaluation: if public personnel systems perform poorly, is it because chief executives and legislators fail to devote sufficient resources and attention to them, or is the failure due to internal systemic dysfunction?

This problem also appears in the form of values trivialization among large groups or large segments of the public, leading to relative apathy toward important values. Madonna earns much more than the president of the United States and the entire physics faculty at MIT. Such conditions illustrate a paradox of importance (the importance of being unimportant) and a paradox of fortune and failure (fame and fortune as failure).

Many people, including their devoted fans, would agree that some of the most generously funded and widely noted persons and activities in our society are not very important. Madonna, the Superbowl, and the Academy Awards are trivial in many senses; they actually derive their value from their unimportance — they are fun, not fundamental.

Thus elements of society ascribe great importance, in certain ways, to people and events that are quite unimportant in relation to major values. Conversely, some of the most important people and events receive little attention and money. This complicates the usefulness of popularity, fame, and financial well-being as indicators of successful performance. It also aggravates the problem of locating causation and rejecting alternatives. Should the members of the Senior Executive Service (SES) appear to perform poorly, do we attribute this to internal characteristics of the SES, or to external factors? (The latter would include the vastly higher levels of compensation available elsewhere, as well as the general squandering of resources on trivial figures and events.)

As an example of this sort of problem, we can point to an incident of the Carter administration, in which the press focused attention on a twenty-one-foot-long chart describing the steps required to fire a federal employee (Kettl, 1989). Before that chart was produced, administration officials had been having difficulty getting the media and the public to pay attention to civil service reform initiatives. Administration officials originally had advanced the reform initiative on a "good government" theme, but media coverage was sharply slanted toward the issue of firing incompetent and unproductive federal employees. The press evidently seized on the long chart because it appealed to reporters' desire to feel that they were attacking the shortcomings of the government and defending the citizenry. Reporters apparently also thought the story would appeal to readers and viewers who were normally apathetic about government administration. Thus important developments in a major reform initiative were influenced by an evaluative process that was disconnected from any carefully grounded evaluation of the problem. In addition, the evaluative process reflected the influ-

ence of the general public's and the media's apathy toward or
inattentiveness to important administrative issues. These developments also helped turn public discussion of the reform
toward a negative campaign against "government bureaucrats."

## The "It's Their Fault" Problem

Blaming is one of the great American pastimes. Various actors
have obvious incentives to blame various systems, institutions,
and organizations for problems that can be ascribed to them.
These blaming games have received much attention in the discussion of bureaucrat-bashing by the media, some academics,
presidents, and other political officials in recent decades. They
also receive attention in discussions of the decline of public confidence in institutions, including the government and its administrative branch (Lipset and Schneider, 1987; Katz, Gutek, Kahn,
and Barton, 1975), and in discussions of whether media coverage tends toward excessive negativism and criticism.

A generally hypercritical and negative context can complicate unbiased evaluation in a variety of ways. It can make
members of the target system defensive. It can create a problem of what might be called "free-floating perfectionism." Some
editorialists, print and electronic media reporters, and oversight
officials in government seem to feel responsible for finding something to criticize or question. Any apparent problem is attacked,
with little attention to placing it in a broader context or grounding it in clearly defined evaluation criteria and comparison levels.

## The "It's Not Their (or Our) Fault" Problem

Just as administrative systems, agencies, and institutions have
their critics, they also have their defenders. If a system appears
to perform poorly, the defenders often argue that the fault lies
outside the system. One of the most common complaints of federal managers is that they have too little authority to reward
and discipline their subordinates. Yet the federal personnel system has also had defenders, who have argued that it was not
impossible to fire or discipline a federal employee and that line

managers in agencies seize on this excuse for their own poor leadership.

## The Self-Promotion Problem

The defenders of a system, agency, or institution typically include its employees and other beneficiaries, who promote their self-interest in defending the system. By their very nature, political and administrative systems mobilize bias in their favor on the part of many employees and clients, who can then become sources of potentially biased evaluative information.

## The Politics Problem

Politics infuses government and its administrative systems, obviously, and contributes at least two general complications.

First, political responsiveness is one of the important values that the systems support, and it serves as a performance criterion in itself. Yet political responsiveness can conflict with other values and criteria, such as efficiency and professionalism. Experts point to various performance problems that may arise from arrangements that promote political responsiveness, such as presidential appointments of top agency officials (Ingraham, 1988). If political officials pursue political responsiveness in a bad or destructive way, they aggravate these problems. If the Senior Executive Service begins to show evidence of malfunction, or if members of it appear to perform poorly, then defenders may argue that the problems do not come from internal dysfunctions or from people within the system but rather reflect the improper use of political appointments by a particular presidential administration.

Second, the political context of administration is inherently contentious. Partisanship and ideology complicate attempts to evaluate administrative systems, even when systematic expert evaluations are conducted. Republicans in the Reagan administration wanted to abolish the Job Corps, even though its defenders pointed to a very favorable long-term analysis of the program by a highly credible evaluation research firm (Wholey, 1986).

*The Parts-and-Pieces Problem*

Various problems of fragmentation in turn lead to problems in aggregation, both in research and in practice. Complexity engenders specialization and reductionism, leading to fragmentation of research and practice. In research, we turn away from complex questions about the general performance of the administrative branch of government or of the public personnel system, and we concentrate on parts of the whole, such as evaluation of pay-for-performance programs. In practice, governments and public agencies vary among themselves in personnel procedures and other matters. Even reform initiatives tend to be specialized, with some focusing on a very limited aspect of the personnel system, or on the budgeting system, or on some other part of the whole (Downs and Larkey, 1986). Public personnel administration is itself only one part of the whole, as critics have pointed out. They argue that public personnel systems are often so isolated and restricted that it becomes difficult to evaluate aspects of them (such as civil service reform initiatives) because so many factors outside a personnel system may influence whether the reforms appear to succeed (Hastings and Beyna, 1986).

This fragmentation creates problems for aggregate or general evaluation. Typically, in a complex system, some parts may work well and some not so well, and this complicates general conclusions about the system's performance. At the federal level, as more authority over personnel has been transferred from the central personnel agency to other agencies, variation among agencies in personnel practices has increased. This makes it harder to draw general conclusions and to evaluate the performance of various parts of the personnel system. If some line agencies have poor personnel procedures, how much does this reflect on the performance of the Office of Personnel Management? Moreover, fragmentation increases the difficulty of mounting comprehensive strategies and reform efforts.

*Avoiding Pessimism*

This listing of difficulties suggests that performance evaluation and enhancement, for such complex systems as public personnel systems, necessarily comes at a high price. The litany also suggests the need for comprehensive approaches and the potential dangers of partial solutions.

One very important point about these complications is that they can obscure effective as much as ineffective performance. Various forms of evidence suggest the likelihood that performance of administrative systems in the United States, including public personnel systems, is relatively successful. A great deal of performance monitoring goes on in government, and agencies collect a profusion of performance indicators (U.S. General Accounting Office, 1992). The positive effects of such efforts are difficult to demonstrate explicitly but are suggested by comparisons with systems in other countries, in past periods, in special studies, and even in the private sector in the United States (Downs and Larkey, 1986; Fried, 1976). Thus, in a more positive sense, the review of problems can serve as a challenge to seek more careful and comprehensive evaluations and reform. The key evaluative questions driving past reforms (for example, whether federal managers' pay is based on her or his performance) have often been sharply limited questions or even the wrong questions.

## Developments in Organization Theory, with Implications for Administrative Performance

One way to pursue this challenge is to examine the literature in organization and management theory on the topics pertaining most directly to performance. In some ways, the following review echoes the foregoing list of problems, but it also illustrates ways in which organization and management theorists have responded to them. Some of those responses, of course, are at odds with trends in public personnel administration and its reform.

### Organizational Effectiveness

Organization theorists have developed an elaborate body of research on organizational effectiveness. These researchers have shown that for all organizations, not just public and nonprofit organizations, effectiveness criteria tend to be multiple, diverse, conflicting, often controversial, and often hard to measure. These researchers have also produced a number of different models of organizational effectiveness. Organization analysts have also produced lists of effectiveness criteria and developed measures of them. These lists and measures indicate that we can indeed assess organizational effectiveness, although to do so with any validity requires extensive resources and care. Moreover, they have also shown that we have no conclusive, universally accepted profile of the effective organization. Rather, organizations, even within the same industry or functional domain, vary widely among themselves (and within themselves, over their life cycles) in the profiles of effectiveness that they pursue.

*The Goal Model*

Illustrative of the complexities that organization theorists have encountered in assessing effectiveness, the goal model of effectiveness served as the earliest candidate for most popular or accepted model. By definition, organizations pursue goals; one only needs to determine those goals and assess the organization's attainment of them.

Organizations have many goals, however, at varying levels of generality and in complex means-ends relations. Tables 5.1 and 5.2 provide examples of effectiveness criteria and illustrate the many criteria required to represent the goals of organizations. Determining all the various important goals and how to measure or assess them presents a major challenge. In addition, different members of an organization, as well as external groups and actors, often differ sharply over the most important goals. For example, labor may differ from management, and different groups of managers or professionals may struggle over which goals should dominate.

*Systems-Resource Models*

In part to avoid the complexities that the goal models encountered, other researchers developed systems-resource models (Yuchtman and Seashore, 1967; Molnar and Rogers, 1976).

Table 5.1. Effectiveness Dimensions for Educational Institutions.

| Perceptual Measures | Objective Measures |
|---|---|
| 1. Student educational satisfaction | |
| Student dissatisfaction | Number of terminations |
| Student complaints | Counseling-center visits |
| 2. Student academic development | |
| Extra work and study | Percentage going on to graduate |
| Amount of academic development | school |
| 3. Student career development | |
| Number employed in major field | Number receiving career counseling |
| Number of career-oriented courses | |
| 4. Student personal development | |
| Opportunities for personal | Number of extracurricular activities |
| development | Number in extramurals and |
| Emphasis on nonacademic | intramurals |
| development | |
| 5. Faculty and administrators' employment satisfaction | |
| Faculty and administrators' satisfac- | Number of faculty members and |
| tion with school and employment | administrators leaving |
| 6. Professional development and quality of the faculty | |
| Faculty publications, awards, | Percentage of faculty with doctorates |
| conference attendance | Number of new courses |
| Teaching at the cutting edge | |
| 7. System openness and community interaction | |
| Employee community service | Number of continuing education |
| Emphasis on community relations | courses |
| 8. Ability to acquire resources | |
| National reputation of faculty | General funds raised |
| Drawing power for students | Previously tenured faculty hired |
| Drawing power for faculty | |
| 9. Organizational health | |
| Student-faculty relations | |
| Typical communication type | |
| Levels of trust | |
| Cooperative environment | |
| Use of talents and expertise | |

Source: Adapted from Cameron, 1978.

Table 5.2. Organizational Effectiveness Dimensions and Measures.

| | |
|---|---|
| 1. Overall effectiveness | 16. Planning and goal setting |
| 2. Productivity | 17. Goal consensus |
| 3. Efficiency | 18. Internalization of organizational goals |
| 4. Profit | 19. Role and norm congruence |
| 5. Quality | 20. Managerial interpersonal skills |
| 6. Accidents | 21. Managerial task skills |
| 7. Growth | 22. Information management and communication |
| 8. Absenteeism | 23. Readiness |
| 9. Turnover | 24. Utilization of environment |
| 10. Job satisfaction | 25. Evaluations by external entities |
| 11. Motivation | 26. Stability |
| 12. Morale | 27. Value of human resources |
| 13. Control | 28. Participation and shared influence |
| 14. Conflict/cohesion | 29. Training and development emphasis |
| 15. Flexibility/adaptation | 30. Achievement emphasis |

Source: Campbell, 1977. Used by permission.

These approaches concentrated on whether an organization could attain from its environment the valuable resources necessary to sustain itself. The researchers examined such criteria as business volume, market penetration, and youthfulness of members. In applying such a model to public agencies, Molnar and Rogers (1976) have assessed the degree to which the agencies attained needed resources from other agencies. The systems-resource perspective, however, does not directly assess the internal utilization of those resources (Daft, 1992) and begs many important questions about the designation and attainment of important goals.

*Internal Process Models*

Other approaches rely on a similar assumption: that the attainment of certain organizational conditions leads to effective goal attainment. Some of these models developed out of the human relations school in the organizational literature. Authors in this school argued the importance of interpersonal trust, teamwork, uninhibited communication, participative decision making, and opportunities for personal growth and development. Accordingly, one assesses effectiveness by determining the degree to which organizations attain such conditions.

These models do not directly assess goal achievement or effective relations with the external environment. Critics further question whether the existence of warm human relations or efficient internal operations necessarily leads to effectiveness. Thus these models, too, have their limits and take their buffeting from critics. (The human relations approaches have strong similarities and connections to some prominent recent arguments about the importance of managing culture in the pursuit of excellence.)

*Stakeholder or Constituency Approaches*

Stakeholder or multiple-constituency approaches respond to a problem mentioned earlier, concerning the multiple parties and interests that seek to influence an organization's goals. For a business firm, a typical listing of stakeholders would include owners, employees, customers, creditors, the community, suppliers, and government. Researchers using these approaches determine the effectiveness criteria important to the organization's stakeholders — for owners, financial return; for employees, pay and effective supervision — and assess stakeholders' satisfaction with the fulfillment of those criteria.

The abbreviated listing of criteria for educational institutions in Table 5.2 contains elements of a constituency approach in that it examines student, faculty, and community concerns. Tusi (1990) has also applied such an approach to human resources agencies. The constituency approach has been gaining popularity because researchers feel that satisfying stakeholders reflects on important dimensions of effectiveness, and organizational members seriously care about their reputations and relations with stakeholders. In addition, researchers use this approach because of their increasing acceptance of the view that effectiveness is a complex, multidimensional concept that requires multiple, complex, and even conflicting measures (Daft, 1992). A problem arises from stakeholders' frequent inability to see eye to eye and from the displeasure of some of them over the pleasure of others. In pleasing some people, organizations often make others mad. How to sort out these disagreements and determine general effectiveness becomes a debatable question.

*The Competing-Values Approach*

Quinn and Rohrbaugh (1983) have developed another approach, which even more explicitly embraces the idea that one cannot eliminate value conflicts from conceptions of organizational effectiveness. Their competing-values approach holds that all organizations pursue multiple and conflicting values and must struggle with the trade-offs among them. These authors argue that the organization must try to achieve both flexibility and consistency. It must also find some balance between an external focus, involving search and surveillance of the external environment and its relations with elements of it, and an internal focus on its own conditions and processes.

Quinn and Rohrbaugh further contend that the extent to which an organization tilts toward one or the other extreme on these two continua depends on a number of factors, such as the organization's stage in its life cycle. For example, younger, smaller, more entrepreneurial organizations usually place a much stronger emphasis on external focus and flexibility than do older, more established, stabilized organizations. This conception of organizational performance contains an important implication: organizational effectiveness inherently involves a complex set of goals and values, many of which stand in mutual conflict. In addition, different organizations pursue different profiles of effectiveness. Thus the competing-values approach rejects the pursuit of a simple, conclusive model of effectiveness for all organizations.

The literature on organizational effectiveness has evolved toward models that emphasize the multidimensionality and conflicting nature of effectiveness criteria, and the existence of multiple profiles of effectiveness. This implies the desirability of diversity among organizations, a theme continued in the following section.

## Recent Developments in Topics Related to Effectiveness

Recent developments in the organization and management literature about such topics as strategic planning, leadership, organizational culture, and individual motivation — all advanced as means of enhancing organizational performance — have interesting implications for the role of public personnel administration. These implications are quite at odds with the orientation of contemporary public personnel administration, including the interest in major reform initiatives. As described at the outset of this chapter, public personnel administration has emphasized standardization and central control. These developments in organization theory stress the need to relax centralization and standardization, in response to such contingencies as uncertainty and complexity, which make it advantageous for an organization to vary from others with greater flexibility. In addition, some of the developments in organization theory stress the value of comprehensive approaches to administrative strategy, change, and effectiveness. This emphasis contrasts sharply with the tendency of public personnel administration to concentrate on personnel matters, in isolation from other dimensions of management and organization. It also contrasts with the tendency of public personnel reforms to concentrate on fragmented, limited aspects of organizations and even of their personnel systems. Thus, for those who seek improved personnel administration, recent developments in organization theory offer insights into major challenges.

*Strategic Planning*

A literature on strategic planning and decision making for public organizations has flourished in the last decade or so (see Bryson, 1988; Nutt and Backoff, 1992). Authors vary in their treatment of the topic, but a fairly typical approach exhorts the executive to appoint a strategic planning team. This team should intensively scan the agency's environment, analyzing threats and opportunities. The team should analyze organizational strengths and weaknesses and develop statements of goals, values, and mission. The team should then develop action plans for achieving the goals and fulfilling the mission, with accompanying plans for implementation and evaluation. Numerous federal, state, and local agencies have developed and published strategic plans.

Strategic planning implies the need for fairly high levels of organizational and executive autonomy. While strategic planning obviously is feasible in the public sector, the constraints of the governmental context, such as a central personnel agency emphasizing jurisdictionwide consistency in personnel rules and procedures, can impede such initiatives. Moreover, similar jurisdictionwide rules — for budgeting procedures, purchasing, financial management, and other functions — overseen by other central administrative agencies further strains the coherence of management functions in large public agencies. Some agency strategic plans say little about matters of personnel administration, although they often mention the motivation of personnel (U.S. Department of Health and Human Services, 1988; U.S. Department of the Treasury, 1984).

This tendency reflects the exclusion of personnelists bemoaned by advocates of strategic human resources management. Just as important, it may also represent ineffectual strategic planning. Writers on strategic change often emphasize the crucial role of comprehensiveness. Tichy (1983), for example, argues that successful strategic change requires coordinated planning and change in all major components of the organization, including the personnel or human resources component. Central personnel agencies applying jurisdictionwide rules and procedures should tend to make it more difficult for strategic planners to incorporate the human resources component into strategic planning and change. For example, some federal scientists considered their peer-review personnel evaluation procedures very effective but gave them up for other, standardized procedures because not to have done so would have made them ineligible for performance bonuses under the standardized system (Sherwood-Fabre, 1986). Some of these units and groups have since asked to be removed from the central jurisdiction, thus indicating that the standardized approach did not work. This situation provides an illustration of the potential conflicts when an agency, in a serious effort at strategic resource management, wants to depart from standard programs or procedures implemented by central personnel agencies.

But weakening the central personnel agency can also impede comprehensive approaches at higher levels, from the perspective of chief executives, legislators, and other oversight officials. From the perspective of the strategic management literature, the problem is not just stimulating more strategic human resources management but also integrating it with other strategic initiatives. Moreover, in the governmental context, this challenge not only perpetuates but also aggravates the longstanding problem of finding the proper balance between agency autonomy and the authority of oversight agencies.

### *Leadership, Organizational Culture, and Empowerment*

In organization and management theory, research and writing on leadership has increasingly touted the effectiveness of transformational leadership or such related orientation as charismatic leadership. Authors vary in their depictions, but they describe the transformational leader as one who motivates exceptional performance and transforms people and organizations (Bass, 1985; Bennis and Nanus, 1985). Such a leader differs from a transactional leader, who emphasizes exchanges with followers and trades benefits for support. A transformational leader leads through the development of a vision and a mission that concentrates attention on a desirable future state to be attained. The leader also invokes important values in an uplifting way, stimulating followers' commitment to common purposes and higher-order values. Transformational leaders stimulate such commitment through their own consistent and reliable commitment. Such leaders invest heavily in their subordinates, engaging them in stimulating and mutual developmental initiatives. In the process, they empower the people around them. Thus they motivate more through shared commitment, loyalty, and individual stimulation than through direct exchange of rewards for specific contributions.

A related and rapidly developing body of research calls on leaders to attend carefully to the cultures of their organizations (Trice and Beyer, 1993; Schein, 1992). Culture includes the shared beliefs and values that guide interpretation and behavior in the organization. Organizational myths, symbols, stories, jokes, procedures, ceremonies, and language, among other

features, express and maintain the culture. Leaders can influence
the culture of the organization through their influence over such
forms and channels of culture and through their own statements,
behavior, and symbolic actions. They can also influence the culture through the development and communication of a vision,
statements of mission, and statements of major values.

Among many other contributions to the rise of this topic,
Peters and Waterman's *In Search of Excellence* (1982) has been very
important. They report that managers in the "excellent" corporations they observed devote much attention to managing organizational culture. The corporations do not emphasize close links
between rewards and productivity as heavily as one might expect. Rather, according to Peters and Waterman, the "excellent" corporations often seek to enhance general motivation and
commitment through the development of a culture of excellence
and innovation. They emphasize empowerment, entrepreneurial behavior, risk taking, and commitment to missions and
values. Rather than emphasizing rewards for the most productive and punishment for the unproductive, these corporations
seek to motivate extraordinary results from ordinary people. As
this description suggests, the literature on leadership, culture,
mission, vision, empowerment, and related themes indicates an
imperative for integration and comprehensiveness. All these
aspects must complement and support one another.

These themes and approaches certainly can be applied
to the public sector. Governmental executives have provided
some truly significant examples of innovative leadership and
fostering of organizational culture (Doig and Hargrove, 1987).
For a long time, writers on governmental agencies have noted
their distinctive cultures (Wilson, 1989). Agencies have issued
a profusion of mission statements and value statements, and
governmental executives have admired the Peters and Waterman book and sought to apply its ideas. *Empowerment* has become a virtual buzzword in public and private management.

Nevertheless, as already mentioned, these recent themes
in organization and management theory and practice have features that appear inconsistent with tendencies of public personnel administration, including some of the reforms aimed at im-

proving it. These recent themes imply the need for relatively high levels of leadership stability, consistency, and autonomy. They also imply the desirability of considerable diversity and variation among organizations. They prescribe flexibility and support for risk taking and entrepreneurial behavior. Agencies and their executives will require considerable autonomy from centralizing and standardizing pressures if they are to tailor their cultures, missions, and visions and empower individuals in the ways they see fit. They will also need to strive for integration and comprehensiveness and will have to weave these themes and initiatives together.

These implications contain particular challenges for public personnel systems. Can they allow and promote even further variation and autonomy among agencies yet still enhance the role of personnel administration as a contributor to internal integration and comprehensiveness? It is quite significant in this regard that some innovative agency executives have sparked controversy and criticism over their power-mongering (Doig and Hargrove, 1987; Lambright, 1993; Lewis, 1980); some writers on agency culture have bemoaned it as an obstacle to innovation and external accountability.

## Individual Motivation

The challenge of enhancing individual motivation further illustrates these conflicting imperatives. As mentioned, some recent trends in organizational theory imply a different motivational pattern from the exchange- or transaction-based patterns that have often predominated in discussions of motivation in the civil service and in the reform of civil service incentive systems. Researchers and organization analysts have developed an elaborate body of theory on motivation, but this work is distinct from the motivational themes of some of the approaches already described in that it analyzes motivation specifically as its primary focus. Here, too, one finds trends and themes that raise similar issues for public personnel administration.

Two decades ago, the most prominent models of motivation included more transaction- or exchange-based approaches.

The expectancy theory of motivation concentrated on the expectations of rewards for performance. Operant conditioning, or behavior modification, concentrated on shaping behavior through reinforcements. The limited empirical success of such models in predicting motivation sent theorists back to their drawing boards. More recent attempts to model the factors that influence motivation have moved toward more integration and comprehensiveness in incorporating concepts from different models (Klein, 1989; Klein, 1990; Pinder, 1984). For example, in addition to reward expectancies, they attempt to incorporate from other bodies of theory perceptions of self-efficacy and self-esteem that can be influenced by job design, leadership, and other factors. They seek to incorporate elements of social learning theory, which have taken issue with models of operant conditioning and superseded them. These social learning–based theories recognize the behavioral influences of factors other than direct external reward and exchange, factors like vicarious learning, learning through observation, anticipatory learning, and self-reward.

These research trends further illustrate the challenges for public personnel administration in that they call for more comprehensive, integrative analyses of motivation. As critics have pointed out, personnel reforms have recently concentrated on the more narrow exchange-based models. Much of the energy in personnel reform has been channeled into pay-for-performance schemes or into more general programs that have pay-for-performance provisions as the central feature. For example, the Performance Management and Recognition System (PMRS) drew on a narrow conception of performance management that heavily emphasized the tying of pay raises to evaluations by a superior.

Even where there is greater decentralization of personnel responsibilities, such as at the federal level in the United States, the residual role for the Office of Personnel Management appears to involve evaluating and inspecting agencies to determine the presence of such procedures and then fostering model programs. Decentralization has often merely taken the form of decentralizing the maintenance of standardized procedures, with continuing central oversight of those procedures.

The objectives include enhancing the contribution of human resources management to the accomplishment of agency missions, but federal employees perceive little progress toward this objective so far (U.S. Merit Systems Protection Board, 1992).

It appears that the long-standing conflict between centralization and standardization of personnel systems, on the one hand, and decentralization to allow for variation, diversity, and autonomy, on the other, is being perpetuated and made even more complicated. The conflicting imperatives of providing for autonomy and variation while seeking to achieve serious involvement of personnel administrators makes striking a balance still more challenging.

## References

Bass, B. M. *Leadership and Performance Beyond Expectations.* New York: Free Press, 1985.

Bennis, W., and Nanus, B. *Leaders: The Strategies for Taking Charge.* New York: HarperCollins, 1985.

Bryson, J. M. *Strategic Planning for Public and Nonprofit Organizations: A Guide to Strengthening and Sustaining Organizational Achievement.* San Francisco: Jossey-Bass, 1988.

Cameron, K. "Measuring Organizational Effectiveness in Institutions of Higher Education." *Administrative Science Quarterly,* 1978, *23,* 604–632.

Campbell, J. P. "On the Nature of Organizational Effectiveness." In P. S. Goodman, J. Pennings, and Associates, *New Perspectives on Organizational Effectiveness.* San Francisco: Jossey-Bass, 1977.

Carroll, P. B. "The Failures of Central Planning—at IBM." *Wall Street Journal,* Jan. 28, 1993, p. A14.

Daft, R. L. *Organization Theory and Design.* St. Paul, Minn.: West, 1992.

Doig, J. W., and Hargrove, E. C. (eds.). *Leadership and Innovation.* Baltimore, Md.: Johns Hopkins University Press, 1987.

Downs, G. W., and Larkey, P. D. *The Search for Government Efficiency: From Hubris to Helplessness.* New York: Random House, 1986.

Fried, R. C. *Performance in American Bureaucracy.* Boston: Little, Brown, 1976.

Goodsell, C. *The Case for Bureaucracy.* Chatham, N.J.: Chatham House, 1985.

Hastings, A. H., and Beyna, L. S. "Managing for Improved Performance: Evaluating the Civil Service Reform Act." In J. S. Wholey, M. A. Abramson, and C. Bellavita (eds.), *Performance and Credibility: Developing Excellence in Public and Nonprofit Organizations.* Lexington, Mass.: Lexington Books, 1986.

Ingraham, P. W. "Transition and Policy Change in Washington." *Public Productivity Review,* 1988, *12,* 61–72.

Ingraham, P. W., and Rosenbloom, D. H. "The New Public Personnel and the New Public Service." *Public Administration Review,* 1989, *49,* 116–126.

Katz, D., Gutek, B. A., Kahn, R. L., and Barton, E. *Bureaucratic Encounters: A Pilot Study in the Evaluation of Government Services.* Ann Arbor: Survey Research Center, Institute for Social Research, University of Michigan, 1975.

Kennedy, P. *The Rise and Fall of the Great Powers.* New York: Random House, 1987.

Kettl, D. F. "The Image of the Public Service in the Media." In The Volcker Commission (ed.), *Leadership for America.* Lexington, Mass.: Heath, 1989.

Klein, H. J. "An Integrated Control Theory Model of Work Motivation." *Academy of Management Review,* 1989, *14,* 150–172.

Klein, J. I. "Feasibility Theory: A Resource-Munificence Model of Work Motivation and Behavior." *Academy of Management Review,* 1990, *15,* 646–665.

Lambright, W. H. "James E. Webb: A Dominant Force in 20th Century Public Administration." *Public Administration Review,* 1993, *53,* 95–99.

Lee, R. D., Jr. *Public Personnel Systems.* Rockville, Md.: Aspen, 1987.

Lewis, E. B. *Public Entrepreneurship.* Bloomington: Indiana University Press, 1980.

Lipset, S. M., and Schneider, W. *The Confidence Gap: Business, Labor, and Government in the Public Mind.* Baltimore, Md.: Johns Hopkins University Press, 1987.

Milward, H. B., and Rainey, H. G. "Don't Blame the Bureaucracy." *Journal of Public Policy*, 1983, *3*, 149–168.

Molnar, J. J., and Rogers, D. L. "Organizational Effectiveness: An Empirical Comparison of the Goal and System Resource Approaches." *Sociological Quarterly*, 1976, *17*, 401–413.

Nau, H. R. *The Myth of America's Decline.* New York: Oxford University Press, 1980.

Nutt, P. C., and Backoff, R. W. *Strategic Management of Public and Third Sector Organizations: A Handbook for Leaders.* San Francisco: Jossey-Bass, 1992.

Peters, T. J., and Waterman, R. H., Jr. *In Search of Excellence: Lessons from America's Best-Run Companies.* New York: Harper-Collins, 1982.

Pinder, C. *Work Motivation.* Glenview, Ill.: Scott, Foresman, 1984.

Quinn, R. E., and Rohrbaugh, J. "A Spatial Model of Effectiveness Criteria: Towards a Competing-Values Approach to Organizational Analysis." *Management Science*, 1983, *29*, 363–377.

Sampson, C. L. "Professional Roles and Perceptions of the Public Personnel Function." *Public Administration Review*, 1993, *53*, 154–160.

Schein, E. H. *Organizational Culture and Leadership.* (2nd ed.) San Francisco: Jossey-Bass, 1992.

Sherwood-Fabre, L. "Achieving Federal Reform." In J. S. Wholey, M. A. Abramson, and C. Bellavita (eds.), *Performance and Credibility: Developing Excellence in Public and Nonprofit Organizations.* Lexington, Mass.: Lexington Books, 1986.

Tichy, N. M. *Managing Strategic Change.* New York: Wiley, 1983.

Trice, H. M., and Beyer, J. M. *The Cultures of Work Organizations.* Englewood Cliffs, N.J.: Prentice-Hall, 1993.

Tusi, A. S. "A Multiple Constituency Model of Effectiveness: An Empirical Examination at the Human Resource Subunit Level." *Administrative Science Quarterly*, 1990, *35*, 458–483.

U.S. Department of Health and Human Services, Social Security Administration, Office of Strategic Planning. *2000: A Strategic Plan.* Washington, D.C.: U.S. Department of Health and Human Services, 1988.

U.S. Department of the Treasury, Internal Revenue Service.

*Internal Revenue Service Strategic Plan.* IRS Document 6941. Washington, D.C.: U.S. Department of the Treasury, 1984.

U.S. General Accounting Office. *Program Performance Measures: Federal Agency Collection and Use of Performance Data.* GAO/GGD-92-65. Washington, D.C.: U.S. General Accounting Office, 1992.

U.S. Merit Systems Protection Board. *Civil Service Evaluation: The Role of the U.S. Office of Personnel Management.* Washington, D.C.: U.S. Merit Systems Protection Board, 1992.

Wamsley, G. L., and others. *Refounding Public Administration.* Newbury Park, Calif.: Sage, 1990.

Wholey, J. S. "The Job Corps: Congressional Uses of Evaluation Findings." In J. S. Wholey, M. A. Abramson, and C. Bellavita (eds.), *Performance and Credibility: Developing Excellence in Public and Nonprofit Organizations.* Lexington, Mass.: Lexington Books, 1986.

Wilson, J. Q. *Bureaucracy: What Government Agencies Do and Why They Do It.* New York: Basic Books, 1989.

Yuchtman, E., and Seashore, S. E. "A System Resource Approach to Organizational Effectiveness." *American Sociological Review,* 1967, *32,* 891–903.

# PART TWO

## *Managing Change Effectively in Public Organizations*

The chapters in Part One examined the changing nature of government work and the extent to which seeking solutions to uncertain problems has become central to many organizational tasks. The five chapters in this section look more closely at the managerial implications of these issues. For many years, it was possible and even realistic to view public managers as administrators — that is, as managers whose primary function was the interpretation and application of voluminous rules and regulations. Contemporary reforms — and, most certainly, the "reinventing government" initiatives — move far beyond that view of public management. The responsibilities of public managers are redefined, as are the skills they must bring to the organization. High on the list of new skills and abilities is the capacity to act in a more flexible way, both inside the organization and in its political environment.

In Chapter Six, Rosenbloom and Ross take a fresh look at the remarkable interrelationship between the political environment and the daily activities of governance and management. They argue that separating politics and administration is a result of executive hegemony, one that misrepresents both the reality of public management and the role of Congress as a major actor in the political environment of public organizations.

O'Leary, in Chapter Seven, analyzes the role of another environmental actor: the courts. Her analysis differs from that of Cooper (Chapter Four) in specifically addressing the constraints that judicial decisions place on daily management activities and the ability to plan for future activities. She notes further that the public manager is no longer primarily a manager but rather a boundary spanner, in the truest sense of that term.

Perry's analysis (Chapter Eight) of the increasingly tenuous relationship between public employees and the organizations that employ them carries the implications of the first two chapters in this section to another level. He notes that while environmental influences have become more complex, employees' relationships with their organizations have become more diverse. When political executives and public managers respond to political demands for increased productivity and accountability, they do so in expedient, symbolic ways. The results, Perry argues, are short-lived, failed solutions. Managing ill-conceived solutions, and causing them to be effective whenever possible, are practical realities of contemporary public management. Public organizations do not operate with a clean slate; they deal both internally and externally with the problems of past reform efforts. Yet, as Perry observes, we have learned remarkably little.

Sanders examines the Senior Executive Service in Chapter Nine. The Senior Executive Service (SES) was intended as a flexible cadre of expert executives who would play an advising, leadership, and management role in governance and government. It has not lived up to its advance billing. Sanders notes that one reason is the "theory" of the SES, which is decidedly at odds with the practical realities of public management. He says that the complexities of managing in the contemporary public environment mandate an "artful blending" of public administration and purposive political advocacy. This mandate must be recognized and accepted if the executives in the Senior Executive Service are to lead and manage effectively.

In Chapter Ten, Wise describes the intricate relationship among public management, public organizations, and governance in another way. Her examination of the role of internal labor markets illustrates the important transitions that are occurring in and for public organizations. Equally important, Wise describes the extent to which the public sector must serve as a model for the rest of society in dealing equitably and effectively with the new labor pools.

In combination, the chapters in Part Two illustrate two important points about effective management and managers: they maintain a delicate balance among competing demands from the organization's environment, and they must also balance the needs of their employees and organizations with those of political and judicial actors whose values and perspectives are quite different from those of the organization. *Reinvention* in this context must mean freeing public managers from these conflicting constraints, as well as providing them with new flexibilities and discretion.

# 6

# Administrative Theory, Political Power, and Government Reform

*David H. Rosenbloom*
*Bernard H. Ross*

Waldo (1948) argues that there can be no comprehensive public administrative theory that is not also a political theory. A variety of works came to support his conclusion, by showing that the core functions of public administration are laden with political questions: decision making (Lindblom, 1959), budgeting (Wildavsky, 1964), organization (Seidman, 1970), personnel (Rosenbloom, 1973; Shafritz, 1975), and implementation (Pressman and Wildavsky, 1973). Failure to note the Waldo theorem is fatal for those seeking to reform government, although reformers and academic advocates of change frequently ignore that lesson. This chapter argues that, historically, there has been a politics of prescriptive administrative theory, and that such theory has often served to enlarge the power of political movements, the presidency, and/or Congress. In some respects, therefore, orthodox public administrative theory has been the political

145

ideology of dominant political groups or of political institutions. (By *orthodox,* we mean the dominant prescriptive theory of a period; the Orthodoxy of the period 1900–1939 was one such orthodoxy.) Current efforts at "reinventing" government (Osborne and Gaebler, 1992) also appear to be an example of political moods and institutions dominating ideas (Goodsell, 1993). Developing market-based public administration at the federal level, however, raises a number of critical issues and faces substantial institutional barriers (Lan and Rosenbloom, 1992). This chapter cautions that academic public administration should devote far more attention to understanding both administrative history and the intellectual history of public administrative thought, in order to strengthen academic public administration's ability to evaluate and understand programs for administrative reform. (In our view, the federal civil service reform of 1978 is an example of a failure that was broadly supported by academic public administration; see Ingraham and Rosenbloom, 1992.)

## The "Prehistory" of American Public Administration

Stillman (1991) may overstate the extent to which the United States was "stateless" throughout the nineteenth century. It is clear, however, that the civilian *administrative* state reached fledgling status only in the 1880s (Skowronek, 1982). Nevertheless, earliest public administrative doctrine was an outgrowth of political dominance. Before 1829, the Federalists and the Jeffersonians treated public administration as an extension of the social elite that dominated American politics at the federal level. As White (1965a) has shown, the basic rules of personnel were those suitable for the treatment of "gentlemen." Selection was from the upper social class, and dismissal was rare. Despite the Decision of 1789 and the Tenure of Office Act of 1820, office was conceptualized essentially as a form of property (Rosenbloom, 1971). In some instances, it was passed down in families. Aronson (1964) found kinship among upper-level appointees to be so pronounced that it would be only a small stretch to say that, in practical terms, the government was owned by the governing class. There were no widespread dismissals accompanying presidential transitions. In fact, President Monroe indicated that he regretted signing the Tenure of Office Act, and neither he nor John Adams implemented it (see Rosenbloom, 1971).

The "Jacksonian Revolution" was fully cognizant of the links between public administration and political dominance. As a field of study, contemporary public administration has reflected the biases of the civil service reform and Progressive movements of the late nineteenth and early twentieth centuries. It has dismissed Jacksonian administration as excess. But contemporary reformers will be sympathetic to Jackson's claims that patterns of recruitment and retention "placed or continued power in unfaithful or incompetent hands" (Richardson, 1896, p. 438), and that, given the primacy of self-interest, "there are, perhaps, few men who can for any great length of time enjoy office and power without being more or less under the influence of feelings unfavorable to the faithful discharge of their public duties" (pp. 448–449). Jackson also advocated what we would now call *diversity:* "Let it be known that any class or portion of citizens are and ought to be proscribed [from holding public office] and discontent and dissatisfaction will be engendered" (Jackson, 1926, p. 32). Jacksonian implementation of these democratic administrative values was highly imperfect. The values eventually became difficult to defend, and they were eclipsed by the civil service reform and Progressive movements.

### The Politics of the Politics-Administration Dichotomy

The idea that public administration can be separated from politics is odd. It was not present at the founding, but later, of course, it became the cornerstone of the public administrative Orthodoxy. It continues to define a good deal of administrative thought, including Osborne and Gaebler's "entrepreneurial" government, in which "steering" is conceptually separate from "rowing" (Osborne and Gaebler, 1992). There is a very stark contrast between the founders' view, as articulated by Alexander Hamilton in *Federalist* no. 72, and the perspective put forth by Woodrow Wilson in "The Study of Administration." According to Hamilton, "The Administration of Government, in its largest sense, comprehends all the operations of the body politic, whether legislative, executive, or judiciary" (Publius, 1961, p. 435). According to Wilson, "The field of administration is a field of business. . . . It is part of political life only as the methods of the counting-house are a part of the life of the society. . . . [A]dministrative questions are not political questions" (Wilson, [1887] 1941, pp. 493–494).

The Wilsonian view is intellectually and governmentally untenable. Wilson himself was unable to sustain it. His essay is filled with contradictions regarding the role of public opinion in public administration and public administration's relationship to constitutional design; in our view, the essay is more instructive for the way in which Wilson wrestled with the contradictions than for his assertions and conclusions. Yet the politics-administration dichotomy has pervaded American public administrative thought, and it continues to be deeply ingrained in American political culture. Why? In part, it is a convenient approach to attempting to retrofit the modern administrative state to our eighteenth-century constitution. Nations with more recent foundings or constitutional change have been able to design their political and administrative arrangements as part of a unified system. In the United States, local governments and, to a lesser extent, state governments have had opportunities to integrate politics and administration comprehensively, but the national government has not. But the grip of the politics-administration dichotomy in America is also due to its relationship to political power.

The politics-administration dichotomy was *installed* in American government and political culture by the Progressive movement. Although their strength varied from place to place, the Progressives were for a time the dominant force in American politics. Their strength was particularly felt at the local governmental level. Adherents included Presidents Theodore Roosevelt and Woodrow Wilson. Administrative reforms at all levels encompassed civil service merit systems, position classification, political neutrality, the development of city management, "rationalization" of budgets through municipal research bureaus, efforts to use "scientific management," and widespread reliance on independent administrative authorities (Doig, 1984) and bipartisan independent regulatory commissions. Concomitantly, the Sixteenth Amendment, which provided for a federal income tax, made it far easier for the federal government to pay for its administrative growth.

Initially, the idea that governmental administration could and should be apolitical was widely opposed by entrenched politicians and their followers. Opponents wondered how apolitical administrations could be responsive to the people and be representative. Wilson himself admitted (or touted) the fact that "civil service reform is . . . not democratic in idea" (Rohr, 1986, p. 231). By the mid-1920s, however, it was a staple of American administrative thought that "the study of administration should start from the base of management" and that public administration was an art being transformed into an applied science (White, 1926, pp. vii–viii; see also Storing, 1965).

The political power struggle underlying the politics-administration dichotomy has been largely ignored or somewhat misunderstood in mainstream public administrative thought. The field's foundations still lie in the reform movement. Along with Wilson, Goodnow (1900) was a most influential public administration scholar of the time; both men were strong advocates of the dichotomy. White's four-volume history of the federal service was not at all insensitive to the politics of administrative change (White, 1965a–d), nor was Van Riper's *History of the United States Civil Service* (1958). Mosher's more accessible and very popular *Democracy and the Public Service* (1982), however, presents the evolution of American civil service concepts as a mix of ideology and practice, in which the relationship between ideas and political developments is often murky at best. Note the following chapter subheads: "1829–83: Government by the Common Man"; "1883–1906: Government by the Good"; "1906–37: Government by the Efficient"; "1937–55: Government by Administrators." The referent of 1829 is Jackson's inauguration. By contrast, that of 1906 is the creation of the New York Bureau of Municipal Research, an event of little political import. The discussion of 1937–1955 does not even mention 1946 as

the year of the Administrative Procedure Act (APA), the Legislative Reorganization (including Tort Claims) Act, and the
Employment Act—three pieces of legislation that strongly coun-
tered the New Deal effort to make federal administration synony-
mous with the executive branch. Along with those who view
public administration as merely science or technology, driven
by ideas alone rather than by political power as well, Mosher
fails to develop coherently the perspective that public administration has been an expression of political power. (In saying this,
of course, we do not intend to detract from Mosher's magnificent
contributions to the field of public administration. His historical discussion was not intended as a substitute for or an alternative to White, 1965a–d, and Van Riper, 1958. In a sense,
it was "boilerplate" for Mosher's discussion of the contemporary
public service.)

Wilson and the other reformers were candid about their
political objectives. Their words speak for themselves. According to Eaton (1880), a civil service reformer who was instrumental in the drafting of the Pendleton Act of 1883, "We have seen
a class of politicians become powerful in high places, who have
not taken (and who by nature are not qualified to take) any large
part in the social and educational life of the people. Politics have
tended more and more to become a trade, or separate occupa-
tion. High character and capacity have become disassociated
from public life in the popular mind." Schurz, a government
official and civil service reformer, had this to say: "The question whether the Departments at Washington are managed well
or badly is, in proportion to the whole problem, an insignificant
question" (1913, p. 123). For Schurz, the purpose of reform is
"to restore ability, high character, and true public spirit once
more to their legitimate spheres in our public life, and to make
active politics once more attractive to men of self-respect and
high patriotic aspirations" (1893, p. 614). And, according to Wilson, the "character of the nation . . . is being most deeply affected
and modified by the enormous immigration which year after
year pours into the country from Europe. . . . We are unques-
tionably facing an ever-increasing difficulty of self-command with
ever-deteriorating materials, possibly with degenerating fibre"

(cited in Rohr, 1986, p. 72). "The only way in which we can preserve our nationality in its integrity and its old-time origina- tive force in the face of growth and imported change is by con- centrating it, putting leaders forward vested with abundant au- thority in the conception and execution of policy," Wilson goes on to say (Rohr, 1986, p. 231, note 61).

Hofstadter (1955, p. 9) refers to "the age of reform" as a clash between "two thoroughly different systems of political ethics." The politics-administration dichotomy was a tool in that struggle. Reformers were able to implement administrative changes in civil service procedures, electoral systems, and rep- resentative models at the local level. These changes, in the end, had a major impact on the political lives of local governments and residents therein.

## Perdurability of the Politics-Administration Dichotomy

There are many reasons why the politics-administration dicho- tomy developed a "perdurable" quality (Waldo, 1984). It be- came institutionalized in civil service systems and other aspects of government, ingrained in the political culture (Waldo, 1961), and viewed as essential to the development of a science of pub- lic administration that would yield the greatest efficiency (Gu- lick and Urwick, 1937). Even after the Orthodox public adminis- tration paradigm was shattered in the 1940s by Simon (1947), Dahl (1947), Waldo (1948), and Appleby (1949), the dichotomy continued to haunt administrative thinking. The widely noted slow-moving crises in American public administrative thought (Ostrom, 1974) are related to a failure to understand the im- pact of political dominance on administrative thought. As a body of thought and practice, public administration continues to over- state the extent to which it is concerned with execution and man- agement, rather than with the confluence of executive, legisla- tive, and judicial constitutional functions (Rosenbloom, 1993).

The politics-administration dichotomy served the interests of executive power. Executives claim independent responsibil- ity for efficient, economical, and effective management of admin-

istrative affairs. When the policies and programs of agencies in
the executive branch fail, blame for untoward political interference in administrative matters is likely to be laid on the door-
step of legislatures and the courts. Perhaps the most influential
example of linking the dichotomy with executive power was the
1937 President's Committee on Administrative Management
(the Brownlow Committee). As Rohr notes, "Applying the principles of scientific management, the committee drew a sharp distinction between policy and administration. This distinction
found its institutional embodiment in Congress, where policy
was made, and in the executive branch, where it was carried
out" (1986, p. 137). In Rohr's view, the committee's perspective was constitutionally flawed: "At the heart of the doctrine
is a fundamental error that transforms the president from chief
executive officer to sole executive officer" (p. 139). In the Brownlow Committee's words, the "canons of efficiency require the establishment of a responsible and effective chief executive as the
center of energy, direction, and administrative management"
(Mosher, 1976, p. 114). Mosher goes on to say, "Accountability is often obscured by Congress itself in imposing upon the
Executive in too great detail minute requirements for the organization and operation of the administrative machinery. . . . We
hold that once the Congress has made an appropriation which
it is free to withhold, the responsibility for the administration
of the expenditures under that appropriation is and should be
solely upon the Executive" (p. 133). In other words, a major
reason for the perdurability of the politics-administration dichotomy is that it supports expansive claims for executive autonomy and power. The dichotomy probably cannot survive where
executive power is under serious challenge. It is a doctrine of
executive domination.

## 1946

The institutional foundations for executive-centered federal administration were established in the late 1930s by the creation
of the Executive Office of the President and the Reorganization
Act of 1939. Congress responded in 1940, with the Walter-Logan

Act, which was successfully vetoed by President Roosevelt. The act was a highly restrictive forerunner of the APA. In Rohr's words, as opposed to allowing agencies to remain extensions of the presidency, it would have made "administrative agencies the wards of the courts" (1986, p. 165) by authorizing extensive judicial review of their activities. In 1946, Congress was more successful in establishing the legal and institutional bases for its contemporary role in federal administration. It enacted the four laws (mentioned earlier) of fundamental, even constitutional, import. The legislative history and purpose of these statutes is treated at greater length elsewhere (Rosenbloom, 1994). Here, it is necessary only to provide a brief summary of how these statutes redefined Congress's role with respect to federal administration.

The APA's rule-making provisions are a stark admission that, in practice, much lawmaking had already passed to the executive branch. Congress found the delegation of legislative power to administrative agencies to be a practical necessity. The Legislative Reorganization Act was intended to restructure Congress so that it could more effectively exercise "continuous watchfulness" over the agencies. It gave birth to the modern system of standing committees and subcommittees, and to a concomitant and increasing political importance of congressional staff members.

The Tort Claims Act, codified as Title IV of the Legislative Reorganization Act, was an open admission that the principal-agent relationship between Congress and the agencies had become attenuated. Previously, neither the principal nor the agent could be held liable for the same types of property damage or personal injuries that a private party might cause. Relief came in the form of private bills or not at all. This followed the common-law approach of *respondeat superior,* under which the principal (or master) was held to answer for the actions of the agents (or servants). The doctrine even made principals liable for "negligent hiring" of incompetents, under some circumstances. The hitch was that neither Congress nor the agencies could be sued because they had sovereign immunity under American common law and constitutional doctrine. Making agencies responsible for their torts was a tacit recognition that the bureaucracy had become so large and pervasively involved in the economy and society that Congress could no longer realistically be expected to redress its wrongs—or prevent them.

The Employment Act made the federal government responsible for promoting "maximum employment, production, [and] purchasing power." Its importance to public administration lay in the fact that much government pump-priming for these purposes would be through federal agencies. Critics correctly predicted that implementation would be "honey combed with political expediency" (Donnelly, 1945, p. 665). Turning pork-barrel politics into a virtuous national economic policy was no small achievement.

The significance of the legislation of 1946 was not lost on Louis Brownlow, a major architect of the modern presidency. In 1947, speaking language familiar to the contemporary ear, he issued the following warning:

> The next step which we the people should take to meet the needs of the Presidency is to persuade the Congress not to yield to the constant temptation to interfere with the administration of the Executive Branch by needlessly detailed requirements for procedures in the execution of the laws it enacts; procedures sometimes so hampering that they almost have the effect of defeating the very purpose for which the Congress has enacted the law. The President is under the Constitutional obligation to "take care that the Laws be faithfully executed," and if we mean to help the President to discharge this obligation we must be sure that his authority to do so is not usurped either by the Congress as a whole, by the House of Representatives or the Senate, and—most important of all—by particular committees of the Congress" [Brownlow, 1949, p. 116].

Correctly foreseeing the potential for micromanagement, however, was easier than gaining agreement that it was illegitimate or undesirable.

The year 1946 also gave birth (or impetus) to the subsystem politics so well analyzed by a number of political scientists (Lowi, 1969; Ripley and Franklin, 1976; Fiorina, 1977; Arnold, 1979). Perhaps Fiorina's description is most concise:

> The growth of an activist federal government has stimulated a change in the mix of congressional activities. Specifically, a lesser proportion of congressional effort is now going into programmatic activities [i.e., legislation and oversight] and a greater proportion into pork-barrel and casework activities. As a result, today's congressmen make relatively fewer enemies and relatively more friends among the people of their districts. . . . Congress does not just react to big government—it creates it. All of Washington prospers. More and more bureaucrats promulgate more and more regulations and dispense more and more money. Fewer and fewer congressmen suffer electoral defeat [Fiorina, 1977, pp. 46, 49].

Micromanagement has been used to political advantage, but it can also be a tool for legislative control of administrative policy making and implementation (Mayer, 1993). Consequently, under the constitutional scheme, it must be viewed, in principle, as a legitimate condition of public administration (protestations by advocates of greater presidential power notwithstanding). Herein lies a difficulty for public administrative theory and for the research informed by it.

The congressional view of public administration does not draw a dichotomy between politics and administration. Conceptually, the two are not really separate. Agencies are expected to make rules, which functionally are supplementary legislation. That being the case, the administrative process should not be left to experts in public management, dominated by a strong president and insulated from the people. The legislative history of the Freedom of Information Act (section 552 of the APA) presents a good example of the difference in outlooks. President Johnson thought Congress was trying to "screw" him with passage of the act; President Ford unsuccessfully vetoed the 1974 amendments that promoted disclosure. See Warren (1992, pp. 202–203).

But public administration is an intensely political process that should be responsive to interested publics and legislators. In consequence, the legislature and the bureaucracy will tend to merge in a political and institutional sense (Seidman, 1970; Ripley and Franklin, 1976; Arnold, 1979), as do special-interest groups and agencies (McConnell, 1966; Lowi, 1969; among others).

In passing, let us note that the parallel development of political science and public administrative thought regarding public bureaucracy in recent decades seems related to political scientists' greater attention to Congress and public administration's heavier emphasis on political and other executives. Although most would agree that bureaucracies are (or should be) agents, our impression is that political scientists are more apt than public administrationists to identify legislatures as the principals.

The Federal Advisory Committee Act of 1972 institutionalizes interest-group representation to a significant extent, as does the APA's formal rule-making provisions. Goodnow's effort (1900) to separate the expression of the people's will from the execution of it, and Osborne and Gaebler's distinction (1992) between "steering" and "rowing," are alien to the post-1946 legislative vision of public administration.

If public administration is viewed as a political process, rather than simply as a managerial one, then in the United States it will be guided by the values of responsiveness, representativeness, and external accountability, which are deeply ingrained in the political culture (Rosenbloom, 1983, 1993). As noted earlier, if it is viewed as an executive-centered, technical, scientific, and apolitical process, it will be guided by some calculation of cost-effectiveness. This difference is fundamentally related to public administration's intellectual and identity crises. After Pressman and Wildavsky (1973) "found" implementation, they were chided by Waldo (1980) for being like children claiming to have discovered a well-known venerable landmark. Nevertheless, the focus on implementation is a fruitful intellectual reconstruction of public administration precisely because it offers no distinction between politics and administration (Bardach, 1977). It moves public administrative thought away from a fixation with overhead institutions and processes, such as those concerned with civil service systems. Lipsky (1980), following the same intellectual path, virtually redefines the field's conceptualization of agencies that deliver services and apply constraints to the public. The focus on implementation also brought greater attention to policy design, and to the concept of the policy cycle. But conventional public administrative scholarship, which has wrestled with the dichotomy by way of either support or rejection, has found it difficult to embrace intellectual perspectives that find the distinction between politics and administration thoroughly irrelevant.

The intellectual impact of legislative-centered public administration has also been pronounced in terms of public choice and other market-based approaches that seek administrative responsiveness to the demands of private individuals and groups. Faith in the neutral expertise of Progressive administrators dissipates when they are considered policy makers (Herring, 1936), as does faith in overhead representative democracy when there are substantial gaps between legislation and implementation. Perhaps nowhere is the contrast greater than in public education. The Progressive public administrative legacy is the bureaucratized, politically insulated school system dominated (in theory) by experts in education and educational administrators, who claim to know what is best for the nation's children. Public choice argues that self-interested behavior in such a structure cannot be discounted and seeks to empower parents to propel the public educational system, through vouchers, magnet schools, and related marketlike mechanisms. Osborne and Gaebler (1992) deride such systems as built on a passé industrial model, which offers "one size fits all" goods and services.

The executive- and legislative-centered concepts of public administration are strongly clashing world views, whose "correctness" will depend ultimately on the political dominance of one or the other. As Dahl (1947) claims, lack of agreement on normative values would seem to doom the universal appeal of prescriptive theories of public administration. It is possible, of course, for prescriptive theorists to develop political support for their values. The civil service reformers and early Progressives did so. Advocates of "social equity" in public administration, such as Frederickson (1987), may yet be successful, although, in our view, those who treat that value as a legitimate guide to independent public administrative action are on very weak ground (Thompson, 1975). It certainly is not on the same plane as well-defined constitutional values. There is no tort of "breach of social equity," although public administrators can be sued personally for financial damages when they violate individuals' due-process rights or other constitutional rights in the course of their official actions (see Rosenbloom and Carroll, 1990).

### Divided Government

If the argument of this chapter holds so far, dominant prescriptive public administration is related to institutional power. It has been bound up with the separation of powers, which complicates administrative change at the federal and state levels more than in local government. Perhaps different visions of public administration are even more deeply embedded in liberalism itself, as Kravchuk (1992) contends. In either case, it is a necessary (if insufficient) condition for substantial administrative reform that executive-centered and legislative views of public administration not diverge so thoroughly. In this regard, divided government has compounded the challenge of developing a politically dominant vision of public administration. Since 1946, Presidents Truman, Eisenhower, Nixon, Ford, Reagan, and Bush have faced a Congress in which the opposition party dominated at least one house (Oleszek, 1991). After presidential and midterm congressional elections, the federal government was divided thirteen times from 1952 to 1992 and unified seven times (Fiorina, 1992). Although divided government was not uncommon in the past, it has been most pronounced since 1952. Moreover, "divided government is not a unique feature of U.S. national government; rather, it has become pervasive in state government as well" (Fiorina, 1991, p. 200). Under these conditions, the prospects for agreement on the desirability of executive-centered public administration are dim, as are those for a new orthodoxy of theory based on legislative public administration. What, then, are the prospects for "reinventing," "refounding" (Wamsley and others, 1990), or even "rebuilding" (National Commission on the Public Service, 1989) public administration in thought and practice?

## "Neopopulist" Public Administration?

Administrative ideas matter, even if they matter most as part of the ideology of a dominant political movement or coalition. As already noted, nineteenth-century civil service reform and the subsequent Progressive administrative reform are the most relevant examples. The reformers and Progressives' ideas eventually became widely enough accepted to be the basis for redesigning the American presidency in 1939. They were able to bridge political parties, institutions, and levels of government. Today, a number of administrative theories, including public choice–based and market-based (or "enterprise") public administration, have an underlying appeal for (and are partly a reflection of) a strong populist strand in American politics. This populism has supported the imposition of tax-and-expenditure limitations on state and local jurisdictions, as well as the imposition of balanced budgets and term limits for legislators. It rejects large-scale, centralized, seemingly ever-expanding public administration dominated by ostensibly politically neutral experts who claim to know what is best for society. It suspects government officials of being motivated by self-interest, and it seeks mechanisms for asserting the primacy of individual citizens' self-interest. It favors decentralization, public choice, deregulation, load shedding, privatization, user fees, and entrepreneurship. Its management doctrine emphasizes "customer service" (see Lan and Rosenbloom, 1992). Osborne and Gaebler's *Reinventing Government* (1992) is its *Common Sense* (Paine, [1776] 1922). At the federal level, efforts to institutionalize it are being led by the National Performance Review, headed by Vice President Albert Gore. Because "reinvented government" is potentially the ideology of a dominant political movement, it has the potential to forge a new orthodoxy. It is intellectually vulnerable—maybe almost vacuous (for example, see Goodsell, 1993)—but so is the Progressive notion that a city can be apolitically "managed."

Neopopulism also embodies a growing distrust of Congress, which tends to be seen as lacking the capacity to identify and solve problems cost-effectively. In view of the constitutional separation of powers and the usefulness of the politics-administration dichotomy to the executive branch, it is not surprising that the National Performance Review is seeking to reinvent federal administration while Congress is separately studying how best to reform itself. The same pattern has been occurring at the state and local levels. The neopopulist mood may well sense the futility of independently reforming two major parts of the same system. It is no wonder that Ross Perot's vow to "get under the hood" and fix the government resonated so strongly with so many voters in the presidential campaign of 1992.

In the federal government, at least, neopopulist and customer-driven public administration faces a substantial obstacle in legislative self-interest. "Reinvented" government would focus on results and customer satisfaction, rather than on processes. In a radical version, agencies would be allowed to manage and to budget and would be held strictly accountable for the results obtained. Process controls related to personnel and human resources management, procurement, and organizational design would be eliminated or severely relaxed. Such public administration would broadly threaten the congressional incumbency system (Fiorina, 1977) in three critical ways. First, legislation would have to be more specific regarding the substantive results desired. There is not likely to be much of a constituency for relaxing process controls while allowing administrators to define the very results for which they will be evaluated. Second, members of Congress would have to forgo much of their micromanagement—and the "pork" so frequently associated with it. Third, the elimination of process controls would reduce both red tape and the casework associated with it. Even if federal administration is reinvented, of course, Congress may manage to reinvent its leverage over the agencies.

## Critical Issues

The connection outlined here between prescriptive public administrative theory and political power raises several critical issues for researchers and would-be reformers. First, academic public administration, which has been in the thick of reform efforts, needs a better grasp of administrative history, the intellectual history of American public administration, and the relationships between ideas and power. In a vitriolic tome with a belligerent tone, Thompson (1975) warns the public administration community that it is in no position to substitute its own values for those of the public, as registered through representative political institutions. Academic public administration plays a valuable role by analyzing, theorizing, and sharing an understanding of administrative phenomena. It is on weaker ground when it advocates reforms that will have substantial political ramifications — especially if it fails to recognize and discuss them. It is on yet weaker ground when it advocates action based on values not strongly shared by the public, or on values that are very imperfectly articulated or understood. The cottage industry in "reinventing" — personnel, budgeting, training, and so forth — has developed largely without adequate discussion of political ramifications and values. Academic research on reform has sometimes been intertwined with advocacy (see Barzelay and Armajani, 1992).

Second, is contemporary public administrative education adequate? Much of it still reflects Progressive values and the politics-administration dichotomy. The term *public administration* seems old-fashioned and is frequently replaced with *public management*. But the latter term can be too narrowly construed (Rosenbloom, 1993). In addition to traditional administrative management and market-based approaches relying on economic analysis, master's degree programs in public administration need to provide students with a firm grounding in the history of their profession, in policy, and in law. These areas are not ignored by the recommended curriculum of the National Association of Schools of Public Affairs and Administration, but they may be underdeveloped. It would be useful for public administrators to know that much of the field's doctrine was developed for such political purposes as weakening political machines, lessening the political clout of immigrants, and enlarging executive power. Policy analysis and bureaucratic politics are important parts of the standard curriculum, but more attention probably should be paid to implementation and contract monitoring. The legal component should include constitutional law, administrative law, personnel and labor law, contracts, and procurement — at least insofar as they are clearly related to typical public administrative activities. Greater accountability to law would seem to go hand in hand with relaxation of traditional process controls. Because litigation is so expensive and cumbersome, a heavy emphasis should be placed on the resolution of disputes (see Fisher and Ury, 1983).

Third, market-based administrative reform raises issues of accountability. The removal of process controls can weaken accountability unless viable substitutes for them are found. Precisely how public administrators will be held accountable for results is not yet clear. Law does hold public administrators personally responsible and liable for knowable failures, and this is an important threshold (Rosenbloom and Carroll, 1990). But some of the jobs currently done by public employees are clearly without adequate support, definition, or gauges for identifying acceptable levels of success. Greater attention and resources will have to be devoted to training if employees are to be held personally responsible for results. Entrepreneurship implies risk. If seemingly rational administrative approaches fail, will those who designed them be punished? How? Who will define what is rational or irrational?

Finally, if public administrative reforms build an "enterprise culture" (Mascarenhas, 1993), and if citizens are expected to perform as customers, what will become of community (Etzioni, 1988)? Customers may not be good citizens. Encouraging Americans to become more self-regarding individuals may be a poor prescription for civic health. If one's fellow citizen is viewed, not as a member of a common civic union with the enlightened purposes spelled out in the Preamble to the Constitution, but rather as a potential free rider, then comity and cooperation may be put at greater risk.

The agenda may be far more complex than many academics realize because it is wrapped up with issues of political power, the character of the polity, and citizenship. Rethinking is a good idea; "reunderstanding" may be even better. Public administration will have much more to offer society when it understands itself far better.

## References

Appleby, P. *Policy and Administration.* University: University of Alabama Press, 1949.

Arnold, R. *Congress and the Bureaucracy.* New Haven, Conn.: Yale University Press, 1979.

Aronson, S. *Status and Kinship in the Higher Civil Service.* Cambridge, Mass.: Harvard University Press, 1964.

Bardach, E. *The Implementation Game.* Cambridge, Mass.: MIT Press, 1977.

Barzelay, M., and Armajani, B. J. *Breaking Through Bureaucracy: A New Vision for Managing Government.* Berkeley: University of California Press, 1992.

Brownlow, L. *The President and the Presidency.* Chicago: Public Administration Service, 1949.

Dahl, R. "The Science of Public Administration: Three Problems." *Public Administration Review,* 1947, *7,* 1–11.

Doig, J. "'If I See a Murderous Fellow Sharpening a Knife Cleverly . . . ': The Wilsonian Dichotomy and the Public Authority Tradition." In J. Rabin and J. Bowman (eds.), *Politics and Administration.* New York: Marcel Dekker, 1984.

Donnelly, J. Testimony before Full Employment Subcommittee of the Committee on Banking and Currency. Senate Hearings 763, August 30, 1945. In *Congressional Record.* Washington, D.C.: U.S. Government Printing Office, 1945.

Eaton, D. *The Civil Service in Great Britain.* New York: HarperCollins, 1880.

Etzioni, A. *The Moral Dimension.* New York: Free Press, 1988.

Fiorina, M. *Congress: Keystone of the Washington Establishment.* New Haven, Conn.: Yale University Press, 1977.

Fiorina, M. "Divided Government in the States." In G. Cox

and S. Kernell (eds.), *The Politics of Divided Government*. Boulder, Colo.: Westview Press, 1991.

Fiorina, M. *Divided Government*. New York: Macmillan, 1992.

Fisher, R., and Ury, W. *Getting to Yes*. New York: Penguin, 1983.

Frederickson, H. G. "Toward a New Public Administration." In J. Shafritz and A. Hyde, *Classics of Public Administration*. (2nd ed.). Belmont, Calif.: Dorsey Press, 1987.

Goodnow, F. *Politics and Administration*. New York: Russell & Russell, 1900.

Goodsell, C. "Reinvent Government or Rediscover It?" *Public Administration Review*, 1993, *53*, 85–87.

Gulick, L., and Urwick, L. (eds.). *Papers on the Science of Administration*. New York: Institute of Public Administration, 1937.

Herring, E. *Public Administration and the Public Interest*. New York: McGraw-Hill, 1936.

Hofstadter, R. *The Age of Reform*. New York: Knopf, 1955.

Ingraham, P., and Rosenbloom, D. (eds.). *The Promise and Paradox of Civil Service Reform*. Pittsburgh, Pa.: University of Pittsburgh Press, 1992.

Jackson, A. *The Correspondence of Andrew Jackson*. Vol. 4. Washington, D.C.: Carnegie Institution, 1926.

Kravchuk, R. "Liberalism and the American Administrative State." *Public Administration Review*, 1992, *52*, 374–379.

Lan, Z., and Rosenbloom, D. H. "Public Administration in Transition?" *Public Administration Review*, 1992, *52*, 535–537.

Lindblom, C. "The Science of 'Muddling Through.'" *Public Administration Review*, 1959, *19*, 79–88.

Lipsky, M. *Street-Level Bureaucracy*. New York: Russell Sage Foundation, 1980.

Lowi, T. *The End of Liberalism*. New York: Norton, 1969.

McConnell, G. *Private Power and American Democracy*. New York: Knopf, 1966.

Mascarenhas, R. "Building an Enterprise Culture in the Public Sector: Reform of the Public Sector in Australia, Britain, and New Zealand." *Public Administration Review*, 1993, *53*, 319–328.

Mayer, R. "Policy Disputes as a Source of Administrative Controls." *Public Administration Review,* 1993, *53,* 293–302.

Mosher, F. (ed.). *Basic Documents of American Public Administration, 1776–1950.* New York: Holmes and Meier, 1976.

Mosher, F. *Democracy and the Public Service.* (2nd ed.) New York: Oxford University Press, 1982.

National Commission on the Public Service (Volcker Commission). *Leadership for America: Rebuilding the Public Service.* Washington, D.C.: National Commission on the Public Service, 1989.

Oleszek, W. "The Context of Congressional Policy Making." In J. A. Thurber (ed.), *Divided Democracy.* Washington, D.C.: Congressional Quarterly Press, 1991.

Osborne, D., and Gaebler, T. *Reinventing Government: How the Entrepreneurial Spirit Is Transforming the Public Sector.* Reading, Mass.: Addison-Wesley, 1992.

Ostrom, V. *The Intellectual Crisis in American Public Administration.* University: University of Alabama Press, 1974.

Paine, T. *Common Sense.* In C. van Doren (ed.), *The Writings of Thomas Paine.* New York: Boni and Liveright, 1922. (Originally published 1776.)

President's Committee on Administrative Management. *Report.* Washington, D.C.: U.S. Government Printing Office, 1937.

Pressman, J., and Wildavsky, A. *Implementation.* Berkeley: University of California Press, 1973.

Publius. *The Federalist.* New York: New American Library, 1961.

Richardson, J. (ed.). *A Compilation of the Messages and Papers of the Presidents of the United States, 1789–1897.* Vol. 2. Washington, D.C.: U.S. Government Printing Office, 1896.

Ripley, R., and Franklin, G. *Congress, the Bureaucracy, and Public Policy.* Belmont, Calif.: Dorsey Press, 1976.

Rohr, J. *To Run a Constitution.* Lawrence: University Press of Kansas, 1986.

Rosenbloom, D. *Federal Service and the Constitution: The Development of Public Employment Relationships.* Ithaca, N.Y.: Cornell University Press, 1971.

Rosenbloom, D. "Public Personnel Administration and Politics: Toward a New Public Personnel Administration." *Midwest Review of Public Administration,* 1973, *7,* 98–110.

Rosenbloom, D. "Public Administrative Theory and the Separation of Powers." *Public Administration Review,* 1983, *43,* 219–227.

Rosenbloom, D. *Public Administration: Understanding Management, Politics, and Law in the Public Sector.* (3rd ed.) New York: McGraw-Hill, 1993.

Rosenbloom, D. "The Evolution of the Administrative State and Transformations of Administrative Law." In D. Rosenbloom and R. Schwartz (eds.), *Handbook on Regulation and Administrative Law.* New York: Marcel Dekker, 1994.

Rosenbloom, D., and Carroll, J. *Toward Constitutional Competence.* Englewood Cliffs, N.J.: Prentice-Hall, 1990.

Schurz, C. "Editorial." *Harper's Weekly,* 1893, *37,* 614.

Schurz, C. *The Speeches, Correspondence, and Political Papers of Carl Schurz.* New York: Putnam, 1913.

Seidman, H. *Politics, Position, and Power.* New York: Oxford University Press, 1970.

Shafritz, J. *Public Personnel Management.* New York: Praeger, 1975.

Simon, H. *Administrative Behavior.* New York: Free Press, 1947.

Skowronek, S. *Building a New American State.* New York: Cambridge University Press, 1982.

Stillman, R. *A Preface to Public Administration.* New York: St. Martin's Press, 1991.

Storing, H. "Leonard D. White and the Study of Administration." *Public Administration Review,* 1965, *25,* 38–51.

Thompson, V. *Without Sympathy or Enthusiasm.* University: University of Alabama Press, 1975.

Van Riper, P. *History of the United States Civil Service.* New York: HarperCollins, 1958.

Waldo, D. *The Administrative State.* New York: Ronald Press, 1948.

Waldo, D. "Organization Theory: An Elephantine Problem." *Public Administration Review,* 1961, *21,* 210–225.

Waldo, D. *The Enterprise of Public Administration.* Novato, Calif.: Chandler & Sharp, 1980.

Waldo, D. "The Perdurability of the Politics-Administration Dichotomy: Woodrow Wilson and the Identity Crisis in Public Administration." In J. Rabin and J. Bowman (eds.), *Politics and Administration*. New York: Marcel Dekker, 1984.

Wamsley, G., and others. *Refounding Public Administration*. Newbury Park, Calif.: Sage, 1990.

Warren, K. *Administrative Law in the Political System*. (2nd ed.) St. Paul, Minn.: West, 1992.

White, L. *Introduction to the Study of Public Administration*. New York: Macmillan, 1926.

White, L. *The Federalists*. New York: Free Press, 1965a.

White, L. *The Jacksonians*. New York: Free Press, 1965b.

White, L. *The Jeffersonians*. New York: Free Press, 1965c.

White, L. *The Republican Era*. (2nd ed.) New York: Free Press, 1965d.

Wildavsky, A. *The Politics of the Budgetary Process*. Boston: Little, Brown, 1964.

Wilson, W. "The Study of Administration." *Political Science Quarterly*, 1941, *56*, 481–506. (Originally published 1887.)

# 7

# The Expanding Partnership Between Personnel Management and the Courts

## Rosemary O'Leary

The public management literature of the last twenty years presents several examples of the "new partnership" (Bazelon, 1976) between judges and public managers. Judges have become administrators of school systems (Wood, 1982; O'Leary and Wise, 1991) and mental health facilities (Yarbrough, 1982, 1985; Rothman and Rothman, 1984). Courts have triggered the redistribution of budgetary expenditures (Fisher, 1975; Allerton, 1976; Hale, 1979; Horowitz, 1983; Straussman, 1986; O'Leary, 1989, 1991, 1993). Entire programs have been initiated, abolished, or temporarily halted in response to court decisions (Melnick, 1983, 1985; O'Leary, 1993). Yet, despite the growing literature on the interaction of courts and public organizations,

*Note:* The author thanks Charles Wise, Jeffrey Straussman, and Heidi Koenig for permission to quote from published work coauthored with her.

researchers, with few exceptions (Shafritz, Hyde, and Rosenbloom, 1986; Rosenbloom, 1983; Nalbandian, 1989; Wise and O'Leary, 1993) largely have neglected an examination of the impact of the "new partnership" on public personnel management.

This neglect is surprising, given the large number of important cases decided by the Supreme Court concerning personnel practices in recent years. Three examples merit highlighting. The *Garcia* v. *San Antonio Metropolitan Transit Authority* decision (1985) made the Fair Labor Standards Act applicable to all state and local employees, triggering a plethora of minimum-wage and overtime provisions, as well as work-week, work-period, and record-keeping requirements for public personnel managers. The *Rutan* v. *Republican Party of Illinois* (1990) case made the promotion, transfer, recall, hiring, and discharging of employees on the basis of their political affiliation a violation of the First Amendment, greatly curtailing the discretion of public personnel managers. In the case of *Martin* v. *Wilks* (1989), the Supreme Court held that white firefighters who worked for the city of Birmingham, Alabama, were not precluded from challenging employment decisions that they felt discriminated against them as whites, even though the employment decisions in question were instigated in direct response to a consent decree, which included goals for hiring and promoting black firefighters. Presumably, state and local governments will now have to involve all potential parties in negotiating such consent decrees or risk protracted litigation, as each party discerns how its interests are affected in successive stages of the litigation, furthering court involvement in public personnel management issues. Again, these are just three of dozens of recent Supreme Court decisions that have concerned public personnel management.

In response to the dearth of research examining the public personnel management implications of court-agency interactions, this chapter examines nine findings, gleaned from research on the impact of the courts on public organizations, through the lens of public personnel management. In each instance, the research in the area is explained, and the explanation is followed by a discussion of the implications for public

personnel management. The final section of the chapter highlights potential lessons learned and suggests an agenda for the
future.

Before we begin, however, two caveats are in order. First,
not all the research on the impact of the courts on public organizations is presented here. This chapter relies heavily on those findings that have been confirmed or generated by research the author
has carried out either alone (O'Leary, 1989, 1991, 1993) or in tan-
dem with other researchers (O'Leary and Wise, 1991; Wise and
O'Leary, 1993; O'Leary and Straussman, 1993; O'Leary and
Koenig, forthcoming). Whenever possible, those findings have
been buttressed with the research of others. Second, this chapter is based on the premise that the courts are a powerful force
in the environment of public organizations. As such, it disagrees
with the conclusion of some researchers (for example, Mashaw,
1983) that the courts do not make a difference. Here, the courts
are viewed as important actors.

### External Control of Organizations

The literature is replete with works by scholars arguing about
the appropriateness of judges' interventions into policy and administrative disputes. With few exceptions (Monti, 1980; Wasby,
1981; Wood, 1990), the literature suggests that judges are becoming increasingly active in their oversight of administrative
agencies (Frug, 1978; Melnick, 1983; Rosenbloom, 1983; O'Leary
and Wise, 1991). In many instances, judges are no longer passive reviewers of agencies' actions but are full participants, shaping litigation and its outcomes (Chayes, 1976).

The public organizational theory literature concerning the
external control of organizations, however, is practically devoid of
references to litigation and the courts. Miles (1980) devotes one
page to applying theories of the external control of organizations
to the court decision *Wyatt* v. *Stickney* (1971), which concerned
mental health facilities in Alabama. Miles's analysis concentrates
on the creation by the court of external bodies, responsible both
to the institution and to the judiciary, to monitor and assess institutional activities. These outside groups directly affected the

structure and operations of mental institutions, changing the environment from stable and placid to turbulent and interactive.

In his recent book on public organizational theory and management, Rainey (1991) devotes only a page and a half to courts and public organizations. It is interesting to note that the topic is included not in the chapter concerning the environment of public organizations but rather in a chapter about the impact of political power and public policy. As Rainey points out, some researchers maintain that courts are "powerful controls on the public bureaucracy," while others see them as "ineffectual" (p. 61). Hence, little can be gleaned from the organizational theory literature concerning the interaction of the courts and public managers.

The literature on the courts includes the work of a few authors who have applied some organizational theory concepts. Baum (1976), for example, examines the impact of court decisions on organizations through the framework of theories of organizational hierarchy and superordinate-subordinate relationships. Another example is Johnson's work (1979a, 1979b), which examines the impact of court decisions on organizations through the framework of theories of organizational culture. This literature, however, tells us nothing about the public management implications of the "new partnership."

An examination of public personnel textbooks and readers is equally disappointing. Ban and Riccucci (1991) barely skim the surface of the public personnel implications of court-agency interactions in their edited volume. Direct discussion of the courts and public organizations in that work is limited to one chapter; the subject is indirectly discussed in chapters on ethics, drugs in the workplace, affirmative action, and labor-management relations. Sylvia (1989) includes no chapter on the courts, but he does very briefly discuss court decisions in chapters on equal employment opportunity and collective bargaining. Shafritz, Hyde, and Rosenbloom (1986) include one chapter on the constitutional issues of public personnel management, and they briefly mention court decisions in other chapters concerning labor relations, sexual harassment, and recruitment, selection, and placement.

Hence, there is a need to examine the research findings concerning the impact of the courts on public organizations, in order to glean implications for public personnel management. The intent here is to stimulate additional thinking and research about the importance of the courts in the external control of public organizations and public managers. Let us now examine nine findings and their implications for public personnel management.

## Findings and Implications

### Finding 1

*Judicial decisions concerning public agencies often include detailed judicial supervision of organizations (including ongoing, affirmative decrees), with frequent judicial interaction with agency staff.*

Public-law litigation does not merely clarify the meaning of the law. It also establishes a regime that orders the future interaction of the parties (and perhaps others as well), subjecting them to continuing judicial oversight (Chayes, 1976; Frug, 1978; Fiss, 1983; Horowitz, 1983). The judge plays an active role in such an endeavor—structuring the suit, assessing the desirability of various potential remedies, and acting as "the creator and manager of complex forms of ongoing relief" (Chayes, 1976, p. 1292). The judge becomes a participant in the affairs of the defendant public organization, its clients, and its whole environment. As Horowitz says, "Monitoring of compliance with the decree becomes essential, liaison with . . . adjunct . . . personnel is common, periodic reporting to the court is generally required, and amendment of the provisions of the decree from time to time may be deemed desirable" (1983, p. 1268). Whereas Fiss (1983) argues that judicial intervention in public management is necessary to remedy constitutional violations, Frug (1978) finds this judicial-administrative interaction particularly troublesome from a managerial perspective: court orders may contain hundreds of specifications, which a public manager must implement, that are simply unworkable, and governmental agencies are said to be too complex to administer under court orders.

O'Leary and Wise (1991) analyzed the impact of the Kansas City school desegregation case on the management of the Kansas City, Missouri, School District (KCMSD). Compliance with the courts' orders became the school district's top priority, at times overshadowing its educational mandate. The courts have dictated which issues get attention in the KCMSD. Administrators have lost control over numerous details of administration. For example, when the plaintiffs and defendants filed a joint motion to request an independent study to determine the extent to which KCMSD was able to meet certain financial obligations under the desegregation plans, the judge said that the study had to include a complete analysis of organizational structure and an assessment of the "leadership performance of key personnel involved in organization development" within the school district (O'Leary and Wise, 1991, p. 323).

Cooper (1988) applies a "decree litigation model" to five case studies involving state and local governments. Drawing on interviews as well as on legal documents, Cooper shows that judges do indeed play a major role in the implementation of remedies. But he also points out that the extent and impact of involvement varies significantly from one judge to another. Indeed, his conclusion about the hard choices facing judges refers to the balance between ensuring the adequacy of remedial action and using prudence in judicial intervention into administrative matters to achieve acceptable remedies. Cooper's study, however, tells us more about judges than it does about the impact of judges' actions on public management.

## Implications

The implications are several. First, for public managers, there will be sharing of supervisory authority and actions with judges. As demonstrated by O'Leary and Wise (1991), this may mean much second-guessing and overruling of public managers by judges. Judicial authority in ongoing affirmative decrees is considerable and may extend to administrative minutiae. For staff people, it may mean divided loyalties. To whom is a staff person ultimately responsible, the court or the manager? For the public, it may mean loss of confidence in the management capacity of nonjudicial public administrators.

Another implication concerns the potential conflict between what is best from the constitutional perspective and what is best from the public management perspective. In the Boston (Wood, 1982) and Kansas City (O'Leary and Wise, 1991) school desegregation cases, clearly the abolishment of a segregated system is a desired outcome from the constitutional perspective. But it would be difficult for a public manager to argue that the *means* of such action — a judge with no administrative training or background taking over as administrator of the school system — is the best option when the case is viewed through the lens of public management. This ever-present tension makes serving as a public manager in such instances an immense challenge.

A final implication for public personnel management has to do with the fact that such decrees are future-oriented, and so public personnel planning is gravely affected. In many instances, the court order becomes the agency's long-range plan, again substituting for the professional judgment of the public manager.

## Finding 2

*Judges often must rely on other courts and other organizations to supervise the implementation of a court decision.*

In their synthesis of the judicial-impact literature, Johnson and Canon (1984) conclude that there is often a wide gulf between a judge's decision and the implementation of that decision. The authors point out that judicial decisions are not self-implementing, nor are judges capable of closely supervising day-to-day operations of government agencies. As a result, judges often rely on other courts (for example, in the case of a remand or an appeal) or on nonjudicial actors in the political system (such as interest groups that threaten to refile lawsuits, court-appointed masters, and oversight committees) to implement decisions. These findings support the early work of Glick (1970), who has concluded that state supreme courts, as interest groups, seek access to other political decision makers in order to urge the adoption of policies that they cannot implement themselves.

In the Kansas City school desegregation case, the school superintendent reported that the largest source of conflict for him came from the thirteen-person desegregation-monitoring committee (DMC) appointed by the judge to oversee all desegregation efforts and to report to the judge. The existence of the committee, which had no statutory limits, yielded a loss of administrative power for the chief administrator, with the committee dissecting or "micromanaging" every major decision, including the width of a creek, key personnel appointments, sites for new schools, the recruitment of students, and advertising for new teachers. A memo from the superintendent to the school board called this particularly "problematic because . . . [the DMC members] question district actions in an area in which the administration traditionally has had wide discretion" (O'Leary and Wise, 1991, p. 324). In the study of the impact of federal court decisions on the policies and administration of the U.S. Environmental Protection Agency (EPA), O'Leary (1993) found that the courts relied heavily on interest groups to monitor the EPA's implementation of the court decisions and at times went so far as to order the plaintiffs to formally monitor the agency and report back to the judge. Wood (1982), in his first-person account of the challenges of managing the Boston school system under a court order, refers to difficulties faced in reconciling the procedures required by the oversight committee with his conception of the realities of managing a large school system. By contrast, Yarbrough's study (1985) of the *Wyatt* v. *Stickney* (1971) case found that a court-appointed oversight committee provided a valuable link between a state agency and a judge. This link, according to Yarbrough, was instrumental in the implementation of the judicial remedy.

*Implications*

Sharing management responsibilities with courts or court-appointed committees and interest groups clearly recasts the role of the public manager. The responsibility of the public administrator is no longer primarily to manage programs or employees but truly to act as a boundary spanner. Public administrators must learn to manage what may be the diverse and sometimes conflicting preferences of interest groups, judges, and oversight committees. Tied in with this is the fact that juggling the demands of internal organizational superiors and external organizational entities can be a formidable challenge.

*Finding 3*

> There are often unintended consequences, unanticipated questions, and unforeseen problems of court decisions involving public agencies.

Horowitz (1977), in his study of the role of the courts in social policy, asserts that although a particular issue addressed by a court is seemingly narrow and insignificant, the policy and administrative ramifications of the decision are often sweeping: "The lawyers' customary search for the 'controlling issue' lead[s] the court to a view of the case . . . that is significantly narrower than the innovation the decision actually imposed" (p. 225). Not considered by the courts, yet of paramount importance to the agencies implementing judicial dcisions, are such issues as the general feasibility of carrying out court orders, monetary costs, and second-order consequences. In this sense, the judge may become a catalyst for unforeseen administrative change.

In their study of the Kansas City school desegregation case, O'Leary and Wise (1991) examine the judge's order to hire new teachers and pay them salaries significantly higher than the national average, and the effect of this order on the human resources division of the school district. They found that the human resources division, unequipped to handle the onslaught of thousands of applications, fumbled the recruiting of new teachers and actually lost some of its highest-quality candidates a a result. Exacerbating the situation was the fact that the human resources division has been operating without a permanent director for nearly two years.

## Implications

The Horowitz and O'Leary and Wise studies highlight some of the implications of the unintended consequences, unanticipated questions, and unforeseen problems of court decisions involving public agencies. Court orders are framed by lawyers' narrow legal issues, not by public management issues. A narrow decision may pose immense public management challenges, but the judge, who usually has no background in public management, may be oblivious to them, and the result is that implementation becomes a nightmare.

It is interesting to juxtapose the different organizational environments of the EPA in O'Leary's study (1993) and the KCMSD in the O'Leary and Wise study (1991). In the EPA case, additional money to implement a court decision was forthcoming only once in twenty years and more than two thousand court orders. The typical EPA response to court decisions is called *reprogramming:* funds and staff are shifted within the agency to the office that is the subject of the court order. In the KCMSD example, millions of new dollars were poured into the district. The KCMSD had the luxury of not having to reprogram or do more with less. Yet in both instances, the management of personnel challenges was formidable.

## Finding 4

*A court order can dictate issues that must be considered by public agencies.*

In her study of the courts and the EPA, an agency plagued by lawsuits, O'Leary (1993) found that the major impact of court decisions on that agency was policy-related. She found that from the "macro" or agencywide perspective, compliance with court

orders has become one of the agency's top priorities, at times
overtaking congressional mandates. The courts shape the agenda
at the EPA. An atmosphere of limited resources, coupled with
unrealistic and numerous statutory mandates, forces the EPA
to make decisions among competing priorities. With few exceptions, court orders have become the "winners" in this competition. From the "micro" or individual organizational unit perspective, compliance with court orders also has become the top
priority of EPA divisions.

When the courts dictate issues that must be considered
by public agencies, that is not the same as actually implementing a decision as conceived by a judge. O'Leary found that the
EPA attempted to implement most judicial orders, whereas
Johnson (1979b), who studied the impact of five decisions on
five Pennsylvania state agencies, concluded that the organizations went to great lengths to avoid dealing with the issues dictated by the court orders.

## Implications

If a public organization is not able or willing to avoid its court-
ordered responsibilities, this finding has important implications
for public personnel management. Public managers already
strive to do more with less in a time of greater public demands
and shrinking resources. It is not unusual for a public organization to have more legislative mandates than funds to implement them. Add to this situation another layer of court-ordered
mandates, usually without additional funds to implement them,
and a potentially explosive public management situation has
been created.

Former EPA administrator Lee Thomas once testified before a congressional committee on the difficulty of implementing both the agency's numerous and unrealistic statutory mandates and the competing court-ordered priorities. His primary
point was that as the number of mandates given to the agency
increases, so does the discretion of the administrator. This
message — that the EPA is overwhelmed and cannot be all things
to all people — is compelling. But the so-called increase in dis-

cretion most likely also means an increase in angry citizens, an increase in demanding members of Congress, and a possible increase in the bewilderment and frustration of beleaguered employees. It also most likely means an increase in lawsuits challenging the public organization's nonimplementation of its mandates.

## Finding 5

*Judicial activity can lead to a reduction in the power and authority of administrators.*

Glazer (1978) predicts that judges' intervention in public management will reduce the power and authority of administrators. O'Leary's research (1993) confirms and extends this hypothesis. From an administrative perspective, the courts have reduced the discretion, autonomy, power, and authority of EPA administrators. New programs often are not implemented because resources are devoted to meeting court demands. Court decisions also affect EPA's planning activities. An agency cannot plan for a court remand.

Court decisions may be broad and vague, affecting more than they need to. An example is an EPA case from 1983, *Monsanto v. Acting Administrator.* In that instance, a judge held that a statute was unconstitutional because Congress had exceeded its regulatory authority and violated the Fifth Amendment's prohibition against the taking of property without just compensation. The court issued a permanent injunction barring the EPA from carrying out four statutorily mandated programs. EPA attorneys agreed that the court could have reached the same conclusion without nullifying all four statutory sections (O'Leary, 1993).

The proliferation of court decisions concerning the EPA has forced what one staff member called "non–user-friendly" regulations. The Office of General Counsel often rewrites regulations, notices, and proposals in anticipation of lawsuits. Lawyers have the last word in most EPA actions, supporting the commonsensical theories of Glazer (1978) and Pfeffer and Salancik (1978): an organization that faces or initiates a number of lawsuits will experience a gain in the power and influence of its attorneys.

From a scientific perspective, the effects of court decisions on the EPA have important implications. The major issue here is not so much that judges make scientific decisions as that judicial decisions interrupt scientific processes. The EPA regulation-development process is what Thompson (1967) calls "long-linked," involving serial interdependence. Certain actions must build on other actions before final products can be issued. For example, scientific studies must be completed, data must be collected, and then the data must be analyzed before technical regulations are developed. There is a need for peer scientific review. Often the EPA either cannot comply with a court decision because these foundational steps have not been completed, or it skips the needed steps, issuing poorly conceived standards. Time constraints are exacerbated.

In the case of *Sierra Club* v. *Ruckelshaus* (1984), for example, the EPA was ordered by a court to issue regulations under the Clean Air Act. The EPA requested nine years to develop a scientific basis for the regulations; a judge allowed 180 days. The agency issued the regulations, bypassing the typical review by its Science Advisory Board (SAB). When the board finally did review the regulations, it found them scientifically flawed. The EPA administrator responded by withdrawing the regulations and was then held in contempt of court. To purge itself of the contempt citation, the agency issued regulations that conformed with the letter of the court's order but undermined the spirit of the Clean Air Act (O'Leary, 1993).

*Implications*

The major implications of reductions in the power and authority of administrators are twofold. First is the issue of human resources planning. Shafritz, Hyde, and Rosenbloom (1986) write that personnel-related costs comprise the majority of a typical public organization's budget, and that personnel resources require "considerable effort, time, and cost to recruit, select, evaluate, train and staff effectively" (p. 95). Planning for adequate staff to implement such decisions becomes difficult, if not impossible. Training of staff to deal with court decisions that may take from six months to twenty years to implement is a great challenge. Finding the funds to hire new employees with the expertise demanded by the court may be impossible.

Second is the issue of employees' motivation. Deci's cognitive evaluation theory of motivation (1975), for example, recognizes the needs for competence and self-determination of employees and states that motivation will be enhanced if feelings of competence are increased. The constant rewriting of rules and regulations may be devastating to employees who take pride in their work, and it may decrease feelings of competence. Fear of litigation or negative communications from the law department may stifle creativity. If scientists are not able to carry out their research carefully and critically, they may leave the public service for private sector jobs, where research can be undertaken at a more scholarly pace. The result could be a "talent hemorrhage" at our public institutions.

## Finding 6

*Judges often refuse to defer to administrators' expertise.*

Melnick (1983, 1985) has been the primary messenger of the conclusion that judges often refuse to defer to administrators' expertise. In his study of the courts and the EPA under the Clean Air Act, Melnick chronicles this fact. O'Leary's EPA study (1993) buttresses this view. O'Leary gives the example of scientists forced to defend their scientific decisions before judges with little or no scientific expertise. In one instance, a judge determined that the EPA did not use the "best scientific . . . data available" as mandated by a statute. At a minimum, the judge held, the EPA should have required that a specific scientific test, a "real-time simulation study," be carried out (*Roosevelt Campobello International Park Commission* v. *United States Environmental Protection Agency*, 1982).

*Implications*

The primary implications here are most likely in the area of morale and retention of employees. It is logical to assume that the greater the number of negative judicial decisions challenging the expertise of members of the organization, the more those individuals will feel threatened in terms of a perceived decrease in power and authority, with potential decreases in morale and potential increases in resignations by frustrated employees. It also is logical to assume that the greater the number of lawsuits in which a judge refuses to defer to the expertise of administrators, the greater the likelihood that other factors will determine future administrative decisions. Examples of additional factors include an assessment of opponents and their power bases, an assessment of the likelihood of getting sued, an assessment of the likelihood of winning in court if sued, and an assessment of the consequences of losing in court. Biases, preferences, and political outlooks of potential judges will probably also be considered more frequently than they are now.

*Finding 7*

> *Often funds must be taken from other programs and channeled into a program that is the subject of a court decision.*

Allerton (1976), writing of the effect of court decisions on Virginia's mental health institutions, has found that the institutions were forced to reorder their priorities in order to make funds available to comply with court orders. The redistributive consequences of court decisions have also been discussed by Horowitz (1983), Hale (1979), and Straussman (1986). As already mentioned, the typical EPA budgetary response to a court order is called *reprogramming,* in which funds and sometimes personnel are moved from program to program within an office, or even from office to office. Here, too, as funds are earmarked for court orders, other and less pressing priorities are halted for lack of funding. "Sometimes it is painful to cut one part of a program for another," a former EPA budget director says, "but it has to be done to comply with the court decision. The Administrator must make tough choices as to where the money will come from. Something in the current year just doesn't get done" (O'Leary, 1993, p. 162).

The EPA also has two funds it has drawn from to meet the expenses associated with court orders: the administrator's discretionary fund, and an "other contractual services" fund. When an award of attorney's fees is made by a court to an environmental group, it is usually paid out of the EPA administrator's discretionary fund. When consulting firms need to be hired to do work to comply with a court order, they are usually paid out of the "other contractual services" fund. EPA staff have reported relying more often on consulting firms to perform the work necessary to comply with court orders, given the lack of specialized internal resources readily available on short notice for such a task.

The observation of Miller and Iscoe (the former was a commissioner of the Texas Department of Mental Health) concerning the judicial imposition of staffing requirements is telling:

> Among the several remedies ordered by the court was imposition of a rigid staffing formula (psychiatric aides to patient ratios of 1:5, 1:5, and 1:10 on the three shifts), although no evidence has been presented at the court hearing to support this or any other ratio. As a result of the court order, nursing personnel and supervisors lost their ability to modify employee levels based on changing needs in the department's eight state hospitals. Because the court-ordered ratios for these psychiatric aides are among the richest in the country, the agency's limited funds have been consumed in meeting the mandate, leaving insufficient dollars to hire adequate numbers of professional personnel such as psychiatrists, registered nurses, and psychologists [Miller and Iscoe, 1990, p. 124].

*Implications*

Miller and Iscoe's observation is an articulate statement of some of the public personnel implications of reprogramming funds in response to court orders. Personnel managers may be forced to place staff in areas of the organization where such placement may not make sense from a managerial perspective. Managers may also be forced to hire unwanted staff while letting other staffing needs go unmet. In either instance, there are clear winners and losers. The program responsible for implementing a court order is the beneficiary of budgetary redistribution. This may exacerbate turf fights and tensions within a public organization.

There are positive and negative consequences of the increased use of consultants to meet the demands of a court decision. On the one hand, it is an expeditious way to meet rapid change in the agency without greatly disturbing the status quo, and experts can be brought in on a short-term basis. On the other hand, as the use of consultants has grown, there has been a gradual erosion of EPA's in-house expertise. In hiring new staff, EPA managers now look less for "technical geniuses" and more for generalists who can oversee and communicate with technical consultants, and this has affected morale, since EPA technical staff at times resent not being able to use their expertise (O'Leary, 1993).

*Finding 8*

> *Court decisions, by transferring budgetary power from an administrator to a judge, may decrease the budgetary discretion of administrators.*

Fisher (1975) studied how the federal courts force the release of funds appropriated by Congress and impounded by the president, severely restricting the discretion of that office. Hale (1979) has found that nearly 50 percent of the largest public organizations operate judicially mandated programs. Among the implications of Hale's study is the conclusion that such action yields a transfer of budgetary power from administrators to judges, decreasing the discretion of administrators. In their study of the implementation of the school desegregation case *Missouri* v. *Jenkins* (1990), O'Leary and Wise (1991) found that the judge in control of the case became a budget czar, reducing architects' fees, for example, from 8 percent to 6 percent, and denying a school district's request for furniture because he was not supplied with the information he wanted about its quality and quantity.

## Implications

The implications of this finding are clear: a transfer of budgetary power from a public manager to a judge leaves the manager with less to work with and more constraints. This can lessen management's alternatives for action. Such budgetary constraint may also serve as a catalyst for creative thinking and offer a chance to develop new modes of operating. Whether the final outcome is restrictive, liberating, or both, yet another budgetary hurdle is placed before the administrator.

## Finding 9

### Court orders affect staff morale.

The ability of the public administrator to manage the organization is in part affected by morale (see Rainey, 1991). Morale in turn may be influenced by court orders; here, there is some case-study evidence from corrections and from the EPA. One line of argument is that court orders have eroded the morale and authority of prison staff (Ekland-Olson and Martin, 1988, 1990). For example, it was found that prison guards resented having to protect the rights of belligerent prisoners in response to a court order, and the guards became angry and dejected. O'Leary (1993), in her study of the EPA, was surprised to find a dichotomy: whereas higher-level political appointees resented what they saw as the intrusion of the courts and disruption of their plans, lower-level career employees reported an increase in morale in response to court orders. As lower-level workers banded together to accomplish the goal of compliance, they became more focused and directed. They expressed great pride about implementing court orders in a timely fashion. In an EPA regional office, for example, staff persons expressed joy when their actions prevented the regional administrator from being thrown into jail for contempt of court.

## Implications

The prison study and the EPA study, viewed together, yield more questions than answers. Under what circumstances does a court order have an adverse effect on staff morale? Under what circumstances does it have a positive effect on staff morale? What can be done to maximize the positive effects and minimize the negative? How can a public personnel manager use a court decision to enhance morale? Another question concerns the priorities of employees. The staff may be motivated to comply with a court order, but what impact does compliance have on the larger organizational objectives and outcomes by which the staff and the organization will be evaluated? Clearly, further empirical research is needed.

## An Agenda for the Future

This chapter has highlighted several management implications of court-agency interaction. In the words of Rosenbloom (1983, p. 224), "a new and heavy burden . . . [has been] placed on public administrators." Supervisory authority and actions may be shared with judges, court-appointed committees, and interest groups, with the result of diverse and sometimes contradictory administrative visions. Public managers may find themselves devoting much time to the task of boundary spanning and less time to internal management. As judges involve themselves in administrative minutiae, staff members may feel a sense of divided loyalty: "Who's the boss?" The public may lose confidence in a nonjudicial administrator who "caused" the problem that had to be "fixed" by the judge and who now struggles with implementation of the court order.

Yet in the midst of these difficult challenges lie opportunities for the most creative managers. The potential problems can be seen as overwhelming burdens or as invitations to daring innovations. The task for researchers and teachers is to translate judicial mandates into catalysts for positive change and development. This means going beyond mere examination of the law or of particular holdings in legal cases. It means understanding the external control of public organizations by the courts, and understanding the managerial consequences of such control. The task is formidable, but it must be tackled if public managers in the future are to thrive in an environment where judges increasingly act as managers of public institutions.

## Cases Cited

*Garcia* v. *San Antonio Metropolitan Transit Authority et al.,* 469 U.S. 528 (1985).
*Martin* v. *Wilks,* 492 U.S. 932 (1989).
*Missouri* v. *Jenkins,* 110 S.Ct. 1651 (1990).
*Monsanto* v. *Acting Administrator,* 564 F.Supp. 522 (1983).
*Roosevelt Campobello International Park Commission* v. *United States Environmental Protection Agency,* 684 F.2d 1041 (1982).
*Rutan* v. *Republican Party of Illinois,* 111 L.Ed.2d 52 (1990).
*Sierra Club* v. *Ruckelshaus,* 602 F.Supp. 892 (1984).
*Wyatt* v. *Stickney,* 325 F.Supp. 781 (1971); 334 F.Supp. 1341 (1971); 344 F.Supp. 373 (1972); 344 F.Supp. 387 (1972); 503 F.2d 1305 (1974).

## References

Allerton, W. S. "An Administrator Responds." In V. Bradley and G. Clark (eds.), *Paper Victories and Hard Realities.* Washington, D.C.: Georgetown University Health Policy Center, 1976.
Ban, C., and Riccucci, N. (eds.). *Public Personnel Management: Current Concerns, Future Challenges.* White Plains, N.Y.: Longman, 1991.
Baum, L. "Implementation of Judicial Decisions: An Organizational Analysis." *American Politics Quarterly,* 1976, *4*(1), 86–114.

Bazelon, D. L. "The Impact of Courts on Public Administration." *Indiana Law Journal,* 1976, *52,* 101–110.

Chayes, A. "The Role of Judge in Public Law Litigation." *Harvard Law Review,* 1976, *89,* 1281–1316.

Cooper, P. J. *Hard Judicial Choices: Federal District Court Judges and State and Local Officials.* New York: Oxford University Press, 1988.

Deci, E. L. *Intrinsic Motivation.* New York: Plenum, 1975.

Ekland-Olson, S., and Martin, S. J. "Organizational Compliance with Court-Ordered Reform." *Law and Society Review,* 1988, *22*(2), 359–385.

Ekland-Olson, S., and Martin, S. J. "*Ruiz:* A Struggle over Legitimacy." In J. J. Dilulio, Jr. (ed.), *Courts, Corrections, and the Constitution.* New York: Oxford University Press, 1990.

Fisher, L. *Presidential Spending Power.* Princeton, N.J.: Princeton University Press, 1975.

Fiss, O. M. "The Bureaucratization of the Judiciary." *Yale Law Journal,* 1983, *92,* 1442–1468.

Frug, G. E. "The Judicial Power of the Purse." *University of Pennsylvania Law Review,* 1978, *126,* 715–794.

Glazer, N. "Should Judges Administer Social Services?" *The Public Interest,* 1978, *50,* 64–80.

Glick, H. R. "Policy-Making and State Supreme Courts: The Judiciary as an Interest Group." *Law and Society Review,* 1970, *5*(2), 271–291.

Hale, G. E. "Federal Courts and State Budgetary Process." *Administration and Society,* 1979, *11*(3), 357–386.

Horowitz, D. L. *The Courts and Social Policy.* Washington, D.C.: Brookings Institution, 1977.

Horowitz, D. L. "Decreeing Organizational Change: Judicial Supervision of Public Institutions." *Duke Law Journal,* 1983, *1983,* 1265–1307.

Johnson, C. A. "Judicial Decisions and Organizational Change: A Theory." *Administration and Society,* 1979a, *11*(1), 27–51.

Johnson, C. A. "Judicial Decisions and Organization Change: Some Theoretical and Empirical Notes on State Court Decisions and State Administrative Agencies." *Law and Society Review,* 1979b, *14*(1), 27–56.

Johnson, C. A., and Canon, B. C. *Judicial Policies: Implementa-*

*tion and Impact.* Washington, D.C.: Congressional Quarterly Press, 1984.

Mashaw, J. *Bureaucratic Justice: Managing Social Security.* New Haven, Conn.: Yale University Press, 1983.

Melnick, R. S. *Regulation and the Courts: The Case of the Clean Air Act.* Washington, D.C.: Brookings Institution, 1983.

Melnick, R. S. "The Politics of Partnership." *Public Administration Review,* 1985, *45,* 653–660.

Miles, R. H. *Macro Organizational Behavior.* Glenview, Ill.: Scott, Foresman, 1980.

Miller, G. E., and Iscoe, I. "A State Mental Health Commissioner and the Politics of Mental Illness." In E. C. Hargrove and J. C. Glidewell (eds.), *Impossible Jobs in Public Management.* Lawrence: University Press of Kansas, 1990.

Monti, D. J. "Administrative Foxes in Educational Chicken Coops: An Examination of the Critique of Judicial Activism in School Desegregation Cases." *Law and Policy Quarterly,* 1980, *2,* 233–256.

Nalbandian, J. "The U.S. Supreme Court's 'Consensus' on Affirmative Action." *Public Administration Review,* 1989, *49,* 38–45.

O'Leary, R. "The Impact of Federal Court Decisions on the Policies and Administration of the U.S. Environmental Protection Agency." *Administrative Law Review,* 1989, *41*(4), 549–574.

O'Leary, R. "Environmental Administration, the Courts, and Public Policy, 1980–1989." *International Journal of Public Administration,* 1991, *14,* 303–314.

O'Leary, R. *Environmental Change: Federal Courts and the EPA.* Philadelphia: Temple University Press, 1993.

O'Leary, R., and Koenig, H. "Toward a Theory of the Impact of Courts on Public Management." *Research in Public Administration,* forthcoming.

O'Leary, R., and Straussman, J. "The Impact of Courts on Public Management." In B. Bozeman (ed.), *Public Management: The State of the Art.* San Francisco: Jossey-Bass, 1993.

O'Leary, R., and Wise, C. "Public Managers, Judges and Legislators: Redefining the 'New Partnership.'" *Public Administration Review,* 1991, *52*(4), 316–327.

Pfeffer, J., and Salancik, G. R. *The External Control of Organizations: A Resource-Dependence Perspective.* New York: HarperCollins, 1978.

Rainey, H. G. *Understanding and Managing Public Organizations.* San Francisco: Jossey-Bass, 1991.

Rosenbloom, D. *Public Administration and Law.* New York: Marcel Dekker, 1983.

Rothman, D. J., and Rothman, S. M. *The Willowbrook Wars.* New York: HarperCollins, 1984.

Shafritz, J. M., Hyde, A., and Rosenbloom, D. H. *Personnel Management in Government: Politics and Process.* (3rd ed.) New York: Marcel Dekker, 1986.

Straussman, J. "Courts and Public Purse Strings: Have Portraits of Budgeting Missed Something?" *Public Administration Review,* 1986, *46*(4), 345–351.

Sylvia, R. D. *Critical Issues in Public Personnel Policy.* Pacific Grove, Calif.: Brooks/Cole, 1989.

Thompson, J. D. *Organizations in Action: Social Science Bases of Administrative Theory.* New York: McGraw-Hill, 1967.

Wasby, S. L. "Arrogation of Power or Accountability: 'Judicial Imperialism' Revisited." *Judicature,* 1981, *65*(4), 208–219.

Wise, C., and O'Leary, R. "Is Federalism Dead or Alive in the Supreme Court? Implications for Public Administrators." *Public Administration Review,* 1993, *52*(6), 559–572.

Wood, R. C. "Professionals at Bay: Managing Boston's Public Schools." *Journal of Policy Analysis and Management,* 1982, *1*(4), 454–468.

Wood, R. C. *Remedial Law: When Courts Become Administrators.* Amherst: University of Massachusetts Press, 1990.

Yarbrough, T. E. "The Judge as Manager: The Case of Judge Frank Johnson." *Journal of Policy Analysis and Management,* 1982, *1*(3), 386–400.

Yarbrough, T. E. "The Political World of Federal Judges as Managers." *Public Administration Review,* 1985, *45,* 660–666.

# 8

# Revitalizing Employee Ties with Public Organizations

*James L. Perry*

The effectiveness of public service is highly dependent on attracting and retaining dedicated, knowledgeable personnel. Without high-quality human resources, most democratic governments would be unable to pursue their constitutionally authorized missions. Woodrow Wilson (1887) recognized this connection over one hundred years ago, when he observed that it was becoming harder to run a constitution than it was to write one.

This chapter focuses on the linkage between public employees and their organizations. By *linkage* is meant the types of connections that individuals have to organizations and the strengths of those connections (Mowday, Porter, and Steers,

*Note:* I would like to thank the editors, Gary Brumback, Sonia Ospina, and Lois Wise for their comments on an earlier draft. I also thank Louis Helling for his helpful research assistance.

1982). Two broad categories are distinguished. The first involves membership—that is, the continuum of relationships, ranging from long-term and direct to short-term and detached (Pfeffer and Baron, 1988). The second category is quality of membership, encompassed conceptually by such ideas as attachment, alienation, involvement, identification, commitment, and loyalty.

The 1980s and 1990s have brought major changes in the nature of public employee–organization linkages. The changes emanate from several far-reaching and interdependent shifts in the environment of public service. One shift involves the declining resources available to the public sector. The redistribution of resources from the public to the private sector has had substantial influence on the attractiveness of the public sector. Resource redistribution, however, is symptomatic of an even more consequential shift—the decline of esteem for public service. Public confidence in and support of public administration institutions has reached post–World War II lows in many parts of the world (Czarniawska, 1985; National Commission on the Public Service, 1989). A third shift concerns the erosion of normative underpinnings for public service. In many parts of the world, the role of government in society is in flux. At a time when government's role is being redefined, few political leaders have been able to articulate a vision that infuses new meaning into public service institutions. A final shift influencing public employee–organization linkages has to do with the constitutional and ideological changes that are occurring throughout the world. These changes are particularly significant for higher-level civil servants, but they affect public service at all levels.

This chapter seeks to document the nature of the shifting public employee–organization linkages. It explores organizational strategies that are being used to manage these linkages, and it offers suggestions to create attachments that are supportive of effective public service. The chapter concludes with a discussion of research that would help answer questions raised by the shifting public employee–organization linkages.

## The Changing Context of Public Service

American public service is currently buffeted by economic, political, and social forces that are worldwide in scope. These forces have altered work environments and, in turn, public employee-organization linkages. One of the earliest and most fundamental changes involves people's work ethic. A periodic Roper Organization survey of Americans' attitudes toward work and leisure shows that more people are working in order to have fulfilling leisure time (Harris, 1990). Although those surveyed in late 1989 indicated a desire to excel in their careers, they also were committed to spending more time with their families and on themselves. The 1989 survey results are consistent with conclusions of the late 1970s, that American workers were increasingly interested in personal self-fulfillment both on and off the job (Kerr, 1979; Katzell, 1979).

The changing character of Americans' work ethic has occurred simultaneously with a growth of cynicism in American life (Kanter and Mirvis, 1989). Americans increasingly have come to believe that the average person is unconcerned with the problems of other people, and that public officials are uninterested in the problems of the average citizen. Cynicism about the public sector is intense. Trust in American institutions generally, and government in particular, declined markedly from the 1960s to the early 1980s, when it reached a new low (Lipset and Schneider, 1987). As we entered the last decade of the twentieth century, only one in four Americans expressed confidence in government to "do what is right" (Lipset and Schneider, 1987). The National Commission on the Public Service (1989) points to the climate of public opinion toward public service as one source of the crisis in U.S. federal service.

Profound demographic changes are also affecting public employee–organization linkages. Among the most prominent trends in the U.S. national work force are the declining numbers of youth entering the labor force, the aging of the work force, and increasing proportions of women, minorities, and immigrants (Johnston, 1988; Johnston and Parker, 1987). Accompanying these recent trends are longer-standing trends that involve rising educational levels, multiple-wage-earner families, and dual-career couples.

An outgrowth of changing demographics is the growing diversity of organizational work forces (Jamieson and O'Mara, 1991; Loden and Rosener, 1991). Women made relatively slow progress attaining upper-level management positions in the 1970s and 1980s; many observers expect women to achieve much greater success as their proportion of the work force grows and as male-dominated organizational cultures become less prominent. Research indicates, however, that women's roles in the family and the workplace often continue to be at odds (Sekaran and Hall, 1989).

In the private sector, global competition has forced corporate restructuring, with its attendant effects on job security and employee loyalty (Carnavale, 1991). The effects of globalization in the public sector are less direct, but global competition undoubtedly has encouraged shifts of resources from the public to the private sector. These shifts have led to declines in relative pay levels for public employees (Wise, 1988). Pressure to reduce regulations and the overhead costs associated with public service has also had a dampening effect on public employment and payrolls. Rising health care costs have created further incentives to control the number of permanent employees.

Private-public resource shifts not only have affected public payrolls but also have influenced the nature of work undertaken by most governments (Levine, 1986). The increase of "government by proxy" has changed the nature of public service work, moving it toward professionalization and administration and away from direct service to citizens and clients (Kettl, 1988). As the constraints on government have grown, and as programs have become more complex, more and more public functions are being carried out by contractors, nonprofits, and other nontraditional providers (Osborne and Gaebler, 1992; see Chapter Two of this volume for further discussion of the "hollow government" phenomenon).

Technological change, particularly the revolution in information technologies, is also altering the work environments that underlie public employee–organization linkages (Bozeman and Rahm, 1989; Perry and Kraemer, 1993). These technologies are incrementally transforming the ways governments at all levels are organized, the activities they perform, how they perform them, and the nature of work itself (Perry and Kraemer, 1993). The importance of knowledge as an input for productivity has made humans critical resources (Drucker, 1969; McGregor, 1988).

## Effects on Public Employee–Organization Linkages

What are the cumulative effects on public employee–organization linkages — that is, on the types of connections that individuals have to public service? One effect is to change *employment relationships*. Employees who once enjoyed long-term attachments under bureaucratic control are now being replaced by employees with weaker connections, in terms of physical location, administrative control, or duration of employment (Davis-Blake and Uzzi, 1993; Garvey, 1993; Pfeffer and Baron, 1988). Moreover, employment contracts are increasingly externalized (see Chapter Ten of this volume for further discussion of this point).

The shift in employment relationships is manifest in a variety of structural arrangements: part-time employment, job sharing, voluntarism, term contracts, contracting out, and political appointments. What was once largely a permanent work force is now differentiated into permanent and contingent components of the public sector.

The shift is not easily documented because available data are sketchy. For example, federal employment data during the last four presidencies provide relatively little support for the notion of a dramatic employment-relationship shift. Table 8.1 presents the numbers of full-time, part-time, and intermittent employees since January 1977. These data are heavily influenced by defense employment, which has varied greatly since the beginning of the Carter presidency. The only trends are that the number of full-time permanent employees has increased, while their percentage of the total work force has declined and the number and percent of intermittent employees has increased

**Table 8.1. Federal Executive Branch Employment at the Start of the Carter, Reagan, Bush, and Clinton Administrations.**

| | Carter January 1977 | | Reagan January 1981 | | Bush January 1989 | | Clinton January 1993 | |
|---|---|---|---|---|---|---|---|---|
| | Number | Percent | Number | Percent | Number | Percent | Number | Percent |
| Full-time permanent | 2,439,241 | 87.97 | 2,442,716 | 84.25 | 2,631,308 | 84.73 | 2,588,384 | 85.20 |
| Full-time temporary | 104,340 | 3.76 | 179,944 | 6.21 | 100,025 | 3.22 | 72,192 | 2.38 |
| Part-time (regularly scheduled) | 165,667 | 5.98 | 214,046 | 7.38 | 208,020 | 6.70 | 166,491 | 5.48 |
| Permanent | | | | | 167,006 | 5.38 | 130,862 | 4.31 |
| Temporary | | | | | 41,014 | 1.32 | 35,629 | 1.17 |
| Intermittent | 63,351 | 2.28 | 62,774 | 2.17 | 106,928 | 3.44 | 144,564 | 4.76 |

*Source:* Data were taken from the monthly release of *Federal Civilian Workforce Statistics: Employment and Trends* (Washington, D.C.: U.S. Civil Service Commission and U.S. Office of Personnel Management) for the dates indicated at the top of the columns.

sharply. If the proposal of the National Performance Review (1993) to eliminate 252,000 positions is implemented, however, then federal employment will shrink, just as it has in many large private corporations.

Nevertheless, the federal employment data fail to reveal the enormous growth in contracting — the "shadow government" (see Chapter Two of this volume). Another segment of the public work force that has probably grown in recent years is part-time employees. Public service industries, such as urban transit and health care, have expanded the ranks of part-time employees. The number of volunteers in public service has also increased enormously (Brudney, 1990).

The official data also do not reflect the growing experimentation with types of employment relationships, a likely precursor of future change. For example, job sharing was first officially promoted in the federal government in 1990. Flexiplace, which involves employees working at remote sites (typically at home), is also becoming more prevalent. Both flexiplace and job sharing have received enormous impetus from the demographic changes already discussed.

More subtle reflections of the externalization of public employment relationships include the benefit changes, such as the mid-1980s change in the federal retirement program. As part of social security reform, Congress approved a portable federal system, to replace one that had functioned as "golden handcuffs," since employees did not become vested until they had accumulated twenty years of service. Although the new system is fair and consistent with reforms in the private sector, it has radically changed the rules binding federal employees to their organizations.

A second effect on public employee–organization linkages involves *psychological attachments*. Hard evidence is again sketchy, but what there is supports the proposition that psychological attachments within the permanent work force have weakened (National Commission on the Public Service, 1989; Peters, 1991). The weakening is not manifest in turnover, which has remained low in the face of poor economic conditions. It is more likely to be seen in employees' work effort. Lane and Wolf (1990)

conclude that the strength of commitment to public employment
has clearly been diminished by value shifts and structural changes
in the wider environment.

A factor contributing to this decline, at least in the federal
government, is greater use of political appointees in positions
historically occupied by careerists (National Commission on the
Public Service, 1989; Peters, 1991). Politicization has several
kinds of impacts on psychological attachments. Most obviously,
it introduces new forms of control over the autonomy of senior
personnel. This may discourage the exercise of the managerial
prerogative to improve performance in accord with institutionalized goals, and it may weaken the commitment of staff to an
agency's mission. The effects of expanded political control are
not unidirectional, however. Enhanced roles for political executives may provide opportunities for increased innovation by introducing new elements into agencies' missions. To the extent
that political actors reinforce or successfully reinterpret an agency's
mission, they may contribute to stronger ties by increasing employees' commitment to core values (Balfour and Wechsler, 1991;
Balfour and Wechsler, forthcoming). But such external influence
may also undermine employees' commitment if it clashes with
personal, professional, or traditional agency norms and values.

Demographic changes also threaten the foundations of
traditional employee attachments. The abundance of postwar
"baby boom" employees in middle- and upper-level posts, together with the relatively slow growth of available promotions,
has produced a "plateauing" phenomenon in many organizations (Wolf, 1983). Both the exit of experienced employees and
the apparent decrease in promotional opportunities for younger cohorts may weaken long-term commitment. In tight labor
markets, where the public service competes with strong demand
in the private sector, maintenance of long-term linkages may
also be impeded by sharper wage differentials.

Positive effects on psychological attachments are also visible. Segments of the public work force, both permanent and
peripheral, have been beneficiaries of the externalization induced
by changing demographics. Job sharing, flexiplace, and flexible benefit programs (often created to provide child-care bene-

fits) have increased freedom and flexibility for many employees. The consequences are frequently very positive. For example, the federal government initiated a flexiplace pilot project in January 1990. An evaluation concluded that flexiplace improved the motivation and performance of participating employees, enhanced the quality of their personal and work lives, and reduced commuting and out-of-pocket expenses (U.S. Office of Personnel Management, 1993).

Environmental changes, then, have had two general consequences for public employee–organization linkages. The first is that employment relationships have grown more diverse. Public organizations are relying less on bureaucratic employment arrangements and more on contingent contracts. One direct public benefit of externalization is lower labor costs. The other general consequence is a decline in the strength of psychological attachments among permanent employees (Leemans, 1987; Jabes and Zussman, 1988; Peters, 1991). This decline may be partially offset by stronger psychological attachments within the peripheral work force.

## Reinvigorating Public Service

If the pessimistic aspects of the foregoing conclusions are taken seriously, then elected officials and public managers face some daunting challenges. What are the long-term implications of changing employment relationships? Can steps be taken to strengthen employees' psychological attachments?

The 1988 and 1992 presidential races were the first in over a decade in which bureaucrat-bashing was not one of the favorite pastimes of the candidates, and President Clinton has been joined in his call for a renewal of public service by other prominent public officials. Despite the positive signs, however, political leaders are easily tempted to pursue civil service controls or lapse into self-serving rhetoric in pursuit of votes. Even when the rhetoric is supportive of civil servants, supportive action frequently does not follow. A politician's call to empower employees becomes meaningless in the face of oppressive controls and arbitrary freezes on wages and hiring.

A central strategic issue for political and appointive leadership is what philosophy and models should guide revitalization efforts. One pattern in American society, often repeated, is to look to business for guidance. The private sector is frequently used as the exemplar of good management, both in the United States and in other Western democracies (Czarniawska, 1985; National Performance Review, 1993; Peters, 1991).

A recent example of the "private is better" philosophy is the practice of paying for performance, which migrated from the private to the public sector in the United States with the Civil Service Reform Act of 1978. Pay for performance is one of a host of utilitarian solutions to the linkage problem, which assume that an employee's psychological ties to an organization are controlled through a calculative process. Romzek (1990, p. 375) calls this an "investment strategy":

> Today most of the current policy proposals to reinvigorate the public service focus on the motivations of and inducements for public employees. The emphasis is usually on an investment approach to employee inducements, such as pay, benefits, and career opportunities available to those who work in the public sector. While these are extremely important facets of the inducements necessary to attract and retain high quality public employees, they are not enough. Nonetheless, nearly all the focus in public debates and proposals is on improving investment-oriented inducements for public employees.

The pursuit of these investment strategies is filled with irony. After more than a dozen years of experience with pay for performance in the U.S. federal service, the system has failed to gain acceptance and, more important, to achieve the goals established for it (Ingraham, 1993; Milkovich and Wigdor, 1991; Perry, 1986, 1992; Performance Management and Recognition System Review Committee, 1991). One reason is structural. Democratic governments have a great deal of difficulty delivering on the implicit commitments associated with contingent pay contracts. The financing of monetary awards is uncertain, given the reliance on public funds. Failure to conform to employees' expectations about financial rewards or performance assessments can fatally undermine pay-for-performance programs (Perry, 1986, 1992). Perhaps the ultimate irony of pay for performance is that it may alienate many public servants, thereby exacerbating rather than solving linkage problems. To make matters worse, pay for performance simultaneously deflects managers' attention from alternative motivational programs because it absorbs so much time and so many organizational resources.

There are clearly alternative strategies, but they may not be readily found in business. Perry and Wise (1990) suggest that public service motivation—an individual's predisposition to respond to motives grounded primarily or uniquely in public institutions—consists primarily of norm-based and affective factors. Norm-based motives are actions generated by efforts to conform to such norms as civic duty and the public interest. Affective motives are triggers of behavior that are grounded in emotional responses, such as compassion and self-sacrifice, to various social contexts. These public service motives are more likely than utilitarian motives to build psychological ties between employees and their organizations that are grounded in shared values—what Romzek (1990) calls *commitment*.

Reinvigorating the commitment of public employees could go a long way toward coping with the shifting public employee-organization linkages. What steps would the commitment strategy require? The specific steps would be contingent on organizational circumstances, but they would include designing and implementing congruent reward systems, developing supportive organizational cultures, creating opportunities for socialization to public service motives, and providing transformational leadership.

*Congruent Reward Systems*

A starting point for a strategy to reinvigorate public service is the organizational reward systems that affect public employees

in their day-to-day interactions with their employers. In the recent past, politicians and top executives in the United States,
driven by public demands for accountability and by concerns
about the public sector's productivity, have opted for the most
politically popular tools (such as contingent pay) as symbols of
their control over the public bureaucracy (March and Olsen,
1983; Perry and Porter, 1982). The solutions have been short-
lived, failing to resolve the long-term strategic problem of reinvigorating public service.

Reward systems can strengthen public employee–organization linkages to the extent that they respond fairly to the
basic needs of employees and promote public service values.
With this general heuristic, what should replace individual monetary rewards as the incentive of choice? A departure from present
trends, although not a full-fledged alternative, would be for
governments to begin to emphasize groups, as opposed to individuals, in the design of incentive systems (National Commission on the State and Local Public Service, 1993; Perry, 1991).
It is difficult to envision such values as civic duty, the public
interest, and communitarianism being nurtured if the values
that the organization promotes in the conduct of its affairs are
highly individualistic. Recent developments in the U.S. federal
government offer some promise. The quality movement, with
its emphasis on teamwork and its antagonism toward individual performance appraisal (even though the antagonism has not
been sufficient to eliminate use of individual appraisals in most
organizations), is one indication of a shift toward group-based
work systems.

Another development is the growing use of gainsharing,
which permits groups of employees to share in revenue increases
or budgetary savings accruing from group efforts. A recently
concluded federal demonstration, PACER SHARE, conducted
at the Directorate of Distribution of the Sacramento Air Logistics Center, illustrates some of the ways in which gainsharing
can be used to reinforce public service values. PACER SHARE
allocated relatively equal shares of budgetary savings to the
Air Force and to participating employees. Individual performance appraisals were eliminated. Although PACER SHARE

permitted employees an opportunity to receive a financial award, it emphasized the group as the level where such results are obtained, and it promoted a reduction in the overall cost of government.

Public organizations must be concerned with providing adequate pecuniary rewards for their members. But because public service is attractive to individuals seeking to satisfy altruistic motives, public organizations need to offer more than pecuniary rewards if they hope to achieve the full potential of their human resources (Knoke and Wright-Izak, 1982; Perry and Wise, 1990). Given Buchanan's research (1974, 1975), another step in a commitment strategy would be to strive to reinforce employees' personal significance. Although public sector work is believed to be socially significant, it is how job incumbents perceive their work that is important. Public managers and reward systems must help organizational members interpret their work in light of such public service motives as civic duty, social justice, compassion, and the public interest. To the extent that organizational rewards are distributed in ways that infuse work with meaning salient to the norms and emotions important to employees, their personal significance and commitment are likely to be enhanced.

Research suggests that building commitment is a reciprocal process (Angle and Perry, 1983). Public organizations cannot expect employees to be committed to their goals and values without a mutual commitment to employees' goals and values (National Academy of Public Administration, 1993). Thus public organizations should seek to develop work systems based on policies of mutuality (Walton, 1985). Employee empowerment is one tactic firmly embedded in mutuality (Brumback, 1993). Removing barriers to trust and creating strong procedural justice systems are additional avenues for strengthening commitment through policies of mutuality. Although public organizations have a reputation for strong procedural justice systems, the existing formal procedures, as many whistleblowers have come to discover (Glazer and Glazer, 1989; Perry, 1993b), often result in substantive injustices, rather than in organizational improvements.

On the whole, reward systems in public organizations could benefit from recent thinking about strategic human resources management (Devanna, Fombrun, and Tichy, 1984; Lengnick-Hall and Lengnick-Hall, 1988; McGregor, 1991; Perry, 1993a). The core principle of strategic human resources management is that organizational effectiveness requires an alignment of strategy, structure, and human resources management practices (Devanna, Fombrun, and Tichy, 1984; Lawler, 1990). Achieving alignment in complex, loosely coupled, polyarchic systems is inherently difficult. It is, however, a goal toward which we should strive.

## Organizational Culture

Organizational culture, the "shared beliefs and assumptions by which individuals operate" within an agency (Romzek, 1990, p. 378), is part of the context of reward systems and therefore an important consideration in their implementation, often representing a constraint on what types of reward systems are likely to be effective (Milkovich and Wigdor, 1991). Golembiewski (1986, p. 15) writes: "Appropriate-culture creation should be viewed as conceptually related to the development and application of formal systems like merit pay, and often as requiring prior attention." But the importance of organizational culture is not solely in its role of facilitating other organizational systems. Shared beliefs and assumptions are important devices in their own right for developing and reinforcing the physical and psychological attachments between individuals and organizations.

Historically, public organizations have had limited control over their missions and administrative systems because they are creatures of legislatures. Given their limited control, public managers have been unable to use organizational culture to reinforce strategies for human resources. Recent trends, however, such as employment externalization and decentralization, may give public managers the latitude to facilitate the creation of strong cultures conducive to high performance. For example, managers may be able to structure the makeup of the core work force and "may find it more convenient to de-emphasize — and perhaps externalize altogether — those functions that are rather peripheral to this core activity of the organization. In the terminology of conventional organizational theory, such an approach reduces structural differentiation, thereby making integration easier to accomplish through a shared set of values, orientations, and activities" (Pfeffer and Baron, 1988, p. 273).

The precise tasks associated with using organizational culture as a means for reinvigorating public service will differ according to circumstances. In general, an organizational culture supportive of high levels of commitment and performance will be developed through rituals, slogans, and shared beliefs, the primary means by which cultures are manifested and sustained. For instance, the ability of the federal government to attract top talent despite the long-standing gap between pay in the public sector and pay in the private sector has been sustained by shared beliefs about the social good of government service. To the extent that recent attacks on government have eroded "social good" beliefs, they have contributed to a decline in the attractiveness of government.

Commitment to the values embodied in public service is still seen by many as an essential element linking individual commitment to organizational culture. Wolf and Bacher (1990) contrast an employee's vocation with her career and her job. They argue that neither the pecuniary (job) nor personal development (career) benefits of public employment are adequate to sustain strong public employee–organization ties; it is the consonance between one's vocation and the agency's mission (externally) and culture (internally) that provides the basis for sustainable commitment.

One implication of the erosion of belief in government as an institution for social good is that it may become necessary to "buy back" interest in top management positions with higher salaries. An alternative course involves the development of new beliefs that support recruitment of talented managers and professionals who are willing to accept salaries lower than those available in the private sector.

*Socialization*

Socialization, the process of inculcating motives (Barnard, 1938), is also an avenue by which to reinvigorate public service. How can public service motives be instilled in potential recruits for government service? National initiatives may serve as a catalyst for activating public service motivation. For example, President Clinton's national service program provides public service opportunities for young people. It is intended to develop normative and affective attachments to public service.

Attempts to recruit and provide incentives for promising entrants into the public service, such as the Presidential Management Intern Program, have been conceived as ways to socialize employees into the broad values and missions of the federal government. The availability of career opportunities, meaningful work, and a sense of belonging and understanding the role of one's efforts in the grander scheme have all been shown to influence the decision of interns to remain in the federal work force. A broad socialization into the world of public service seems important, in addition to commitment to agency goals (Johnson, 1991).

Given that services are increasingly being delivered by nonprofit organizations (Smith and Lipsky, 1993), the value commitments of individuals to such organizations as churches, community action agencies, and philanthropic organizations should also be harnessed as a means of reinvigorating public service. The value commitments of members of the third sector provide an avenue for reinvigorating public employee–organization linkages. These value commitments should be formally recognized in the design and evaluation of third-party delivery systems.

One way in which government organizations have already tapped in to the value commitments of nonemployees is through volunteers (Brudney, 1990; Ilsley, 1990). But using volunteers in public service is not without problems. From the perspective of permanent employees, the integration of volunteers may be difficult because of the threat that volunteers pose to permanent employees. Heavy reliance on volunteers' efforts may detract from the very reasons underlying their involvement — volunteering as a value, and the opportunity to enhance a basic level of service.

*Leadership*

Many of the ideas just discussed depend for their success on leadership, both political and managerial. Leaders must be able to articulate the values that will bind people to public service. As already noted, recent efforts to reinvigorate public service have relied predominantly on appeals to rational or calculative motives, which ignore the importance of shared values. Although calculative ties are partially substitutable for value commitments, they cannot fully replace the strength of ties growing from shared values.

The role of leaders is twofold. First, leaders must recognize that the erosion of ties to public service is a cyclical process involving the decay of public service–based values over time (Gardner, 1990; Hirschman, 1982). The cyclical process requires reaffirmation, not abandonment, of historical relationships (that is, of the importance of shared values as the basis for integrating individuals into public service). As Gardner (1990, p. 13) has written, "Values always decay over time. Societies that keep their values alive do so not by escaping the processes of decay but by powerful processes of regeneration."

The second role of leaders follows from the first: to initiate the processes of regeneration that strengthen ties to public service. This may require taking the lead in developing some of the organizational and institutional programs already discussed here. It also requires leaders to reach out to their followers and articulate, in ways appropriate to today's context, the values that give meaning to their lives. Leaders cannot be content to manage transactions with followers; instead, they must engage followers in a transformational process that lifts their aspirations (Burns, 1978).

## Questions and Issues for the Future

This chapter has described a commitment-based strategy for revitalizing public employee–organization linkages. The commitment strategy, in contrast to a calculative or investment strategy, seeks to integrate institutional and individual values. The mechanisms for achieving integration are reward systems geared toward public service motives; organizational culture; socialization; and transformational leadership.

The issues addressed in this chapter reveal a variety of research needs, many of which have not been addressed seriously.

The most central need revolves around the changing nature of public employment relationships. As more of the public sector shifts from traditional bureaucratic control to other types of employment systems, we are moving outside the experience for which we have good empirical data. We have some evidence about the interactions of volunteers and permanent staff (Brudney, 1990), but it is confined to smaller, less complex organizational settings. New research should focus on evolving employment relationships in large, complex public organizations.

In addition to developing a better understanding of evolving public employment relationships, we need to know more about employees' psychological attachments and about effective interventions. Much of what we now know about psychological attachments is drawn from empirical research in business organizations. Although this research may provide insights into general processes, it is no substitute for empirical research on public institutions. Further empirical research is absolutely essential to an understanding of the complex interplay of the rational, normative, and affective motives that operate in public organizations (Knoke and Wright-Izak, 1982). Understanding the interplay of these motives is essential to an understanding of the dynamics and efficacy of the commitment strategy discussed in this chapter.

What we do not know about employment relationships, psychological attachments, and reinvigoration strategies raises a host of practical questions that merit investigation. How does the mix of employment relationships in an organization affect employees and the organizations that employ them? How can the line between careerists and political appointees be redrawn with minimum deleterious effects? Is a commitment-based strategy feasible in the unstable political environment of most public agencies? How can organizational members of varying statuses best be integrated?

Important as answers to these questions are, they are secondary to an even more basic set of research issues. What effects will the shifting public employee–organization linkages, and the responses of managers and political leaders, have on other important public values? An immediate concern is the implication of employment externalization for accountability (see Chapter Eleven of this volume for further discussion of accountability and flexible personnel systems). This concern can be framed starkly as a question: Can government, particularly the federal government, become just another "peripheral firm"? The implications of the shifting public employee–organization linkages intersect other institutional values, among them representativeness and social equity. These value issues, and the instrumental questions just posed, encompass an agenda for scholars in public administration and public personnel for years to come.

## References

Angle, H. L., and Perry, J. L. "Individual and Organizational Influences on Organizational Commitment." *Work and Occupations,* 1983, *10,* 123–146.

Balfour, D., and Wechsler, B. "Antecedents and Outcomes of Commitment in Public Organizations." *Public Productivity and Management Review,* 1991, *14*(4), 355–368.

Balfour, D., and Wechsler, B. "A Theory of Public Sector Commitment: Towards a Reciprocal Model of Person and Organization." *Research in Public Administration,* forthcoming.

Barnard, C. I. *The Functions of the Executive.* Cambridge, Mass.: Harvard University Press, 1938.

Bozeman, B., and Rahm, D. "The Explosion of Technology." In J. L. Perry (ed.), *Handbook of Public Administration.* San Francisco: Jossey-Bass, 1989.

Brudney, J. L. *Fostering Volunteer Programs in the Public Sector: Planning, Initiating, and Managing Voluntary Activities.* San Francisco: Jossey-Bass, 1990.

Brumback, G. B. "The Continuing Evolution of MBR and Related Developments." *Public Administration Review,* 1993, *53*(3), 213–219.

Buchanan, B. II. "Building Organizational Commitment: The Socialization of Managers in Work Organizations." *Administrative Science Quarterly,* 1974, *19,* 533–546.

Buchanan, B. II. "To Walk an Extra Mile: The Whats, Whens, and Whys of Organizational Commitment." *Organizational Dynamics,* 1975, *4,* 67–80.

Burns, J. M. *Leadership.* New York: HarperCollins, 1978.

Carnavale, A. P. *America and the New Economy.* Alexandria, Va.: American Society for Training and Development, 1991.

Czarniawska, B. "The Ugly Sister: On Relationships Between the Private and Public Sectors in Sweden." *Scandinavian Journal of Management Studies,* 1985, *2,* 83-103.

Davis-Blake, A., and Uzzi, B. "Determinants of Employment Externalization: A Study of Temporary Workers and Independent Contractors." *Administrative Science Quarterly,* 1993, *38,* 195-223.

Devanna, M. A., Fombrun, C., and Tichy, N. "A Framework for Strategic Human Resource Management." In C. Fombrun, N. Tichy, and M. A. Devanna (eds.), *Strategic Human Resource Management.* New York: Wiley, 1984.

Drucker, P. S. *The Age of Discontinuity.* New York: HarperCollins, 1969.

Gardner, J. W. *On Leadership.* New York: Free Press, 1990.

Garvey, G. *Facing the Bureaucracy: Living and Dying in a Public Agency.* San Francisco: Jossey-Bass, 1993.

Glazer, M. P., and Glazer, P. M. *The Whistleblowers: Exposing Corruption in Government and Industry.* New York: Basic Books, 1989.

Golembiewski, R. T. "OD Perspectives on High Performance: Some Good News and Some Bad News About Merit Pay." *Review of Public Personnel Administration,* 1986, *7,* 9-26.

Harris, M. "What's Wrong with This Picture?" *Working Woman,* 1990, *15,* 72-76.

Hirschman, A. O. *Shifting Involvement: Private Interest and Public Action.* Princeton, N.J.: Princeton University Press, 1982.

Ilsley, P. J. *Enhancing the Volunteer Experience: New Insights on Strengthening Volunteer Participation, Learning, and Commitment.* San Francisco: Jossey-Bass, 1990.

Ingraham, P. W. "Of Pigs in Pokes and Policy Diffusion: Another Look at Pay-for-Performance." *Public Administration Review,* 1993, *53,* 348-356.

Jabes, J., and Zussman, D. "Motivation, Rewards, and Satisfaction in the Canadian Federal Public Service." *Canadian Public Administration,* 1988, *1,* 204-225.

Jamieson, D., and O'Mara, J. *Managing Workforce 2000: Gaining the Diversity Advantage.* San Francisco: Jossey-Bass, 1991.

Johnson, G. *Recruiting, Retaining, and Motivating the Federal Workforce.* New York: Quorum, 1991.

Johnston, W. B. *Civil Service 2000.* Washington, D.C.: U.S. Office of Personnel Management, 1988.

Johnston, W. B., and Parker, A. H. *Workforce 2000: Work and Workers for the 21st Century.* Washington, D.C.: U.S. Department of Labor, 1987.

Kanter, D. L., and Mirvis, P. H. *The Cynical Americans: Living and Working in an Age of Discontent and Disillusionment.* San Francisco: Jossey-Bass, 1989.

Katzell, R. A. "Changing Attitudes Toward Work." In C. Kerr and J. M. Rostow (eds.), *Work in America: The Decade Ahead.* New York: Van Nostrand Reinhold, 1979.

Kerr, C. "Introduction: Industrialism with a Human Face." In C. Kerr and J. M. Rostow (eds.), *Work in America: The Decade Ahead.* New York: Van Nostrand Reinhold, 1979.

Kettl, D. "Government by Proxy and the Public Service." *International Review of Administrative Sciences,* 1988, *54,* 501–515.

Knoke, D., and Wright-Izak, C. "Individual Motives and Organizational Incentive Systems." *Research in the Sociology of Organizations,* 1982, *1,* 209–254.

Lane, L. M., and Wolf, J. F. *The Human Resource Crisis in the Public Sector.* New York: Quorum, 1990.

Lawler, E. E. III. *Strategic Pay: Aligning Organizational Strategies and Pay Systems.* San Francisco: Jossey-Bass, 1990.

Leemans, A. M. "Recent Trends in the Career Service in European Countries." *International Review of Administrative Sciences,* 1987, *53,* 63–88.

Lengnick-Hall, C. A., and Lengnick-Hall, M. A. "Strategic Human Resource Management: A Review of the Literature and a Proposed Typology." *Academy of Management Review,* 1988, *13*(3), 454–470.

Levine, C. H. "The Federal Government in the Year 2000: Administrative Legacies of the Reagan Years." *Public Administration Review,* 1986, *46,* 195–206.

Lipset, S. M., and Schneider, W. *The Confidence Gap.* Baltimore, Md.: Johns Hopkins University Press, 1987.

Loden, M., and Rosener, J. B. *Workforce America: Managing Diversity as a Vital Resource.* Homewood, Ill.: Business One Irwin, 1991.

McGregor, E. B., Jr. "The Public Sector Human Resource Puzzle: Strategic Management of a Strategic Resource." *Public Administration Review,* 1988, *48,* 941–950.

McGregor, E. B., Jr. *Strategic Management of Human Knowledge, Skills, and Abilities: A Handbook for Leaders.* San Francisco: Jossey-Bass, 1991.

March, J. G., and Olsen, J. P. "Organizing Political Life: What Administrative Reorganization Tells Us About Government." *American Political Science Review,* 1983, *77,* 281–296.

Milkovich, T. G., and Wigdor, A. K. (eds.). *Pay for Performance: Evaluating Performance Appraisal and Merit Pay.* Washington, D.C.: National Academy Press, 1991.

Mowday, R. T., Porter, L. W., and Steers, R. M. *Employee-Organization Linkages.* San Diego, Calif.: Academic Press, 1982.

National Academy of Public Administration. *Leading People in Change: Empowerment, Commitment, and Accountability.* Washington, D.C.: National Academy of Public Administration, 1993.

National Commission on the Public Service. *Leadership for America: Rebuilding the Public Service.* Washington, D.C.: National Commission on the Public Service, 1989.

National Commission on the State and Local Public Service. *Hard Truths/Tough Choices: An Agenda for State and Local Reform.* Albany, N.Y.: Nelson A. Rockefeller Institute of Government, 1993.

National Performance Review. *From Red Tape to Results: Creating a Government That Works Better and Costs Less.* Washington, D.C.: U.S. Government Printing Office, 1993.

Osborne, D., and Gaebler, T. *Reinventing Government: How the Entrepreneurial Spirit Is Transforming the Public Sector.* Reading, Mass.: Addison-Wesley, 1992.

Performance Management and Recognition System Review Committee. *Advancing Managerial Excellence: A Report on Improving the Performance Management and Recognition System.* Washington, D.C.: U.S. Office of Personnel Management, 1991.

Perry, J. L. "Merit Pay in the Public Sector: The Case for a Failure of Theory." *Review of Public Personnel Administration,* 1986, *7*(1), 261–278.

Perry, J. L. "Linking Pay to Performance: The Controversy Continues." In C. Ban and N. M. Riccucci (eds.), *Public Personnel Management: Current Concerns, Future Challenges.* White Plains, N.Y.: Longman, 1991.

Perry, J. L. "The Merit Pay Reforms." In P. W. Ingraham and D. H. Rosenbloom (eds.), *The Promise and Paradox of Civil Service Reform.* Pittsburgh, Pa.: University of Pittsburgh Press, 1992.

Perry, J. L. "Strategic Human Resource Management: Transforming the Federal Civil Service to Meet Future Challenges." *Review of Public Personnel Administration,* 1993a, *13*(4), 59–71.

Perry, J. L. "Whistleblowing, Organizational Performance, and Organizational Control." In H. George Frederickson (ed.), *Ethics and Public Administration.* Armonk, N.Y.: M. E. Sharpe, 1993b.

Perry, J. L., and Kraemer, K. L. "The Implications of Changing Technology." In F. J. Thompson (ed.), *Revitalizing State and Local Public Service: Strengthening Performance, Accountability, and Citizen Confidence.* San Francisco: Jossey-Bass, 1993.

Perry, J. L., and Porter, L. W. "Factors Affecting the Context for Motivation in Public Organizations." *Academy of Management Review,* 1982, *7*, 89–98.

Perry, J. L., and Wise, L. R. "The Motivational Bases of Public Service." *Public Administration Review,* 1990, *50*(3), 367–373.

Peters, B. G. "Morale in the Public Service: A Comparative Inquiry." *International Review of Administrative Sciences,* 1991, *57*, 421–440.

Pfeffer, J., and Baron, J. N. "Taking the Workers Back Out: Recent Trends in the Structuring of Employment." *Research in Organizational Behavior,* 1988, *10*, 257–303.

Romzek, B. "Employee Investment and Commitment: The Ties
That Bind." *Public Administration Review,* 1990, *50,* 374–382.

Sekaran, U., and Hall, D. T. "Asynchronism in Dual-Career
and Family Linkages." In M. B. Arthur, D. T. Hall, and
B. S. Lawrence (eds.), *Handbook of Career Theory.* Cambridge,
England: Cambridge University Press, 1989.

Smith, S. R., and Lipsky, M. *Nonprofits for Hire: The Welfare
State in the Age of Contracting.* Cambridge, Mass.: Harvard
University Press, 1993.

U.S. Office of Personnel Management. *The Federal Flexible Workplace Pilot Project Work-at-Home Component, Final Report.* Washington, D.C.: Career Entry Group, Staffing Policy Division,
U.S. Office of Personnel Management, 1993 (Photocopied).

Walton, R. E. "Toward a Strategy of Eliciting Employee Commitment Based on Policies of Mutuality." In R. E. Walton
and P. R. Lawrence (eds.), *HRM Trends and Challenges.* Boston:
Harvard Business School Press, 1985.

Wilson, W. "The Study of Administration." *Political Science Quarterly,* 1887, *2,* 197–222.

Wise, L. "Dimensions of Public Sector Pay Policies in the United
States and Sweden." *Review of Public Personnel Administration,*
1988, *8,* 61–83.

Wolf, J. F. "Career Plateauing in the Public Service: Baby Boom
and Employment Bust." *Public Administration Review,* 1983, *43,*
160–165.

Wolf, J. F., and Bacher, R. N. "The Public Administrator and
Public Service Occupations." In G. L. Wamsley and others
(eds.), *Refounding Public Administration.* Newbury Park, Calif.:
Sage, 1990.

# 9

# Reinventing the
# Senior Executive Service

*Ronald P. Sanders*

They number only eight thousand, yet their work affects every citizen of this country. They are responsible for a federal budget that exceeds $1 trillion and funds thousands of complex and arcane programs. Over three million people, in and out of uniform, depend on them for direction and leadership. They do glamorous things, like searching for a cure for AIDS and putting satellites and space shuttles in orbit. They also audit tax returns, build dams, pay Medicare bills, and process the countless forms that fuel the engines of government. They are members

*Note:* The opinions expressed in this chapter are solely those of the author and do not represent the official views or position of the Department of Defense or the Senior Executives Association (SEA). The author wishes to express his appreciation to SEA's Professional Development League, which sponsored and funded the research described here.

215

of the federal Senior Executive Service (SES), archetypal bureaucrats called on to lead and manage the unbelievably complex
organizations that deliver public goods and services. Their excellence is undeniably essential to effective governance.

This chapter is about them, the mandarins of our nation's
career civil service, who labor at the interface of the deciding
and the doing in government. The premise of this chapter is
simple: the ability of these individuals is vitally important, and
the efficacy of many of our public institutions (especially but
not exclusively federal) depends in large part on their skills and
expertise. This is particularly the case if the federal government
is ever to be "reinvented" (see Osborne and Gaebler, 1992), a
prospect that would seem to depend on the competence of career
executives. In this regard, the 1978 Civil Service Reform Act
promised a Senior Executive Service composed of the federal
government's best and brightest, developed and deployed to meet
the challenges of modern public administration. But has it kept
that promise?

That question serves as the central focus of this inquiry.
I will begin by reviewing the promise of the SES, as embodied
in the law and the legislative history of its enabling statute. That
promise is considerable, but it is insufficient in and of itself. It
must be operationalized in the day-to-day management of what
are arguably the federal government's most "strategic" human
resources, and I will evaluate that prospect in some detail by
examining how senior executives are developed and deployed
by the federal government. This preliminary empirical assessment reveals that promise and practice appear to be two very
different things. The chapter concludes by suggesting some reasons for this disparity and then offering systemic and structural
recommendations that may serve to realize the full potential of
the SES.

## The Promise of the SES

The promise of the Senior Executive Service is implicitly grounded
in the dichotomy of public administration's classical paradigm,
its underlying purpose purely instrumental: to ensure that the

executive management of the United States government is responsive to the nation's needs, policies, and goals. This is hardly a surprise. That paradigm was implicit throughout the SES's parent legislation, the Civil Service Reform Act, with its emphasis on bringing an unresponsive and poorly performing civil service under control.

In the case of the SES, the act established a government-wide system for "selecting, assigning, developing, rewarding, and managing the men and women who administer the hundreds of federal programs that are vital to the nation" (Campbell, 1979). The personnel rules that comprise that system serve as a common and defining denominator intended to bind those men and women. The members of the SES, as progeny of that system, are characterized in law by a number of classical metrics that purport to define executive competence: efficiency, effectiveness, service quality, continuity, accountability, compliance, and the like. Taken together, these metrics suggest that competence in the SES is neutral, instrumental, and intended to be value-free. In this regard, the service's enabling statute promises characteristics without context, neglecting to articulate a larger institutional role for its members among the various actors in our political system. This may have been deliberate, perhaps even a political expediency, given the objectives of the act (it was hardly a celebration of the historical effectiveness of the civil service). Nevertheless, the neutral instrumentality of the SES is presumed to be reason enough for its existence. But governance is inherently value-laden; thus the "theory" of the SES may be at odds with the practical realities of public management.

Those practical realities may serve to clarify this institutional ambiguity and, in so doing, offer some insight into a redefinition of career executive competence. The Senior Executive Service acts as the interface between political appointees at the top of a government agency and the career civil servants below them who deliver its services. Although never expressly spelled out in law or regulation, the hierarchical nature of government tends to position career senior executives at the confluence of policy and execution. This is not intended to suggest a dichotomy in this regard (indeed, it is precisely this confluence that sweeps away the classical paradigm) but rather more of a continuum, with the "deciding" at one end, the "doing" at the other—and the senior career executive squarely in the middle.

If this is true, one may begin to posit an institutional role for the service that goes well beyond the promise of neutral competence and administrative instrumentality. It is a role that revolves around a notion of "political" management: the exercise of traditional (and largely generic) executive leadership competencies in the pursuit of various institutional, political, organizational, and even individual interests. It is a role that is explicitly value-laden, an artful blending of public administration and purposive political advocacy, and it must be fully acknowledged and understood if the full potential of the SES is to be realized in a reinvented federal government.

## The Practice of Federal Executive Resource Management

Has the instrumental promise of the Senior Executive Service, as set forth in its enabling statute, been kept? Has its full institutional potential (to include dimensions that are inherently political) been realized in the day-to-day management of the federal government's executive resources? If one accepts the premise that effective governance at the federal level turns at least in part on career executive leadership, then these issues become a matter of strategic importance, to the public as well as to any particular presidential administration.

A sample of career senior executives was surveyed in order to examine these issues empirically. Using the institutional framework of the SES (posited previously) as a benchmark, the survey sought to answer three broad questions concerning the day-to-day workings of the Senior Executive Service:

1.   Do senior executives demonstrate common managerial competencies, regardless of agency or functional specialty, that are consistent with their instrumental role?

2.   Do members of the SES also demonstrate mastery of competencies that can be characterized as political management, in a nonpartisan sense?

3.  How have these competencies been developed and utilized?
    In other words, what kinds of career development and executive assignment strategies have been employed to ensure that SES members have been appropriately developed and deployed to optimize these competencies?

   To answer these questions, the survey attempted to elicit data from SES respondents in four areas: personal characteristics and career history, position type, general day-to-day activities (managerial and political), and relationships with various political actors. It was administered to a sample of some 300 career members of SES. These executives were randomly selected from the SES membership of the Senior Executives Association (SEA), a nonprofit professional association representing the interests of federal executives. A sample of 207 executives responded, for a return rate of 67 percent. Of the approximately 8,000 career members of the SES, 2,402 (or 30 percent) are dues-paying members of SEA, which introduces some bias into the sample, precluding statistical inference from the population as a whole. Nevertheless, the results have practical utility in better understanding the SES.
   To establish a baseline for this examination, the respondents indicated their primary functional responsibilities (legal issues, personnel, budget, agency operations, general administration, and so on). Responses were then collapsed into three type-clusters, for purposes of more detailed examination. Of the total sample, 31 percent occupied line positions involved in delivering an agency's principal product or service (such as health care in the case of Veterans Administration hospitals); 46 percent performed a variety of more specialized staff functions, such as in public affairs, personnel, procurement, and so on; and 23 percent performed general administrative duties that dealt with management support of agency operations but were not directly involved in the principal products or services. In the subsequent analysis, position types were treated as an independent variable.
   As noted, the empirical study was principally concerned with the various competencies demonstrated by career members of the Senior Executive Service. In this regard, one of the assumptions implicit in the service's enabling statute is that "man-

agement is management"—in other words, that there are certain instrumental activities common to the executive function. (Indeed, these activities are generally thought to be inherent in executive positions, regardless of setting; see Rainey, 1991, for a review of the literature in this regard). The survey attempted to evaluate this assumption by asking respondents to indicate the amount of time they spent on a number of generic management activities during a given period.

Those activities, adapted from Gulick's classic PODS-CORB typology (1937), were reportedly performed with considerable regularity (see Table 9.1). SES members, regardless of

Table 9.1. SES Managerial Activities
(Reported by 207 Respondents).

| Activity | Average Percentage of Time |
|---|---|
| Directing | 38 |
| Organizing | 13 |
| Coordinating | 13 |
| Planning | 10 |
| Managing people | 10 |
| Managing money | 10 |
| Managing information | 6 |

position type, spent the bulk of their time directing operations, but they also reported spending considerable time organizing work groups and assignments and coordinating efforts among other parts of their organizations. Somewhat less time was reportedly spent on planning, dealing with human resources, and financial and budget matters. Thus, as a practical matter, SES members seem to demonstrate a common set of managerial competencies. This observation suggests that they may be deployed with considerable flexibility within and among federal agencies.

These results are consistent with the reported self-image of career executives, who tended to describe themselves in similar terms (see Table 9.2). In this regard, respondents were given a list of executive roles, adapted from the work of Mintzberg

Table 9.2. Executive Self-Image
(Percentage of 207 Respondents Indicating "Most/Least Descriptive").

| Management Role | Most Descriptive | Least Descriptive |
|---|---|---|
| Leader | 33 | 1 |
| Administrator | 31 | 2 |
| Implementer | 8 | 11 |
| Coordinator | 8 | 8 |
| Mediator | 7 | 8 |
| Coach | 9 | 7 |
| Technical expert | 3 | 31 |
| Regulator | 1 | 32 |

(1972), and were asked to indicate which roles were most (and least) descriptive of their responsibilities as SES members. "Leader" was the most frequent choice, with 33 percent of the sample identifying this as the single word that best described their executive responsibilities. Only 1 percent of the sample chose this as the least descriptive. For 31 percent, "administrator" best described the nature of their duties, while 2 percent said this term was least descriptive. Conversely, 32 percent of the respondents said that "regulator" least described their responsibilities (only 1 percent chose this as the best descriptor), while an additional 31 percent indicated that "technical expert" was least descriptive. Thus the self-image of the federal career executive seems to be consistent with the broad executive competencies that he or she reportedly applies. Members of the Senior Executive Service, or at least those in this particular sample, do not see themselves as narrow technocrats or "green eyeshade" government regulators, but rather as leaders and general managers whose responsibilities transcend the specialized technical aspects of particular agencies or programs. This is consistent with the competencies they report, competencies that may be more or less common to any executive position. This is quite different from the stereotyped bureaucrat sometimes conjured up by politicians and public.

These findings suggest that the first, explicitly instrumental promise of the SES has been kept. According to the data,

SES members seem to exhibit the various competencies and qualitative characteristics envisioned by the law's definition of executive excellence, narrow as that definition may be. In this regard, the results support the notion that members of the SES generally employ similar skills, and that these skills may be compared broadly to those employed by executives outside the federal government. Note that these various generic managerial competencies are implicitly "neutral" and apolitical in nature, and they are thus consistent with the intellectual and legal underpinnings of the service.

Survey results also suggest that there are other dimensions of the federal senior executive's job that are not so purely instrumental. In this regard, the survey attempted to measure the extent to which SES members demonstrated managerial competencies that could be characterized as political—that is, purposive dealings with actors and/or processes that are part of our political system. For example, an SES member's attempt to persuade a congressional staffer to draft and introduce a particular piece of legislation that supports his or her agency or program (via the staffer's elected superior, of course) may be characterized as political management.

According to the survey, such competencies were prevalent among SES members (see Table 9.3). For example, 67 percent of survey respondents indicated that they had given public speeches advocating a particular position of their agencies, and 46 percent stated that they had been called on to testify before Congress. Another 31 percent actually drafted legislation and

Table 9.3. Political Management Activities
(Percentage of 207 Respondents Reporting Activity Performance).

| Activity | Percentage |
| --- | --- |
| Public advocacy | 67 |
| Congressional testimony | 46 |
| Legislative drafting/advocacy | 31 |
| Regulatory/policy development | 28 |
| Agency strategic planning | 25 |
| Acting in a political capacity | 19 |

actively worked for its passage, while 19 percent of the respondents had even acted for a political appointee or served in a political position for an extended period. If these competencies can be construed as political, in a strictly nonpartisan sense, then the survey suggests that career senior executives regularly practice them.

This observation is supported by additional empirical evidence. Survey results revealed frequent and extensive interaction with various political actors, the institutions and organizations that are our government. For example, respondents reported weekly or monthly dealings with the executive branch's central management agencies (the Office of Management and Budget, the Office of Personnel Management, the General Services Administration, and so on), and with senior political leaders, defined as agency heads or their immediate staff members. Similar interaction frequencies were reported with respect to Congress, in dealings with elected officials (state and local as well as federal) and congressional committees. SES members also indicated monthly interaction with other political actors, such as lobbyists, public interest groups, and the media. Surprisingly, respondents reported weekly exposure to private citizens in matters related to their official duties.

These competencies surely go beyond neutral instrumentality and apolitical administration. Indeed, they seem to indicate just the opposite: the intimate involvement of career senior executives in political activities that are inherently value-laden without necessarily becoming partisan. Moreover, while these competencies may be unique in a governmental setting, it appears that they are more or less common to members of the career executive corps that manages in that setting. These competencies are consistent with the larger institutional role of the Senior Executive Service posited by this chapter, and their presence among members of the SES suggests that its second, implicit promise has also been kept in that regard.

One may infer from these data that as a corps, career senior executives possess the broad executive and political competencies essential to effective public management. But are these competencies effectively developed and deployed by the federal government and its various agencies? In other words, has the potential of the SES, as adduced by the characteristics ascribed to its members, been fully realized? There is evidence that the current SES corps was drawn from a high-quality candidate pool, whether developed deliberately or otherwise. Nevertheless, if the relatively insular career paths of career executives (once they enter the SES) is any indication, that corps has been underutilized.

In this regard, survey respondents had surprisingly varied backgrounds before becoming senior executives. About 20 percent had held management positions in other federal agencies, over 17 percent had prior managerial experience in the private or not-for-profit sector, another 12 percent had worked in state and/or local government, 24 percent had completed some kind of formal SES candidate development program, and 97 percent had supervised five or more employees before entering the SES.

The sample also reported considerable mobility before having entered the SES. Over half (56 percent) had moved two or more times during their federal careers, and 53 percent had held positions in two or more functional specialties (such as budget, personnel, acquisition, and so on). These results indicate that most current members of the SES came to the service with broader and more varied experience than might have been expected. Thus their development is consistent with the competencies they have been asked to demonstrate. It is somewhat problematic that their development may have been less than deliberate (National Academy of Public Administration, 1992), but the fact remains that at least this part of the service's third promise has been kept.

Career development strategies have been adequate (and may be getting more attention), but utilization is a different story altogether. Most executives had demonstrated a fair amount of functional, geographical, and organizational mobility before becoming members of the SES, but their mobility actually declined afterward. Fewer than 25 percent had moved to another geographical location after appointment to the SES, and only 29 percent had been reassigned to another functional area (44 percent of the sample had moved to a new position, but in the same functional area). Moreover, movement among federal agencies, regardless of dimension, has been almost nonexistent. The most recent annual figures from the U.S. Office of Personnel Management (1992) indicate that only about 1.4 percent transferred from one agency to another during 1991.

By law, mobility is a condition of appointment to the SES, but members of the SES are not very mobile. This may be because of their resistance to the turmoil associated with movement among functions, organizations, and especially agencies, or it may be that SES members are just not asked to move (except perhaps in the case of a purge). Whatever the reason, this apparent immobility is significant in at least two respects. First, it stunts the growth of career executives, limiting their perspectives and hence their potential. Second, and more important for the purposes of this chapter, it means that the collective competence of the Senior Executive Service is being suboptimized. The prospects for reinventing the federal government are lessened as a consequence.

## Why the Promise Has Not Been Kept

These results suggest considerable disparity between theory and practice. The practice of career executive resource management in the federal government today does not correspond to the promise of the SES. The competencies exhibited by SES members suggest that the service has great potential, but that potential seems to be limited by a number of factors. In part, the institutional ambiguity surrounding the SES impedes the emergence of a strategic framework for its utilization. Clearly, there are political impediments as well: to the public and to many a politician, senior career executives symbolize "big government" and the status quo.

Perhaps the greatest impediment to the potential of the SES is the apparent Balkanization of the service itself. Survey data suggest that SES members generally possess generic, crosscutting competencies that could be applied to a variety of organizational settings, but their utilization may be impeded by rigidities inherent in the present structures of government. These rigidities, perpetuated by the human resources management policies that circumscribe the service, have both horizontal and vertical dimensions.

Across government, federal agencies sometimes resemble a loose confederation of feudal fiefdoms, rather than interlocking, interdependent parts of a larger, "corporate" whole. This seems to be particularly true of the Service, with its disappointing statistics on mobility. At the executive level, agency boundaries are virtually impermeable to SES members — to the extent that any members even want to cross those boundaries. These horizontal barriers also appear to exist within departments and agencies, although to a lesser extent. According to the survey data, there was somewhat greater intraagency mobility except between general administrative positions and other line and specialized staff functions (such as procurement and personnel). This lends additional support to the observation that the SES is more myth than reality, composed of multiple, agency-specific corps, each with its own set of functional career paths.

Horizontal boundaries may be somewhat more permeable to senior executives within a particular federal agency, but that venue still presents formidable vertical ones. For the most part, SES career paths are truncated, limited by a political-career "glass ceiling" that is virtually unbreakable. At one time, agencies traditionally reserved at least one or two subcabinet positions for career executives (for example, assistant secretaries of administration; see Heclo, 1977); those positions increasingly are filled by political appointees (National Commission on the Public Service, 1989). Career executives are thus bound from above and on the flanks by well-guarded organizational borders. Taken together, these borders limit mobility and undermine the coherence of a governmentwide SES corps.

There may be a self-fulfilling prophecy at work here as well. Part of the political culture's inherent bias against career bureaucrats (and its reluctance to put bureaucrats in charge) may stem from the conventional wisdom that bureaucrats represent the status quo. Senior executives who have traveled a narrow, insular career path within a function or an organization may not have the perspective or the experience to do otherwise. If some senior career executives are myopic or unduly parochial, it may be because they know nothing else; there is empirical evidence that they were brought up that way. As members of the SES, few have traveled beyond their own particular territories, perhaps because, paradoxically, they are perceived as lacking the vantage point that comes from such travel.

The borders are perpetuated by the personnel policies that govern the service. A few agencies do deliberately develop and manage their career executives to meet agency goals (National Academy of Public Administration, 1992), but the goals are not linked to an overarching human resources management strategy that supports larger national ends. Without that link, the SES corps has no governmentwide strategic context, a potentially fatal flaw. The U.S. Office of Personnel Management (OPM) certainly does not provide that link, serving not as the federal government's "corporate" personnel department but rather as a keeper (and overseer) of the processes that control the SES.

This may even overstate OPM's role in SES matters. It prescribes selection guidelines, most notably a set of executive competencies that serve to screen SES candidates. It also provides a measure of quality control through ad hoc qualifications-review boards that exercise final approval over SES selections. And it details procedures concerning the periodic recertification of SES members, to include very general certification criteria. But it does not specify mechanisms or even standards for SES candidate development or performance management, nor does it establish any policies or procedures dealing with such central features of the SES as mobility and rank. These issues are left to individual agencies and ensure fragmentation.

Seen in this light, the federal government may be bound together by an overarching civil service system, but it clearly does not act as a single employer with an overarching human resources management strategy. Its personnel policies are almost exclusively concerned with process accountability (Ingraham, Rosenbloom, and Knight, 1992) at the expense of outcome — that is, with how jobs are filled, rather than with who fills them and why. This is especially the case with career executive management. Each cabinet department and agency — and, in some cases, each subcabinet bureau — is left to devise its own executive resource management strategy in keeping with its particular mission.

Is there anything wrong with this from a normative stand-point? Not especially, so long as each agency is considered in isolation, although it does make the promise of the SES hard to keep. Compare this approach with the highly centralized senior executive assignment systems employed by other Western civil services (the United Kingdom, Canada, France), as well as with practice in private industry among multinational corporations and conglomerates, which may be as organizationally complex (if not as large) as the federal government (National Academy of Public Administration, 1992). Almost without exception, these very diverse organizations manage their senior "career" executives as a corporate resource, with central assignment, development, and succession strategies.

Thus the Senior Executive Service is doubly damned, bereft of both content and context. Without a substantive foundation of governmentwide human resources management policies that articulate, manifest, and, most important, operationalize the underlying values, purposes, and practicalities of the SES, there is no corps. And without a link to some larger human resources management strategy that contributes to—and changes with—the national agenda, the SES has no context. Does this matter? Yes. If the Federal government is to be reinvented for real, and not just for rhetoric, the Senior Executive Service must be reinvented as well.

### Reinventing the SES

How, then, do we realize the promise of the SES? How does the federal government as an employer better utilize these human resources as it contemplates fundamental changes in the various organizations they manage and lead?

The answer is quite simple. The federal government must create a new managerial culture among its most senior (and most influential) career employees. In so doing, it must redefine executive excellence. In this regard, it must first make the SES into a true corps—a cohesive body deliberately bound together by shared values, experiences, and opportunities—and deliberately shape it into one that is willing and able to serve as the "shock troops" of administrative revolution. Otherwise, the revolution may fail (Schein, 1985).

This chapter proposes a set of interrelated reforms that deal with the framework of the SES managerial culture, and the human resources management policies and practices that reinforce the shared values that comprise it (Schein, 1985). The reforms rest on a condition: at least with respect to its executive cadre, the federal government must begin to act as a single employer — an admittedly diversified organization (indeed, with various ends that may compete and conflict), but one with executives who are bound by certain core administrative values that support larger political ends.

This condition is not especially difficult to meet, as far as the Senior Executive Service is concerned, for many of those values are codified into law and (according to the data) already manifest in its members. And the condition has been met in other cases (for example, the military's commissioned officer corps, or the State Department's Foreign Service). This will not happen by accident, however. As in any other organization's cultural revolution, it will begin with leadership and vision from the top (Schein, 1985). In the case of the federal government's executive branch, this means the president, for only the individual who occupies that office has the wherewithal to initiate the human resources management reforms that follow. But the leadership cannot stop there. Each cabinet secretary and agency head must reinforce it, treating the SES corps not as a parochial property but as a corporate resource.

A strategic context is also required. A corporate approach to executive resource management is meaningless unless it is clearly and expressly linked to and contributing to the overarching goals of an administration. This link is essential (National Academy of Public Administration, 1992); indeed, it may be the single most important goal of an organization's human resources management function, one that rises above the preoccupation with process administration to focus on outcomes designed to complement a "specific business strategy" (Schuler, 1990; see also Perry, 1993).

In the federal government, this link must be clearly established by political (and career) leaders who represent — and, more important, chart the course for — an administration. This may very well disqualify OPM, which has been criticized for its apparent inability to deal with crucial human resources management problems (National Academy of Public Administration, 1992; U.S. General Accounting Office, 1989; Perry, 1993). Traditionally, OPM has treated civil service policies and procedures in isolation, as ends in themselves rather than as means to the larger program and policy objectives of an administration. Indeed, OPM evaluates policies and procedures, not in terms of their contributions to organizational outcomes, but rather in terms of compliance.

But if not OPM, then who? The most obvious candidate for the federal government's strategic human resources planner is the Office of Management and Budget (OMB). As an institution, OMB is ideally suited to this role, inasmuch as it serves to translate an administration's substantive agenda into an annual budget submission, the closest thing the federal government has to a strategic plan. Budget submission establishes overall agency staffing levels, based on substantive program and policy decisions that represent the priorities of a particular administration. Executive resources deserve similar treatment.

In this regard, OPM is legally empowered to establish the number of SES positions allocated to federal agencies, as part of its biennial review of executive resource requirements. In so doing, however, it makes no attempt to identify, much less link, the strategic considerations that should drive those determinations. As a practical matter, OPM does secure informal OMB clearance before making those determinations, but OMB usually just "ratifies" them; rarely does it attempt to change the requirements, and then only at the margins.

Thus, at least indirectly, an administration's program and policy priorities already have some influence on government-wide executive resource decisions. Contrast this, however, to the sort of rigorous scrutiny that an agency's budget submission receives from OMB. Clearly, if the federal government is to take full advantage of its career executives, the relationship between them and administration priorities must be much more explicit and direct. In other words, OMB must take on a more affirmative role in purposively managing executive resources, allocating them according to an administration's program and policy initiatives, just as it does with budget dollars.

This set of prioritized resource allocations represents an administration's "demand" for senior career executives (note the emphasis on administrationwide requirements, rather than narrow agency ones). What about the supply side of the equation — the individual career executives who must meet those requirements? Here again, current practice must change. Now, each agency is left to its own devices in filling executive requirements, with certain basic procedures serving as the only common denominator among them. Compare this practice with that of large multinational corporations, or even the armed forces, where key executive placements are made centrally by those who direct the entire enterprise.

The prospect of reinventing the federal government requires a governmentwide approach to managing executive resources more strategically. Such an approach would first identify the several hundred key positions most critical to an administration's agenda, and then seek to place the most talented of the career SES corps against those requirements. Such a process would resemble the one typically used to place political appointees except that it would be based on performance and potential rather than on politics and patronage (and, one hopes, would be more systematic).

This kind of approach would ensure the proper ends-means relationship between an administration's strategic agenda and the allocation of career executive resources to implement it. In so doing, it would build commitment and trust among career SES members by acknowledging their pivotal role as an essential part of the solution. To put this more bluntly, it would co-opt the career executive by giving him or her a personal stake in the success of an administration.

To ensure a true corporate perspective, such an approach could be managed by OMB, as the closest thing to the government's strategic planner, in conjunction with OPM, as the government's personnel process manager. Placements, or career executive "appointments," could be made by multidisciplinary executive-search committees modeled after the transition teams that manage the placement of political appointees. Ideally, to avoid inbreeding and ensure a governmentwide perspective, they would be composed of officials, both career and appointed, from within and outside the target agency or organization, and they would be chaired by senior administration officials.

These internal executive-search committees would first determine (with technical assistance from OPM) the particular requirements of the key position, and then they would seek to identify the SES members judged to be best able to meet the requirements. This search could start with the elite of the SES corps: those awarded presidential-rank awards. Career executive appointees, like their political counterparts, would serve "at the pleasure" of the president or in time-limited terms that could be renewed periodically (National Academy of Public Administration, 1992). They would also be afforded placement rights within the SES corps and some protection against arbitrary action.

This strategic approach to career executive management would fundamentally change the culture and value system that underlies today's SES corps. First, by singling out the best of the corps for placement, it would establish mobility as a reward for excellence (if you are really good, you will be asked to be part of the administration), whereas today mobility is seen as a punishment, a means of dealing with poor performance, personality problems, or political purges. Second, by severing a career executive's ties to a particular agency or program, it would erode the self-fulfilling prophecy of bureaucratic inertia and parochialism, which are engendered by those ties. In so doing, it would undermine some of the misconceptions that politicians, appointees, and the political culture generally may have about career bureaucrats.

As noted, this scheme is not without risk. Career senior executives would be asked to give up the relative stability of the status quo for a periodic "free-agent draft" conducted by a new political administration every four years or so — in effect, a sanctioned, systematic purge of at least a portion of the career executive ranks. Such a prospect is sufficiently disconcerting to cast doubt on the likelihood of the reforms advocated by this chapter. Thus this new system must have built-in protection against abuses if it is to be at all viable. Such protection would have to strike a balance between, on the one hand, the flexibility needed by an administration to make strategic executive resource decisions and, on the other, the necessity of guarding against arbitrary (that is, politically punitive) action. This is no mean feat.

What would such protection entail? In order to dispel the legitimate suspicion that more flexibility would further politicize the senior civil service, a reinvented SES would have to raise the political-career glass ceiling, with the statutory designation of certain key subcabinet positions (for example, that of an agency's deputy secretary or assistant secretary for administration, or the equivalent) as career-reserved. These positions were once almost the exclusive domain of the career civil servant; lately they have fallen into the domain of patronage, largely from fear of powerful, permanent bureaucratic mandarins who are impervious to political control. Under the system proposed here, this fear would be mitigated by an administration's discretion to reassign a career assistant secretary and choose a new one (albeit from the ranks of the career SES).

By poking a few holes in the glass ceiling, an administration would send a powerful signal to the career SES corps — a quid pro quo for added flexibility — and it would also begin to resolve some of the institutional ambiguity surrounding the corps. As an additional protection, the career incumbents of these subcabinet positions should also serve as the "directors general" for the senior executives (and other civil servants) in their respective agencies, much as the director general of the Foreign Service does for the State Department: as a combination "godfather/godmother" for the career employees under his or her purview, and as their voice to the agency's political hierarchy.

Such career executive godfathers/godmothers exist informally in agencies today, but their ability to influence senior executive personnel's actions (or protect SES members from actions that may be improperly motivated) is typically based on

personal stature, which must be institutionalized if career executives are to trust the system proposed here. As part of their
institutional role, agency directors general would be intimately
involved in the placement of career executives to and/or from
their respective organizations, serving on the aforementioned
executive-search committees and otherwise ensuring that placements were not tainted by nonmerit considerations.

Within-agency protection is not sufficient, however. Some
form of formal institutional oversight is also necessary if senior
executives are to accept greater political influence over their
working lives. In this regard, career directors general collectively could comprise a senior executive career board (Newburg,
1991) to oversee SES appointments and reassignments across
agency lines. That board would not have an operational role.
Career appointments would still be made on behalf of an administration by its Office of Management and Budget, and those
appointments would still be designed to link career placements
with the administration's program and policy priorities. The
career board would be empowered to review those appointments
under certain conditions, serving as a "court of last resort" for
an SES member who believed that his or her placement was
punitive or motivated by improper (as opposed to legitimate)
political considerations. The board would also be empowered
to effect, or block, the reassignment or appointment of a career
executive in certain exigencies.

Obviously, in a system expressly designed to tie the placement of senior career executives to political priorities, improper
political considerations by definition would be very difficult to
discern, and the board's actions to overrule an administration's
personnel decisions could not be taken lightly. But an oversight
board made up of career executives in key positions — career executives placed in those positions by the administration itself —
just might have enough credibility with both to make such judgments successfully.

### Toward a More Empowered SES

This chapter began with the premise that leadership by senior
career civil servants is essential to effective governance, partic-

ularly during a period of fundamental change in government's structure and operations. In this regard, any prospective reinvention of the federal government will turn on the willingness and capacity of its Senior Executive Service to lead and manage that challenge—to not just accept it (waiting out attempts at change is a familiar and effective tactic in the bureaucracy), but actively make the commitment to bringing reinvention about.

Is the SES up to it? That was the central question of this inquiry, and the answer is "It depends." Clearly, the service's enabling statute envisioned a corps of career executives with the competencies necessary for managing such a task, and it established an administrative framework for the service's development and utilization. Those instrumental competencies, stretched by the practical realities of executive management in an inherently political context, promise a corps of senior federal executives who have the potential both to govern and to serve as change agents.

Has practice lived up to that potential? Yes and no. There are two prerequisites to realizing the full potential of the service. First, its members must have the qualities necessary for leading and managing change. Second, and more important, the SES corps itself must be managed strategically, in a way that reflects and contributes to an administration's priorities. The preliminary data reported in this chapter suggest that SES members generally possess and apply the managerial and political competencies required to meet the challenge. Thus the quality of the SES corps is evident. It is significant that most of the surveyed senior executives saw themselves as leaders, rather than regulators or technical experts. By anyone's definition, leadership entails a willingness to confront the status quo.

These qualities notwithstanding, however, there is evidence that the SES corps has been seriously suboptimized by the human resources management policies that govern its members. Those policies do not treat the SES as a governmentwide "strategic" resource, nor do they establish a link between the development and assignment of senior executives and the program and policy goals of an administration. SES career paths appear to be insular, perhaps dysfunctionally so. By almost every account, federal senior executives seldom move among functions and rarely among agencies. If their mobility before entering the SES is any indication, their current stasis is not a result of their unwillingness to move. It is more likely that they are unable to move.

To put the matter simply, the SES corps is not managed, at least not across agency boundaries. Mobility, in that sense, is typically seen as the responsibility of the executive branch, not of the federal government at large. But from that individual vantage point, organizational boundaries appear impenetrable. This must change, not for the sake of change (this, too, can be dysfunctional), but to ensure that the reinvention of government will be more than just rhetoric. The federal government's feudal approach to senior career executive management is obsolete.

If experience in the private sector is any guide (see, for example, Peters, 1992), we will solve complex problems only by thinking outside the traditional organizational boxes. From the standpoint of human resources management, we need flexible policies and practices that deal with complexity by developing, identifying, bringing together, and managing individuals who have leadership ability, varied interdisciplinary competencies, and broad multiorganizational and multifunctional perspectives. To that end, this chapter proposes a new, strategic way of managing the federal government's Senior Executive Service, one that goes beyond the narrow confines of instrumentality and neutral competence to fully engage career executives in the politics of leading government.

These proposals, taken together, may be characterized as suggesting a revolution in the culture of the federal civil service, a combination of systemic and structural change that treats the career Senior Executive Service as an institutional (and, by definition, a national) resource and manages it accordingly. These proposals, if adopted, would fundamentally change the relationship between an administration and the senior careerists who can help make or break its agenda. Adequate safeguards must be established to protect against abuses on both sides. Once in place, the reforms advocated by this chapter may make the prospect for enterprising, entrepreneurial, and empowered federal government more likely. At a time when government is being called on to do more and better with less, these proposals are worth the risk.

## References

Campbell, A. "Civil Service Reform and Reorganization." In F. J. Thompson (ed.), *Classics of Public Personnel Policy.* Oak Park, Ill.: Moore, 1979.

Gulick, L. "Notes on the Theory of Organization." In L. Gulick and L. Urwick (eds.), *Papers on the Science of Administration.* New York: Institute of Public Administration, 1937.

Heclo, H. *A Government of Strangers: Executive Politics in Washington.* Washington,D.C.: Brookings Institution, 1977.

Ingraham, P., Rosenbloom, D., and Knight, J. P. "The State of Merit in the Federal Government." In P. Ingraham and D. Kettl (eds.), *Agenda for Excellence: Public Service in America.* Chatham, N.J.: Chatham House, 1992.

Mintzberg, H. *The Nature of Managerial Work.* New York: HarperCollins, 1972.

National Academy of Public Administration. *Paths to Leadership.* Washington, D.C.: National Academy of Public Administration, 1992.

National Commission on the Public Service (Volcker Commission). *Leadership for America: Rebuilding the Public Service.* Washington, D.C.: National Commission on the Public Service, 1989.

Newburg, A. *Rank-in-Person: Making the Promise a Reality.* Unpublished manuscript, 1991.

Osborne, D., and Gaebler, T. *Reinventing Government: How the Entrepreneurial Spirit Is Transforming the Public Sector.* Reading, Mass.: Addison-Wesley, 1992.

Perry, J. "Strategic Human Resource Management: Transforming the Federal Civil Service to Meet Future Challenges." *Review of Public Personnel Administration,* 1993, *13*(4), 59–71.

Peters, T. *Liberation Management.* New York: Knopf, 1992.

Rainey, H. *Understanding and Managing Public Organizations.* San Francisco: Jossey-Bass, 1991.

Schein, E. *Organizational Culture and Leadership.* San Francisco: Jossey-Bass, 1985.

Schuler, R. S. "Repositioning the Human Resource Function: Transformation or Demise?" *Academy of Management Executive,* 1990, *4,* 49–60.

U.S. General Accounting Office. *Managing Human Resources: Greater OPM Leadership Needed to Address Critical Challenges.* Washington, D.C.: U.S. General Accounting Office, 1989.

U.S. Office of Personnel Management. *The Status of the Senior Executive Service 1991.* Washington, D.C.: U.S. Office of Personnel Management, 1992.

# 10

# Rethinking Public Employment Structures and Strategies

## *Lois Recascino Wise*

An important component of the contemporary reform toward decentralization and greater managerial discretion in public organizations is the emphasis it places on internal labor-market systems as determinants of the way human resources are used and organizational rewards are distributed. An internal labor market (ILM) is a formal component of an organization's management system, which establishes the policies for allocating and pricing the value of human resources used by an organization. The question of whether an organization principally relies on an internal or an external labor-market system is a management decision that defines the relationship between employees and managers within an organization.

*Note:* Special thanks to Pat Ingraham, Jim Perry, and Barbara Romzek for their comments.

In the absence of centrally determined rules and regulations for personnel management, each organization or responsible division develops its own procedures and policies for selecting and allocating human resources (Siahpush, 1991). Consequently, the systems for regulating personnel management within the public sector are likely to become less uniform and more responsive to local norms and organizational constraints (Buitendam, 1991). At the same time, differences between governmental and nongovernmental organizations should become more distinct as personnel decisions within government are insulated from external market forces.

In this sense, as public agencies are sheltered from the market environment, and as rules and regulations for personnel management are determined locally, segmentation within the labor market between governmental and nongovernmental employers becomes sharper. At the same time, because of their training or career experiences, some employees may be characterized as members of either the private or the public sector, with limited movement between the two sectors. The way employees are used and developed within organizations will send distinct cues to the work force about the kinds of skills and work histories workers should acquire. These cues affect the quality of the public work force and have spillover effects on the external market as well, to some degree. In this sense, the environment for and results of employment status may become more distinct between the sectors. To the extent that work-force composition in the public and private sectors is significantly different, the consequences of labor-market segmentation affect the level of equality in society.

The membership of the public work force does in fact differ from that in the private sector, and it is expected to become increasingly diverse over the next decade. Overall, governmental employees are older than the general work force and are disproportionately nonwhite and female (although women are slightly underrepresented at the federal level). These demographic differences, coupled with longer job-tenure rates in governmental organizations, magnify the effects of differences between the sectors in work-force composition and capacity.

Prospective workers from disadvantaged groups may think that they will obtain a better overall return for their labor in government than in business or industry; and, typically, the public sector offers members of minority groups better conditions of employment (fair selection and equitable pay) than they can obtain in the private sector (Smith, 1979; Venti, 1987). The pattern of women clustering in the public sector is repeated in many different countries and governments (Rose, 1985; Hale and Kelly, 1989). Although the affinity of disadvantaged groups for public sector employment is rational in an economic sense, it raises questions about the role of the civil service as a vehicle for enhancing possibilities for social equity within a society.

Equal employment opportunity (EEO), which involves equal access to jobs among population segments or groups, requires a certain balance between government's activities as an employer and its ability to influence employment patterns in nongovernmental organizations, or else it may produce a form of segmented equality. Government may become the employer of the disadvantaged when it pursues policies that provide members of certain groups better rates of pay or conditions of employment than they would receive in the private sector. Similarly, to the extent that other management philosophies (like managing for diversity, or new public management) shoulder out EEO as a primary orientation, the flow of workers between the sectors and the pattern of recruitment or mobility within a sector may be altered.

There has been concern that the achievement of equal representation in the public bureaucracy may serve as a symbol of social equity that deflates further demands for equality and establishes a form of segmented equity: the pursuit of equal representation in itself may undermine efforts to achieve other, broader goals (Outshoorn, 1990). There is also the possibility that movement away from EEO and affirmative action, toward more management-oriented (in contrast with employee-oriented) policies, may undermine progress toward social equity in public employment.

The impact of ILMs on occupational mobility and, in turn, on social equality has been an important area of research among economists and sociologists. Studies indicate that the rules and regulations controlling vertical and horizontal mobility within organizations determine the extent to which managerial and upper-level positions are open and accessible, creating a more pluralistic governmental agency and a less elitist decision-making structure. A question of interest is whether current developments in management practice and organizational rules and policies will create a situation wherein one group or class holds the elite and decision-making positions, while another group or social class tends to do the work at the bottom of the organization's hierarchy. Concerns for democratic representation within the issue of internal labor-market theory are thus significant.

The issue of work-force capacity is closely tied to ILM systems. The way jobs are structured determines the extent to which organizations are able both to utilize the full range of employee skills available to them and to send appropriate signals to employees about which skills and competencies to acquire. When employees see little commitment from the employer, or when their own level of organizational loyalty is low, their motivation for attaining new skills is diminished. A perceived decline in job security, related to real or rumored reductions in force, changes an employee's belief in the utility of responding to the cues an agency might send. At the same time, policies that do not emphasize the development and retention of good employees may leave an organization in short supply of needed knowledge and competencies. Organizations relying on temporary employees, for example, are unlikely to function as learning organizations, as Kettl describes them in Chapter One. Without some continuity in the employment of key personnel, organizations lack the needed history to learn from past experience.

This chapter attempts to contribute to an understanding of the connection between internal labor-market structures and work-force capacity, particularly in the context of a national civil service system. The following section offers a discussion of the issues related to ILM theory and then begins to make a connection between current reforms in public management and the consequences of those changes for internal labor-market systems.

## Challenges to Human Resources

Broad changes that are already under way appear to offer certain challenges to human resources managers. Three key trends seem to affect ILM systems. The first involves individualized pay schemes, which are often linked to pay for performance and to demands for greater efficiency and accountability in public organizations. The second pertains to changes in the systems for establishing rank and status in government organizations. The third trend discussed here involves changes in employment contracts, reflected in the expanded use of temporary and noncore employees, a reduction in job security, and changes in emphasis away from the legalistic protection of employees' rights and toward greater emphasis on management's needs.

### *Toward Individualized Pay Schemes*

The first trend has surfaced on each continent and has broad ramifications for changing the pattern of human resources management. It poses a particular challenge to subsystems of human resources management because, in its link with efficiency, it assumes a fair and accurate appraisal system, which in fact may not exist in a public organization. Moreover, the trend toward pay for performance represents a shift in the reward structure for civil service employment. It has the tendency to dilute the value of normative and affective incentives as a basis for public service employment and to place emphasis on monetary and material rewards.

This shift affects the way the incentive structure operates, both in recruiting and in retaining workers. It implies that different kinds of people will be attracted to public service from those who were when other rewards were emphasized—for example, the opportunity for public service, the opportunity in policy making, the desire to promote a social good, and so on (Perry and Wise, 1990). Some research also argues that the movement toward pay for performance reflects a loss of legitimacy for public employees and a movement away from job security and pay equity, toward a more arbitrary reward system.

A decentralized decision-making process and a nonuniform system for determining pay setting, as well as pay increases, should produce greater disparity in wage profiles. Ironically, however, managers are often unwilling to accept the burden of discretion and are much more conservative in the way they allocate rewards, thereby creating a more narrow wage profile than the former systems used (Wise, 1992).

## Changing Systems of Rank

The second trend is a movement away from narrow-banded rank-in-position systems. In the case of the United States, the Civil Service Reform Act of 1978 introduced the Senior Executive Service, a rank-in-person system, and placed it at the elite level of the federal civil service. The trend toward rank-in-person has proceeded rather slowly in the United States, but it has been put into practice more rapidly in other national civil service systems. A case in point is the Swedish national civil service, which converted all white-collar posts rather abruptly to a rank-in-person system, after having operated under a thirty-five-grade white-collar pay schedule until 1990. Other European and Anglo-American systems are making similar overtures toward rank-in-person systems. Moreover, to the extent that employees negotiate independently for salaries, and managers have discretion for setting earnings of individual employees, a de facto rank-in-person system can exist, even though in principle a rank-in-position system remains on the books and provides guidelines for pay setting and status.

## Toward Contingent Workers

The third broad transition that seems to be under way in human resource management is the shift away from permanent career staff and toward temporary and other peripheral employees. Since the 1980s, temporary employment has become increasingly popular in the United States and other countries (Boyle, 1991; Wise, 1988). In the past, temporary employment was not of significant scale in the United States, but in recent years hiring of full-time temporary employees has expanded. About one million persons work full-time in temporary jobs through the temporary-help industry.

According to government estimates, the temporary work force doubled between 1978 and 1985, and expansion of temporary jobs accounts for a significant share of the total growth in jobs in the United States. Historically, growth in industry has been cyclical, reflecting changes in the business cycle. The great majority of temporary jobs are in clerical and administrative support occupations.

This trend toward contingent workers is significant in the public sector. In 1985, the U.S. government expanded the authority under which federal agencies could hire temporary workers and increased the duration of temporary appointments to four years. This change led to more than 7,000 additional temporary appointments in one year, an increase of 22.4 percent in the size of the federal temporary work force. In 1985, there were 42,118 temporary appointments in the U.S. federal civilian work force. The great majority of these positions (66 percent) involved clerical work. In the federal sector today, about 157,000 workers can be classified as temporary, representing about 7 percent of the federal work force (Arnold, 1993).

A preference for contingent workers may reflect uncertainty about future labor needs and unwillingness to make a commitment to permanent positions. Instead, employers pursue a short-term hiring strategy that protects them from overexpansion of the labor force by using temporary, "discardable" workers. In addition to being able to shed these workers quickly in the event of an economic downturn, management makes little investment in training or incentives to enhance organizational commitment among these workers (Wise, 1989).

Temporary workers are generally a cheap source of labor. Many work part-time; others sporadically work a full day. Already without job security, temporary employees usually do not receive the benefits normally obtained through employment, such as health insurance or retirement benefits, although they may be eligible to purchase their own policies through their jobs. This applies to temporary employees in government as well as to those working in the private sector. In that their services are easily terminated during economic downturns, temporary workers insulate the bulk of the work force from cyclical swings in the economy. Given the fact that temporary workers are disproportionately female, young, and black, their disadvantageous employment conditions give cause for concern (Wise, 1989).

Nevertheless, temporary employment arrangements are attractive to many people. Those who prefer temporary employment cite variety in work assignments, as well as the greater compatibility of work schedules with personal obligations. Women with family responsibilities are key candidates for temporary jobs, since their employment can be adjusted to meet both daily and cyclical family responsibilities. Persons reentering the work force who are unsure of their skills and employability may find temporary employment preferable, since it allows them to test the market and facilitates changes in an unsatisfactory career or job situation (Wise, 1989).

## Implications of the Three Trends

The three trends under way in public personnel management have clear implications for at least four subsystems of human resources. They affect the composition and capacity of the public work force and have consequences for the achievement of broader democratic goals and the attainment of representative democracy.

### ILM Rules for Establishing Status and Position

Internal labor markets are composed of series of job ladders, which may be well developed for certain occupational groups but underdeveloped for others. Managerial ILMs, for example, are more likely to be found in large organizations with closed systems emphasizing promotion from within. ILMs thus have an impact on the rate of movement between organizations or sectors. ILMs also have an impact on mobility within an organization in that they may facilitate or impede movement within departments or between departments. The way a job ladder is structured, and the relationship of one job to another in terms of the specificity of work difficulty and job requirements, will affect upward progress within an organization. To the extent that inconsistent job requirements exist between relatively similar positions, and variations in job titles or grading systems occur, the chances for upward mobility within an organization are impeded by the rules and regulations affecting advancement. At the same time, informal rules and customs may play an important role in explaining how people move within public agencies. For example, the extent to which managers take advantage of the discretion available to them is affected by organizational customs, as is formal adherence to existing rules.

From management's perspective, the way job tasks are structured within an organization, and the rules and regulations that determine how people are placed, affect management's ability to take full advantage of organizational members. Job evaluation systems are integrally related to the job ladders that determine the kinds of mobility within organizations (DiPrete, 1989; Doeringer and Piore, 1971). Job ladders can be seen as conveyor belts, moving people with entry-level skills upward through the organization as time progresses and as they increase their skills and their knowledge of the things important to a particular organization. Job ladders can provide managers with an increasingly trained and sophisticated work force that has a special understanding of the tasks related to achieving organizational goals.

Rank-in-position systems, which have been so popular in the public sector, organize employees into job categories that may not have common attributes for establishing status. In this sense, they can be seen as placing a barrier against employees' growth and development. White-collar work, for example, can be organized into many separate categories, so that clerical workers, technicians, professional workers, and top administrative personnel each form a unique job category, with its own job factors and ranking system. In such a structure, there may be little opportunity for movement among job categories in that "bridge" jobs may not have been carefully developed and attended to, as is sometimes done in affirmative action and upward-mobility systems. In the same way, such arbitrary job requirements as those involving education, state licensure, or certification may also serve as impediments to movement between job categories. Many employees, although qualified to do the work, may not have had time or opportunities to attain specified certificates or degrees.

One issue to be considered in the development of future human resources management systems is the extent to which common factors are used in evaluating jobs. This issue has been given substantial consideration by those who advocate comparable-worth wage policies. I will not comment here on the desirability of using job evaluation systems as a way of minimizing the social disparities caused by occupational segregation and uneven access to positions of power and authority. I will say only that the issue of using common factors in job evaluation has clear relevance to how flexible management can be in allocating people within organizations and taking advantage of available human resources. To the extent that an organization hopes to nurture and grow its own labor pool, the use of unique factor systems or unique ranking systems for different categories of work can be seen as an impediment to that goal, because unique systems confine employees to certain categories and overlook the potential for cross-training and skill utilization between different areas of work.

Another issue concerns the extent to which bands or classes for grouping jobs together for status and pay are broadly or narrowly defined. More narrow systems tend to favor equity and fair treatment, since they limit managerial control over how employees can be moved within an organization. These narrow bands can be fairly extreme in public sector organizations. A broad-banded system seems compatible with the notion of greater efficiency and decentralization, which is part of the broad trend toward a new public management and is endorsed by the National Academy of Public Administration (1991). Although the shift has a management orientation, it is not unfriendly toward employees, since it opens more doors for lateral and vertical mobility and may identify areas for cross-training and development.

## *ILM Rules for Mobility and Deployment*

Movement within an organization is determined by rules affecting career advancement, as well as by an organization's policies for and investments in staff training and development. Opportunities for promotion and job training can be seen as distributive functions of ILMs. From the organization's perspective, these are nonmarketable resources. They are also scarce provisions of ILM systems. The scarcity of these resources increases the importance of ILM rules and regulations in determining their allocation.

Deployment rules are those policies and practices that determine opportunities for career advancement and for staff training and development within an organization. Thus deployment rules can be seen as part of the distributive function of ILM systems, and they can also be seen as having a redistributive effect within a society when governments, as employers, provide equal opportunity in staff training and development for advancement. These opportunities for advancement are scarce. Consequently, the way ILM rules and regulations affect their allocation is an important concern for democracy and equal opportunity. Mobility rules have an impact on a person's status and career advancement, as well as on his or her economic well-being. Mobility rules may also have an impact on a person's psychological well-being and sense of personal growth and accomplishment, to the extent that individuals invest a certain amount of self-esteem in the progress of their careers and the status they occupy. Opportunities for both horizontal and vertical movement within an organization are important vehicles for expanding the career horizons of the work force, since deployment rules define who is eligible for mobility and the criteria by which candidates are assessed. They have a clear impact on the advancement of equal employment opportunity within organizations.

In this context, the establishment of affirmative action or upward-mobility programs in public agencies recognizes the extent to which deployment rules may serve as barriers to advancement for people who have been socially or economically disadvantaged. The choice between educational and experiential criteria for placement, for example, affects socially advantaged and disadvantaged groups differently, as does the use of achievement and aptitude tests for hiring and promotion. Broad job classifications, as noted, may increase individual mobility. Similarly, the identification or construction of "bridge" jobs between career ladders establishes alternative routes for mobility that extend the career horizons of public employees. In the same sense, distinctions between clerical and administrative jobs also affect mobility.

Training opportunities are critical for growth and upward mobility. Firms vary in their emphasis on human resources development, and these differences have effects on employment patterns (Osterman, 1984), but in the federal government there is a strong emphasis on in-service training. An emphasis on training and retraining reflects a willingness to invest in people. Civil service systems based on patronage may view employment as a short-term relationship and see little value in long-term investment. When jobs are given out purely for their reward value, the complexity of the work and the need for training may go unrecognized, even on a short-term basis. The notion of long-term employment, which characterizes many national civil service systems, is compatible with policies for investing in the training and development of employees, not only for job-specific skills but also for long-term career development within the organization.

Greater reliance on ILMs for allocating human resources within organizations would be compatible with long-term interest in employees' education and development. To the extent that public employees enter professional jobs with undergraduate and graduate degrees in hand, public organizations need to identify new incentives for educational achievement and lifelong learning, but managers generally have not begun to address this issue, even in organizations with a strong emphasis on employee development. The fact that, unlike European educational systems, the U.S. system focuses on degrees, rather than on educational credit hours or points earned, can be seen as an impediment to postgraduate education. Moreover, the absence of a midlevel degree between the master's degree and the Ph.D. means that no realistic educational goal exists for the great majority of persons in public service already holding a master's degree.

A challenge to human resources management in the twenty-first century will involve the increasingly popular trend toward managing for diversity. Discussion of the impact of a culturally diverse work force is not limited to the United States (Boyle, 1991). Managing for diversity means fully utilizing the potential skills and resources of people from different backgrounds, including racial and ethnic groups, religious groups, age groups, and groups of people with different handicaps. Managing for diversity is a positive concept that champions the uniqueness and special qualities of people, but it does pose a risk for affirmative action and equal employment opportunity, being based on the assumption that achievement of these goals is at hand. A system that first puts forward management's ability to use employees does not primarily protect employees' rights. It is a clear movement away from the legalistic system that has characterized American personnel management. Managing for diversity seeks to be creative and risk-taking, as opposed to standardized and secure. It gives managers more discretion in using people within an organization. By the same token, it enhances job opportunities for organizational members.

### ILM Rules for Job Security

Civil service systems typically offer employees more job protection than jobs in the private sector do, but there are important exceptions to this general pattern. Patronage-based personnel systems do not promise lifetime employment and may encourage turnover among employees. Government cutbacks over the last decade have been associated with reductions in force at all levels of government and with more emphasis on peripheral workers. What is of interest in these cases are the criteria for establishing tenure rights and the trade-off between individual employees' seniority and their perceived value, in terms of performance ratings or other indicators of productivity.

Since there is a growing trend toward a more politicized civil service structure and greater reliance on contingent employees in the public work force, these nonprotected positions give an organization greater flexibility in using human resources and reducing costs. They facilitate efforts to "downsize" or "right-size" organizations by eliminating people who have no job permanency or job protection and therefore have no right to severance pay. In this sense, expansion of the contingent work force enhances managerial flexibility, as well as an organization's ability to survive demands for restructuring.

Changes under way in core-peripheral work-force dynamics, especially in white-collar organizations, are also important for understanding the role of internal labor markets. Core workers are those who are promised job security and career advancement within a firm. Peripheral workers are those members of the contingent work force who offer their services on a part-time or temporary basis, often working without fringe benefits or any pledge of job security. Osterman (1988) suggests that the increased use of temporary workers can be viewed as management's attempt to transform the ILM status of an occupational group, from stable employment with job security, training opportunities, and career development to a simple hire-fire relationship. Elements of the ILM may be used as an inducement by management to make certain changes more palatable to the work force. For example, plans to widen job classifications and increase managerial discretion in placing employees may be accompanied by more opportunities for training or by opportunities for greater earnings through productivity incentives.

In testimony to a U.S. House of Representatives civil service subcommittee, Office of Personnel Management director James B. King spoke against the trend toward more peripheral workers and proposed a two-year limit on temporary positions. He stated, "The misuse of temporary appointments sends a very negative message to our work force: that the government wants the services of these workers as cheaply as it can get them and with no investment in the employees' career development. . . . This is not the message we ought to be sending to our public servants" (cited in Arnold, 1993, p. A15). This position is supported by federal employee union representatives and some members of Congress. Others, however, view temporary appointments as an element of a flexible organization and a less costly public payroll.

## ILM Rules for Wages and Salaries

Salaries for public employees may be attached to specific positions that employees happen to occupy or to individual workers, and pay may be based on training, competency, experience, productivity, or some other attribute. The connection between ILM systems and wage differentials has been examined by many researchers. Internal labor markets may create wage structures that are very different from those in the external market. But the extent to which ILMs favor people with employer-specific knowledge or skills, as well as those with skills in great demand in the external labor market, appears to be indeterminate. In highly segmented labor markets, where government is the only employer for specific professional groups, employees are often disadvantaged in salary setting and wage development. Nurses and teachers, for example, may lag behind the wage rates of those with similar training and experience who are working in the private sector, in other jobs. Nevertheless, employers in both sectors appear to offer premium wages to employees with valued organization-specific knowledge whom they are unwilling to lose to another employer. This practice became popular in national civil service systems during the 1980s, when governments began to implement different market supplements as bonuses over fixed salary levels, to recruit and retain valued employees. People at the top of a promotion ladder and those with access to organizational decision makers may have an advantage over others in gaining a wage premium for organization-specific knowledge (Cappelli and Cascio, 1991).

A central theme in the movement toward a new public management is emphasis on pay for performance and efficiency in compensation. The expectation is that greater discretion among managers in setting wage levels for employees and in allocating fringe benefits and bonuses will increase the poten-

tial for inequity in compensation practices. A central idea in
the movement toward a new public management is to make
government more cost-efficient and thereby reduce operating
costs while still providing adequate services of sufficient quality. This expectation rests on a number of assumptions, which
researchers have pointed to as faulty (Perry, 1986). One potential
shortcoming, for example, is the assumption that rewarding individual employees for greater performance or greater efficiency
will cause some aggregate benefit to accrue to the organization
and make the organization more efficient in producing services.
But there is evidence to suggest that individual benefits for performance and efficiency have the result of raising organizational
costs. One concern here is that a reaction within an organization will distort the wage system and the way wages are allocated. A trend toward disalignment of the wage structure — as
a result, for example, of offering high wages for new or low-
level employees — generates inequity between upper- and lower-
level employees, or between incumbent and new workers, that
may be attached to ideological conflicts about the way payroll
funds should be distributed (Cowherd and Levine, 1992). ILMs
may attempt to legitimize perceived inequities in how rewards
are distributed and, in the process, distort other management
functions.

Pay-for-performance systems pose a threat to the internal alignment of wages and salaries within organizations. Each
increment that has a substantial impact on the total compensation
of employees changes the level of variance and the standard devi-
ation among employees in their wage profiles. In rank-in-position–based systems, the safety or security of internal alignment,
and of equal pay for equal work as an underlying principle, cannot be guaranteed when total compensation is the standard for
measuring wage equity. Base pay may remain equitable, but
in fact total compensation may offer significant variations from
some preset position or status standard. To the extent that
performance-based pay systems are not integrated into an overall
strategic human resources management plan, they may send
conflicting signals to employees about what behavior or competencies are valued.

It would be unfortunate if discretionary pay systems were found to increase the possibility of wage discrimination, given government's role as an EEO employer and the redistributive impact of public sector payrolls. Some research supports the idea that pay-for-performance systems are discriminatory in nature, and that performance is really not the key determinant of wage variations among employees in such systems. Wise (forthcoming), for example, studied two federal agencies in the United States and shows that variables unrelated to performance (such as age, sex, and race) are significant explainers of variations in the size of bonus awards. Some research suggests that pay-for-performance systems tend to have discriminatory effects related to the type of work that a person does, or to the sort of job evaluation system or personnel system in which he or she is situated. Management employees, as opposed to professional specialists, may have either more or less access to the rewards distributed in a pay-for-performance system (Wise, forthcoming; U.S. General Accounting Office, 1989). As a consequence of these and other dysfunctional results, the federal Performance Management Recognition System was not renewed. A decentralized system, providing agencies more discretion in determining criteria for appraisal and methods of management, has been recommended by public management reformers (National Academy of Public Administration, 1991).

## Toward a Careful Balance

Current trends in public management put emphasis on internal labor-market systems as determinants of how human resources should be valued in public organizations. The values of local managers, as well as local organizational norms, replace centrally set rules and practices for personnel management. These trends provide opportunities for greater flexibility in public management and may also increase opportunities for employees' development and growth. At the same time, they remove many of the legalistic policies that have dominated public personnel management in the United States. ILM systems raise important concerns, not only for the dynamics of economic systems within a society but also for the level of social, political, and economic equality within a system. Opportunities for upward mobility and access to elite positions in government are important indicators of the level of democracy and social equity in a system, and they are clearly affected by the structure of ILM systems. To the extent that ILMs facilitate or impede efforts toward occupational mobility, they affect the current status of socially disadvantaged groups, as well as their future prospects for improving their standard of living.

As employers, governments need to remain competitive with the prevailing labor market in formulating employment policies and setting wage rates, so that the flow of labor between the sectors is not directed in terms of group membership or class. This calls for a careful balance in the way human resources are used and motivated in public organizations. The shift toward management's interests in the use of human resources increases flexibility and may enhance organizational efficiency and survival. In redefining the relationship between employees and employers, however, managers must focus not only on short-term adjustments but also on the long-term consequences of such policies for employees' motivation, competency, and organizational commitment.

## References

Arnold, M. S. "Abuse of Temporary Workers." *Washington Post,* June 23, 1993, p. A15.

Boyle, R. "Civil Service Management Trends: Challenges for the 1990s." *Administration,* 1991, *39*(3), 234–247.

Buitendam, A. *Decentralization and the Governance of Employment Relationships: Human Resource Management Between Labour Market and Organization.* Research memorandum no. 413. Institute of Economic Research, Faculty of Economics. Groningen, Netherlands: University of Groningen, 1991.

Cappelli, P., and Cascio, W. F. "Why Some Jobs Command Wage Premiums." *Academy of Management Journal,* 1991, *34,* 848–868.

Cowherd, D. M., and Levine, D. I. "Product Quality and Pay Equity Between Lower-Level Employees and Top Management: An Investigation of Distributive Justice Theory." *Administrative Science Quarterly,* 1992, *37,* 302–320.

DiPrete, T. A. *The Bureaucratic Labor Market: The Case of the Federal Civil Service.* New York: Plenum, 1989.

Doeringer, P., and Piore, M. *Internal Labor Markets and Manpower Analysis.* Lexington, Mass.: Heath, 1971.

Hale, M. M., and Kelly, R. M. (eds.). *Gender, Bureaucracy, and Democracy: Careers and Equal Opportunity in the Public Sector.* New York: Greenwood Press, 1989.

National Academy of Public Administration. *Modernizing Federal Classification: An Opportunity for Excellence.* Washington, D.C.: National Academy of Public Administration, 1991.

Osterman, P. (ed.). *Internal Labor Markets.* Cambridge, Mass.: MIT Press, 1984.

Osterman, P. *Employment Futures.* New York: Oxford University Press, 1988.

Outshoorn, J. "Is That What We Wanted? Affirmative Action as Issue-Perversion." Paper presented at the annual meeting of the European Consortium of Political Research, Paris, Apr. 10–15, 1990.

Perry, J. L. "Merit Pay in the Public Sector: The Case for a Failure of Theory." *Review of Public Personnel Administration,* 1986, *7*(1), 261–278.

Perry, J. L., and Wise, L. R. "The Motivational Bases of Public Service." *Public Administration Review,* 1990, *50*(3), 367–373.

Rose, R. (ed.). *Public Employment in Western Nations.* Cambridge, England: Cambridge University Press, 1985.

Siahpush, M. S. "Empowering Structures in Organizations: Toward a Specification of the Resource Perspective." *Social Science Research,* 1991, *20,* 122–149.

Smith, S. "Compensating Wage Differentials and Public Policy: A Review." *Industrial and Labor Relations Review,* 1979, *32,* 339–352.

U.S. General Accounting Office. *Pay for Performance: Interim Report on the Performance Management Recognition System.* Washington, D.C.: U.S. General Accounting Office, 1989.

Venti, S. F. "Wages in the Federal and Private Sectors." In
   D. A. Wise (ed.), *Public Sector Payrolls*. Chicago: University
   of Chicago Press, 1987.
Wise, L. R. "Dimensions of Public Sector Pay Policies in the
   United States and Sweden." *Review of Public Personnel Adminis-
   tration*, 1988, *8*, 61–83.
Wise, L. R. *Labor Market Policies and Employment Patterns in the
   United States*. Boulder, Colo.: Westview Press, 1989.
Wise, L. R. "Approaches and Strategies for Setting Public Sector
   Pay." Paper presented at annual meeting of the Association
   for Public Policy and Management, Denver, Oct. 1992.
Wise, L. R. "Factors Affecting the Size of Performance Awards
   Among Mid-Level Civil Servants in the United States." *Public
   Administration Quarterly*, forthcoming.

# PART THREE

## *Governance and the Public Sector*

The chapters in the earlier parts of this volume examined the nature of government work and of managing changes in the public sector. The chapters in Part Three examine the implications of these issues for the management of change and accountability in the American public service and system of governance.

For the past century, the American public service has been structured with an eye to eliminating favoritism and constraining managerial choices. The result has been a large accumulation of administrative rules and regulations concerning acquisition, allocation, development, and sanction functions. Implicitly, these rules and regulations condone a trade-off between administrative accountability and administrative efficiency. Fiscal stresses facing governments at all levels of the federal system have rendered this conventional trade-off unacceptable. The diminished legitimacy of the American system of governance has generated calls for increased accountability.

Both supporters and detractors of the American public service agree that change is essential. American public service systems are too slow and cumbersome to provide effective management in this era of rapid change. Government at all levels in the United States must find new ways to function in the face of increasingly complex problems and declining confidence in government's ability to serve the needs of its population.

Undoubtedly, change is in the offing for both the structure of the American public service and for the role that public agencies and employees will play in the country's governance processes. Calls for reform emphasize more decentralization and increased flexibility for management. The chapters in Part Three explore the issues of flexibility and change in relation to the public service and governance.

In Chapter Eleven, Romzek and Dubnick focus on what happens to accountability when management systems are designed for increased flexibility. They explore whether proposed reforms in public service systems are compatible with the polity's expectations for accountability. They also note the key values and ecological factors that influence the American system of governance and challenge the functioning of its accountability systems. Romzek and Dubnick identify four different types of accountability systems that are widely used and equally legitimate within the American political system: bureaucratic, legal, professional, and political. They propose an ideal alignment between accountability systems and personnel management systems and functions, observing that if administrative reforms are blind to these dynamics of accountability, they are not likely to contribute to the long-term viability of the American public service.

Peters, in Chapter Twelve, notes the changing context within which the public service operates and explores the implications of these changes for governance, taking governmental reform as a given and reminding us that planned change is an element of governance in all political systems. Considering alternative models of the state, Peters ponders their implications for the structure of public sector organizations, workforce acquisition and management, and the role of the public service in the policy process. He draws comparisons between the traditional model of administration, with its clear separation of roles between administration and politics, and such alternatives as the market model, the participatory state, and the temporary organization. Fully formed or not, the alternative models do inform the dialogue on governance and reform. Peters contributes to that dialogue by articulating the structural, workforce, and policy-process differences that governments face in choosing among alternative models of reforming the state.

# 11

# Issues of Accountability in Flexible Personnel Systems

## Barbara S. Romzek
## Melvin J. Dubnick

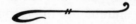

How does the democratic polity ensure that government employees do what they are supposed to do? The short answer to this question is that the polity ensures responsible behavior by holding public employees accountable for their performance. A more complete answer requires an examination of the role expectations public employees face and the range of mechanisms available for managing public sector accountability relationships (Friedrich, 1940; Finer, 1941; Krislov and Rosenbloom, 1981; Mosher, 1982; Yates, 1982; Gruber, 1987; Romzek and Dubnick, 1987; Rourke, 1992; Dubnick and Romzek, 1993).

The challenge for public agencies and employees is to manage the multiple, diverse, and sometimes conflicting expectations they face in their jobs. The challenge for the political system is to design institutional mechanisms that help achieve those values for which it seeks to hold the public service accountable, without creating unnecessary obstacles to effective and efficient administration. Historically, those values have varied over time (see Kaufman, 1969). Nevertheless, the American system has consistently come down on the side of accountability, accepting administrative inefficiencies as a necessary price to be paid. At times, more energy may be spent in demonstrating compliance than in completing the actual management tasks themselves.

Those dynamics and the dysfunctions they create form the basis of the widespread interest in rethinking the federal public service. Of particular interest are the structures and operating principles on which our contemporary federal public service is founded (Rosenbloom, 1971a; see also Ingraham and Rosenbloom, 1990). For several years, discussions about the federal public service have decried the lack of flexibility in merit systems, which have emerged as the most cumbersome of the public service employment systems. These ponderous rules and regulations were originally designed as intentional efforts to constrain partisan political influence in personnel matters (White, 1958; Skowronek, 1982), but in recent decades the limits they placed on the power of political partisans have curbed managerial discretion as well. The resulting gap this system has created between personnel administration and the expanding managerial needs of government has become a widely accepted fact of public life, subject to criticism both from within and from outside the public service profession (McGregor, 1982; President's Private Sector Survey on Cost Control, 1984; Levine, 1985; Osborne and Gaebler, 1992).

Since this and associated problems are products of the dynamic relationship between employees' efforts to deal with expectations and the polity's requirements for accountability, the movement toward greater flexibility raises a variety of important issues about that relationship and its role in reforming the federal public service. The central issue, as we argue here, is whether such reforms can succeed if they ignore or are indifferent to the accountability systems that form the institutional context of American public administration. Efforts at reform that fail to address these issues are unlikely to succeed, at best. At worst, they may aggravate an already deteriorating situation.

## Challenges Facing the American Public Service

According to Macy (1982, p. 309), "The systematic constraints which have been growing in the government through the years need to be loosened so that human judgment and intelligence can be brought into play in arriving at decisions in the public interest." The federal public service in the United States has evolved over the past two hundred years in a discontinuous pattern reflecting, in part, the tensions between accountability and management that have arisen at various points in American history (Ingraham and Rosenbloom, 1990). Earliest concerns regarding the American public service were for personal integrity and commitment to the young nation. At the outset, George Washington sought individuals on the basis of fitness of character and loyalty to the new government, but his immediate successors placed great weight on partisan political factors in the appointment of officials. Removal from office tended to be more resistant to partisanship through the administration of John Quincy Adams (Rosenbloom, 1971a). Responsiveness to elected officials, however, became the central theme under the spoils system that emerged during the Jackson presidency. Regarded at the time as a means of reforming an elitist public service, the stress during this period was on creating a partisan link between political leaders and administrators (Ingraham and Rosenbloom, 1990; Rosenbloom, 1971a).

In reaction to the excesses of responsiveness, government reformers of the late 1800s passed legislation requiring that merit criteria be considered paramount for public employment. Individuals were to be hired solely on the basis of their knowledge, skills, and abilities. Initially, these efforts were intended as a means of "cleansing" democratic administration by eliminating partisanship from the public service. Eventually, however, they aimed at improving the efficiency of government by segregating politics from administration (Waldo, 1984; Skowronek, 1982). More recent efforts to render the federal service more responsive to the presidency have reflected still another major shift in what seems to be an ongoing dynamic relationship between management needs and accountability demands (Ingraham and Rosenbloom, 1990). The cumulative result of these various reforms was development of a hybrid public service, incorporating components that serve a variety of regime values developed over two centuries.

## Values

When one looks at the totality of public employees, it becomes apparent that the public service does not seem to have a single coherent organizing concept (although many observers tend to assume that merit provides that organizing principle), nor does the American public service have an obvious direction in which it logically should develop. There is no consensus among political leaders regarding how best to utilize the public service (Stillman, 1991; Ingraham and Rosenbloom, 1990). This is not to say, however, that there has been a lack of alternative values to help prod, push, and pull American public administration in different directions at different times.

Four values of particular interest to us for the present analysis are those that are manifested in the range of accountability mechanisms available in the American public service: political responsiveness, efficiency, rule of law, and deference to professional expertise (compare Kaufman, 1969; Fried, 1976; Meier, 1993).

*Political responsiveness* is manifested in the provision for political appointees to fill the highest levels of governmental management posts, subject to removal at the will of the elected officials who appointed them. Assuming that they are able to exercise effective management over their subordinates in an agency (see Heclo, 1977), these appointees are the primary vehicles through which political responsiveness is achieved.

*Efficiency* is reflected in the notion that agency resources should be deployed so as to maximize agency performance on the basis of available resources. This value is manifested in merit systems, which are organized around the principle that personnel functions are based on knowledge, skills, and abilities (Klingner and Nalbandian, 1993). A widely used mechanism to promote efficiency is the specification and standardization of acquisition, development, and sanction procedures.

*Rule of law* is manifested in the proliferation of organizations responsible for oversight and monitoring for compliance with public service directives (for example, the Equal Employment Opportunity Commission; the Merit System Protection Board, or its precursor, the Civil Service Commission; the Federal Labor Relations Authority; and judicial rulings regarding agencies' and employees' rights).

*Deference to professional expertise* is reflected in the Senior Executive Service and similar innovations, representing a growing interest in tapping the management skills of public employees without the typical constraints of merit systems.

## Ecological Factors

We cannot fully appreciate the accountability challenges facing the public service without recognizing the influence of ecological factors. Changes in the fiscal health of government, the managerial climate, and the work force combine to exacerbate problems with structures and processes in the public service. Economic forces, and demographic and attitudinal changes in the work force, have constrained government's ability to recruit and retain high-quality public servants. Worsening economic conditions have dictated that governments reduce expenditures. These reductions often result in low salary increases (if any at all) and staff cutbacks (Levine and Kleeman, 1992).

Shifting demographics indicate that the "baby boom" generation is plateauing at middle management and fewer young people are entering the labor force. These groups represent a significant proportion of public employees. They bring to their work different ideas from those of their parents' generation regarding the balance between work and personal life (Romzek, 1992). These employees are more resistant to making personal-life sacrifices for career advancement. The cumulative impact of these forces creates new challenges for the public service, challenges that require a rethinking of current policies and procedures. Old structures and procedures that emphasize gatekeeping and constraints on managerial discretion put the public service at a disadvantage in recruitment and retention.

The complexity of the public service and the rigidity of merit-system procedures and rules hinder government's ability to respond to ecological changes. Historically, the responses have been piecemeal. The lack of flexibility in public service personnel procedures constrain most experimentation. The source of many of the current problems facing the public service is often traced to the cumbersome nature of the various civil service rules and regulations that have developed through incremental reforms over the past century: "One hundred years of accumulated rules and regulations are the baggage of merit. They do not clarify and define; they obscure" (Ingraham and Rosenbloom, 1992, p. 293).

The result is an accumulation of rules and regulations that are complex, confusing, and often counterproductive. Recognition of the problems with public service personnel practices is not new. Efforts to reconsider and reform the public service have sprung up sporadically over time. Most reforms since 1978 have focused on issues of compensation and merit pay (Glenn, 1990; Fay, Risher, and Hempel, 1991; Levine and Kleeman, 1992). More comprehensive concerns are reflected elsewhere (National Commission on the Public Service, 1989). These various efforts have emphasized the challenges facing the public service, including recruitment, turnover, productivity, politicization, decentralization, and competitive compensation packages.

What all these efforts to rethink and reinvent the public service have in common is an emphasis on increasing the flexibility of civil service systems and on a shift from managerial control to managerial support (Osborne and Gaebler, 1992; Barzelay and Armajani, 1992). To succeed at such changes, reforms must be as attentive to accountability concerns as they are to their technical design and political attractiveness. Reformers and those who benefit from the reforms must "sell" the polity and the public service on the position that personnel support is as important as the need to control personnel decisions. Otherwise, the accountability dynamics are likely to undo whatever short-term success is achieved (Dubnick, 1994).

## Accountability and the Public Service

"The action of administration . . . is so important that it is impossible for any country possessing constitutional government to allow the administration a perfectly free hand in the discharge of its duties" (Goodnow, 1893, p. 135). Questions about accountability and the American public service take a variety of forms regarding who does what, to whom, how, when, and where (Krislov and Rosenbloom, 1981; Mosher, 1982; Yates, 1982; Gruber, 1987; Caiden, 1988). For half a century, scholars have been discussing accountability within the confines of the Friedrich and Finer dialogue (Finer, 1941; Friedrich, 1940), a normative debate about whether internal or external accountability mechanisms are preferred. Our work on accountability seeks to move beyond the normative debate, to develop a framework that characterizes some of the mechanisms and dynamics of accountability in the public sector (Romzek and Dubnick, 1987; Dubnick and Romzek, 1991). These accountability relationships are two-way; that is, while they can be used by others to hold public employees and agencies answerable for their performance, the same relationships can be used by employees and agencies themselves to influence the quantity, content, and intensity of the expectations generated by the accountability mechanisms (Gray and Jenkins, 1985).

We postulate that accountability mechanisms in the United States vary along two dimensions: source of control, and degree of control. These dimensions combine to reflect the range of mechanisms by which public employees can be held accountable for their actions and the range of mechanisms available to public employees as they try to manage the expectations and accountabilities they face in their work.

The dimension of source of control relates to the origin of the expectation(s), whether internal or external, and the relationship of the stakeholder(s) to the agency or individual. (To this extent, we build on both Finer, 1941, and Friedrich, 1940.) Internal sources of control originate from within the agency — say, a supervisor, a co-worker, or a standard operating proce-

dure. At the individual level, internal sources of control may
be manifested in personal attitudes that the individual has in-
ternalized, perhaps from professional standards or codes of
ethics. For example, Wheat (1991, p. 391) notes that some au-
ditors may literally or figuratively "carry about a little book of
publicly acknowledged and professionally agreed upon principles and standards to which they feel obligated to adhere." Similar dynamics may occur for any number of other professionals
in the public service. External sources of control originate outside the agency (for example, elected officials, clientele groups,
media, and oversight bodies).

The second dimension of accountability is the degree of
control present in the accountability relationship (see Hood,
1976). Degree of control can vary from high to low. A high degree
of control involves close specification of duties and intense scrutiny of actions across a wide range of issues. A low degree of control involves much less scrutiny, in much less detail; instead, the
agency or employee is granted a great deal of discretion in deciding whether and how to respond to expectations.

The combination of these two dimensions yields a typology of four categories of accountability mechanisms in the public
sector: bureaucratic, legal, professional, and political (see Figure
11.1). Each type emphasizes different values and different bases
for the accountability relationship. Bureaucratic mechanisms
are characterized by a high degree of scrutiny from an internal
source, typically a supervisor or rules of operation; the prevailing value is efficiency. Legal accountability involves a high
degree of scrutiny from an external source (for example, a court
or an outside auditor); the prevailing value is rule of law. Professional accountability is characterized by a low degree of scrutiny and an internal source of control; the prevailing value is
deference to expertise. Political accountability involves a low
degree of scrutiny from an external source (typically a clientele
group, a citizens' group, or elected officials); the prevailing value
is responsiveness. In bureaucratic and legal accountability mechanisms, the actor has less flexibility regarding behaviors; actions are constrained by standard operating procedures, rules,
legislative mandates, and court rulings. In professional and polit-

Figure 11.1. Accountability in Public Administration.

| | Source of Agency Control | |
|---|---|---|
| | **Internal** | **External** |
| **High** | 1. Bureaucratic<br><br>Superior/subordinate<br><br>Supervision, rules, standard operating procedure | 2. Legal<br><br>Principal/agent<br><br>Fiduciary Oversight monitoring |
| **Low** | 3. Professional<br><br>Layperson/expert<br><br>Deference to expertise | 4. Political<br><br>Constituent/representative<br><br>Responsiveness to stakeholders |

*Degree of Control over Agency Actions* (row label applying to High/Low)

ical accountability, the actor or agency has the flexibility to choose whether to respond to the expectations and the discretion to decide how best to respond.

Each of the four types of accountability mechanisms is equally legitimate, and all may be present simultaneously. Under conditions of "perfect administration" (Hood, 1976), a single accountability system will dominate to the exclusion of the other four. In practice, however, an agency or individual will typically operate in a context where at least two types of accountability mechanisms actively compete for the agency's or individual's attention, with the other types in place but latent. In times of crisis, the less frequently used or dormant forms of accountability typically are activated; but even under conditions of less severe environmental turbulence, the administrator or agency may contend with pressures (expectations) generated by a variety of alternative accountability mechanisms.

Ironically, when more than one type of accountability system is active, individuals and agencies may have some degree of influence on the type of accountability mechanisms most frequently used. The choices made under these circumstances are at the very heart of the tasks of "management" in public agencies (Barnard, 1938; Simon, 1957). The choice of which accountability mechanisms to engage or trigger is typically a function of environmental context, managerial strategy, and the nature of the core task.

The environmental context of public administration is multidimensional, encompassing physical, technological, demographic, cultural, economic, governmental, personal, and policymaking features of the ecological setting (Dubnick and Romzek, 1991). Changing demographics, advancing technologies, a globalized economy, and growth in governmental institutions are several ecological factors that have influenced the expectations facing today's federal public service. The same factors also influence managerial choices related to the accountability mechanisms used to contend with the multiple, diverse, and often contradictory expectations that challenge most public administrators today (Hargrove and Glidewell, 1990).

It is hard to generalize about managerial strategy for the American public service because of the sheer number of agencies and individuals involved in federal, state, and local governmental administration. In very general terms, managerial strategy involves decisions about how an agency or program positions and structures itself in relation to its surroundings and mission. In terms of action, it is the job of aligning an organization's resources and capabilities to its current situation, in order to meet current expectations and future goals (Summer, 1980; Kilmann, 1984). Traditionally, public sector organizations have been managed strategically to deal with four types of expectations: those related to resource use (inputs); those focusing on process; those concerned with outputs;

and those seeking to achieve outcomes. To the extent that generalizations can be made, managerial strategies in the federal service have reflected a need to meet accountability expectations focused on personnel inputs and process. In fact, bureaucratic and legal accountability mechanisms are often so closely intertwined in public employment systems that they are nearly impossible to disentangle, even when they are clearly in conflict. Current efforts to create a more flexible federal service represent a growing clamor for policies and rules that will promote output-outcome strategies (Nigro, 1990). Conscious efforts to move in that direction would probably entail major adjustments in how the public service relates to alternative accountability systems.

Just as managerial strategy varies from agency to agency, so does core task vary. The more technical the agency's core task, and the more specialized the skills that are required, the greater the likelihood that the accountability relationship will involve deference to expertise. For example, the Social Security Administration and the U.S. Postal Service might find it easier to contend with a situation where bureaucratic accountability expectations and mechanisms were dominant because the core tasks of these agencies are easily routinized and our knowledge about their tasks is well settled. Some agencies deal with greater degrees of uncertainty. One such agency is the National Aeronautics and Space Administration (NASA). The economic and political pressures that pulled the agency away from its primary reliance on expertise (professional accountability) may have contributed to the *Challenger* tragedy and other major administrative problems. In the *Challenger* case, the bureaucratic and political accountability mechanisms in use were ill suited to the technical nature of the agency's core task and to the level of knowledge and certainty that NASA had regarding this task (Romzek and Dubnick, 1987). In the case of the Los Angeles Police Department's beating of Rodney King, we find overreliance on professional accountability mechanisms and an inconsequential role for a key conventional bureaucratic accountability mechanism: individual performance evaluation (Romzek and Dubnick, 1991).

*Patterns of Accountability Mechanisms*

Within this context of four accountability systems, and at any point in time, the federal public service would clearly benefit from achieving a rough alignment between its personnel management systems and the dominant accountability mechanisms. The likelihood that this will occur seems low at this time, but an evaluative baseline could prove helpful in understanding the relationship between personnel management and accountability. To form that baseline alignment, we can transpose two of the three factors (management strategy and core task) relevant to shaping the relationship between public administrators and accountability systems (see Figure 11.2). Environmental dynamics, such as level of turbulence or stability, have been noted as affecting organizational structures and efforts to control (Emery and Trist, 1965; Thompson, 1967).

The managerial strategy factor is represented along the vertical axis by the alternative focal points already mentioned: inputs, process, outputs, and outcomes. In personnel management, the concern for inputs is a reflection of an institutional need for government agencies to contribute to the wider purposes of collective action in society. Those adopting this strategic position focus on the selection and allocation functions of public personnel management. Adherents to this perspective "include the rule making and enforcement bodies which advocate the political neutrality of the . . . civil service, elements involved in the formulation of national human resource policy (e.g., veterans preference, . . . affirmative action), those who promote the goal of efficiency and productivity in government, and, finally, those who control fiscal capacity and program priorities" (Nalbandian and Klingner, 1981, p. 542).

The interest in process as the primary strategic focus of public personnel management is partly a product of the "constitutionalization" of the public employment relationship that has taken place in recent decades (Rosenbloom, 1971a, 1971b, 1994; Shafritz, Riccucci, Rosenbloom, and Hyde, 1992). It also represents a concern with enforcing many of the policies and rules emerging from concern for inputs. The results have been

Figure 11.2. Accountability and Personnel Management: An "Ideal" Alignment.

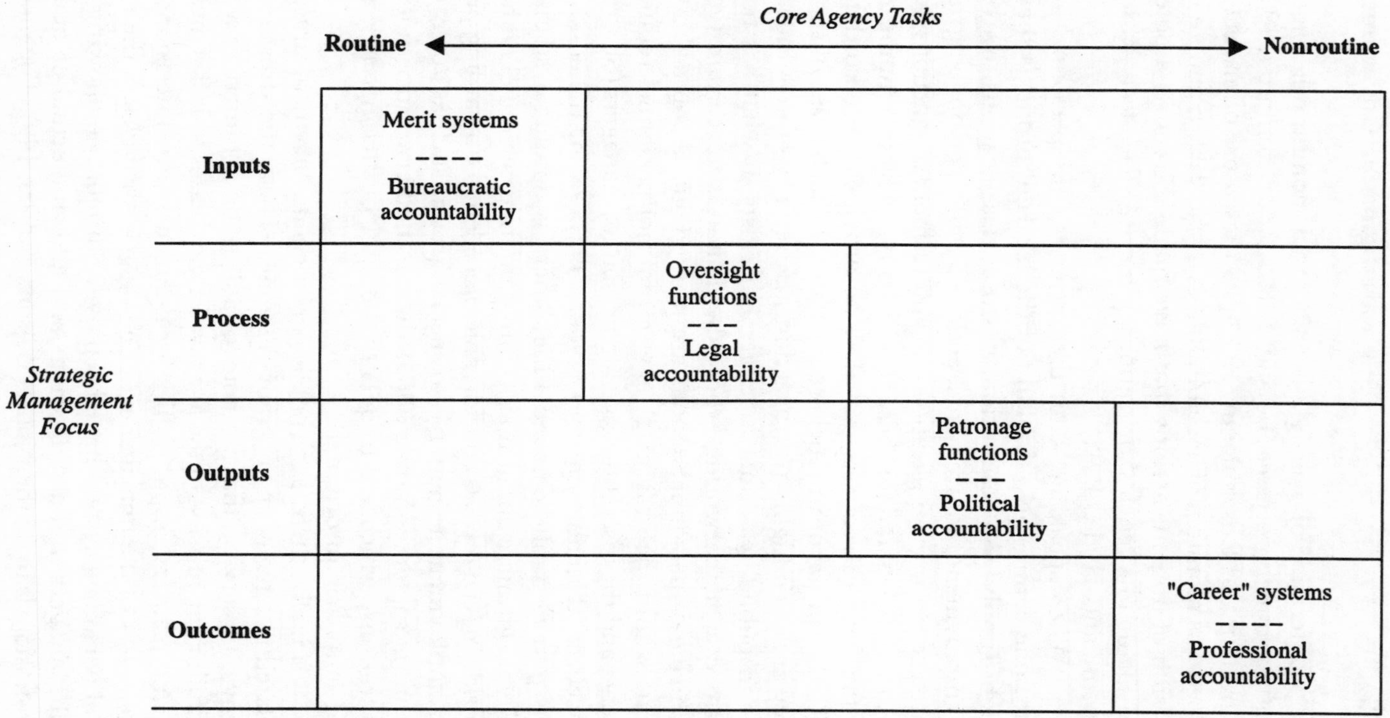

Routine ← → Nonroutine

Core Agency Tasks

Strategic Management Focus

| | Routine → | | → Nonroutine |
|---|---|---|---|
| Inputs | Merit systems<br>– – – –<br>Bureaucratic accountability | | |
| Process | | Oversight functions<br>– – –<br>Legal accountability | |
| Outputs | | | Patronage functions<br>– – –<br>Political accountability |
| Outcomes | | | "Career" systems<br>– – – –<br>Professional accountability |

the proliferation of oversight agencies that monitor other agencies' personnel processes (Levine, Peters, and Thompson, 1990; Ingraham and Rosenbloom, 1992); increased use of inspectors general as monitors of accountability (Light, 1993); and an explosion of litigious actions that have made the courts a potential factor in agencies' operations (Shafritz, Riccucci, Rosenbloom, and Hyde, 1992).

When speaking about the outputs of the personnel system, one cannot help thinking of the kinds of products that it might supply: job description, position classifications, waivers of employment requirements, actions against personnel, grievance proceedings, application and enforcement of sanctions, and so on. The demand for these services is typically communicated in the form of requests that they be provided, in accordance with the special or unique circumstances of each case. In short, they are often highly politicized in nature. Thus the output focus in public personnel management exists in what has been termed a "netherworld," where the demands for certain types of hiring or personnel actions are worked out as political decisions within the gray area between formal personnel requirements and the discretion given to personnel managers (Shafritz, Riccucci, Rosenbloom, and Hyde, 1992). As for the ethics of this part of public personnel life, "there is nothing systematically illegitimate about maintaining a public personnel netherworld. Indeed there is considerable precedent for awarding public employment advantages to special groups such as veterans. What is so contemptible about the . . . netherworld is not its operations, which are frequently benign, but its *hypocrisy*" (p. 73; emphasis in original).

Finally, there is the public personnel management strategy related to agency or program outcomes. Here, the stress is on providing services that promote (or at least do not interfere with) fulfilling the mission of the agency. In most cases, this has meant giving primary responsibility for major personnel decisions to managers of the line agency: "The biggest struggles in the federal personnel system have been over autonomy — allowing local managers to make decisions and allowing actual or quasi-professionals to do their jobs" (Wilson, 1989, p. 149). The model for this plan was the China Lake demonstration project conducted by the U.S. Department of the Navy under the little-used provisions of the Civil Service Reform Act (CSRA) of 1978 (Wilson, 1989; Nigro, 1990; Ban, 1992). What that much-cited project demonstrated was the potential benefits to be gained from a personnel management approach that facilitated, rather than controlled or regulated, the work of the client agency.

On the horizontal axis of Figure 11.2 we establish a continuum, representing the range of one significant characteristic of the core tasks performed by federal agencies: routineness. Although this is an oversimplification, the characteristic of routineness does provide a shorthand correlate for a number of other factors: simplicity, repetition, specialization, narrowness, formalization, and programmability (see Mintzberg, 1979; March and Simon, 1958). In terms of human resources, agencies or programs engaged in more routine tasks clearly require a qualitatively different set of skills and resources from those required by agencies dealing with more complex, nonroutine tasks. The resulting matrix reflects a hypothetically appropriate alignment of accountability systems with major functions and comprehensive forms of public service personnel systems (Klingner and Nalbandian, 1993, p. 27). Bureaucratic accountability mechanisms seem most relevant where the stress is on inputs and the agency's core tasks are routine, and where there is clear hierarchy to enforce accountability. Being accountable in these circumstances means being answerable to some hierarchically positioned supervisor who is able both to monitor and to correct (if necessary) the actions of the organizationally subordinate. Given these needs, a merit system such as those operating today (Ingraham and Rosenbloom, 1992) is probably best suited to the situation.

A focus on process is most likely to find favor under mechanisms that emphasize legal accountability. Here, the stress is not on routine actions but on the availability of procedures that can be activated, as necessary, to enforce rules and regulations. Access to the courts, active oversight by regulatory agencies (such as the Equal Employment Opportunity Commission), and internal enforcement of agency rules and procedures aimed at promoting and protecting the rights of employees are all suitable solutions in such conditions. While not in the model of a personnel system, these mechanisms can be grouped together as oversight functions.

Whether hypocritical or not, it would be difficult to ignore the role (although intermittent) of the so-called netherworld in public personnel management, especially when political accountability systems are active and in a potentially dominant position. To some degree, the actions taken in the netherworld resemble those that are expected of traditional patronage systems. Since the federal patronage (political appointee) system is rather limited in scope, and since the netherworld has a more pervasive presence, we use the label *patronage functions* to designate those personnel management activities most relevant to political accountability mechanisms.

Finally, where outcomes take priority and tasks are not routine, it would be most appropriate for professional accountability mechanisms to dominate. It is under such mechanisms that the implied ideal of "flexible" personnel administration is likely to thrive. The logic underlying the federal "career" systems fits these circumstances, for the systems were originally designed and given autonomy from the merit systems in order to allow certain agencies (for example, the State Department and the U.S. Forest Service) to enlist or develop "professional" cadres suitable to distinct jobs.

With these "ideal" arrangements in place, a question remains: What determines the real alignment of accountability systems with personnel management systems and functions? In our model, the answer is found in the variable ecological setting that comprises the third factor shaping the relationship between public administration and the four accountability systems. The role played by environmental factors in that relationship is a critical one, but it would be extremely difficult (if not impossible) to do more than speculate on the nature of that role. As the source of the multiple, diverse, and often conflicting expectations that simultaneously energize and constrain public administrators and their agencies, the ecological setting is a central factor in generating the efforts of public employees to manage expectations through their attempts to manipulate or control accountability systems (Dubnick and Romzek, 1993). Further complicating this relationship is the fact that accountability systems are themselves a major institutional component of that ecological setting.

But our inability to know the specific forms of the relationship between public administration and accountability systems has little to do with the insight this model provides into the operations of the public service within its complex institutional setting. To the extent that we have a baseline model for an "ideal" alignment between accountability systems and personnel management systems and functions, we can assess the implications of the various problems facing today's public personnel management system and analyze specific actions and proposals for reform that have emerged in recent years.

For example, the movement for a more flexible public personnel system is certainly high on the agenda of public administrators here and abroad (Organisation for Economic Cooperation and Development, 1990). Applying our framework, we can see that the issue of inflexibility represents more than mere stubbornness on the part of personnel managers unwilling to change old habits. The continued strength of the merit system, as an operating system and as an obstacle to much-needed reform, is an indication of the strength and dominant position of the bureaucratic accountability system in matters related to personnel at the federal level. From time to time over the past two decades, that dominance has been challenged, but only with temporary success.

During the 1970s, for instance, the initial commitment to affirmative action in the federal service resulted in immediate increases in the employment of protected groups at the middle and highest levels of government, but those advances soon vanished, in many cases. A number of reasons have been cited to explain that pattern (Kellough and Rosenbloom, 1992), many of them associated with shifts in political and fiscal conditions that were not conducive to sustaining affirmative action. In terms of accountability, the retreat from affirmative action was facilitated by the continued preeminence of bureaucratic accountability systems. Had affirmative action in the Equal Employment Opportunity Commission and other agencies been accompanied by an effort to strengthen the legal accountability system and associated oversight functions, the strong initial success might have been sustained.

In another test of the dominance of bureaucratic accountability systems in the federal public service, the Reagan administration developed a strategy for using the 1978 Civil Service Reform Act to its advantage in establishing effective control over the highest levels of the civil service. Putting the personnel system to work for partisan and ideological purposes did pay off, to some degree. The Reagan administration quickly expanded the netherworld of political accountability, in part by appointing noncareer personnel to high-level career positions through provisions in the CSRA (Newland, 1983). But the challenge had its limits, as indicated in the findings of a study by Ban and Ingraham (1990). Reviewing the records of noncareer Senior Executive Service appointees between 1979 and 1985, they found that members of this highly politicized group served an average of 1.7 years, and that at least 40 percent left government after less than one year. Once again, there are a number of explanations, but we should not overlook the role played by a dominant bureaucratic accountability system and the inability of the Reaganites to sustain their attempt to change the upper levels of the federal service into a more politically accountable cadre. For all the damage the Reagan administration did, the traditional system — and all its flaws — proved resilient (see Durant, 1992).

### The Need for Flexibility in Public Personnel Systems

The federal personnel system is structured to cover millions of employees who work in hundreds of agencies spread across the United States and beyond its borders. Many of the problems that have arisen in the operations of the federal civil service system derive from rigidity and from the poor fit between the current dependence on highly bureaucratized merit systems and the needs of federal agencies and employees. As a result, numerous agencies and classifications have petitioned to be exempted from cumbersome merit systems (Ingraham and Rosenbloom, 1992; Bowsher, 1992).

Balkanization of the public service is not likely, however, given the fact that requirements are imposed on government agencies and go well beyond the parochial needs of agencies and employees (Mainzer, 1973; Rainey, 1979; Nalbandian and Klingner, 1981). Rather than see agencies that are strong enough or savvy enough opt out of the personnel system, it would be better to redesign the structure and processes of the public service system to introduce enough flexibility to accommodate diverse agencies' management strategies and core tasks, as related to personnel needs. A key needed change is to shift public agencies and political institutions away from an emphasis on negative controls and regulatory oversight as primary vehicles for accountability.

When flexibility is sought, what one typically wants is relief from negative controls and a shift toward personnel systems that facilitate managerial discretion and professional responsibility. Time and again, despite the desire for such relief, we see in this country a willingness to sacrifice the goals of efficiency and effectiveness for accountability. We cannot ignore fundamental mistrust of government as a factor in the prospects for success of any proposal for flexibility (Dubnick, 1994); there are things that we allow in the private sector that simply are not tolerated in the public sector (Rainey, 1979). As we seek flexible personnel practices, we need to reassure the polity that flexibility does not mean lack of accountability. Rather, flexibility will mean managing human resources more strategically in the context of multiple accountability systems. It will mean relying on more kinds of accountability mechanisms, not necessarily on less accountability.

The key to increasing flexibility in public sector personnel systems is acknowledging their dependence on multiple accountability systems. The explicit development of a strategic approach to the existence of multiple accountability systems would be tacit recognition that public employees face multidimensional mandates. It would also allow for more appropriate matches between expectations and accountability mechanisms. For example, personnel practices related to Senior Executive Service members, given their experience and expertise, primarily should be designed and managed in the context of professional and political accountability systems. To the extent that emphasis is placed primarily on bureaucratic and legal accountability mechanisms holding SES members answerable for their performance, such mechanisms will not be taking full advantage of SES members' talents. In short, flexibility must be cultivated and nurtured through the strategic management of expectations and accountability mechanisms.

The unanswered question is whether these multiple accountability systems will be configured in a form that will facilitate such a strategic approach. Multiple accountability systems represent both opportunities and constraints for public sector managers. The current configuration of multiple expectations and multiple accountability mechanisms creates zones of discretion for administrators and agencies. Within these zones of discretion, public managers have latitude over how to manage expectations. The current arrangements, however, do bias the exercise of discretion in the direction of bureaucratic and legal accountability approaches. The possibility of greater flexibility will be improved when this bias is reduced or shifted to favor professional and political accountability norms.

What are the prospects for such changes? The current situation in federal personnel management is so dominated by pressures for bureaucratic and legalistic accountability that movement toward greater flexibility seems unlikely. Under the current preoccupation with merit systems and oversight functions, strategic concerns for outputs and outcomes are often ignored or treated with indifference. In the rare instances when output and outcome needs are allowed to surface, innovative solutions are narrowly applied, and their impact is generally short lived. A more common scenario is the development of solutions acceptable to bureaucratic or legalistic standards that typically prove inappropriate. When this occurs, accountability expectations are more constraining and require more effort to meet, and they detract thereby from efforts directed at reaching the program goals of the organization.

## Flexibility in Personnel

The movement toward flexibility could involve reforms at all four strategic focus levels. Let us examine some recent personnel policies and their prospects for success in light of this recognition of the role that accountability dynamics play in public personnel management. Flexibility may entail many different things. It may mean (1) less centralized control and oversight of basic personnel functions; (2) fewer and less detailed rules and regulations regarding how line agencies promote and protect employees' rights; (3) greater empowerment to line agency personnel, allowing them to adapt their human resources policies to their agencies' needs, which may be political as well as administrative; and (4) greater deference to the capacity of professional public servants (workers more than managers) to shape the quality of their work in order to improve productivity. Each of these things is acceptable and desirable in theory — that is, each is legitimate in some accountability scenario — but the long-term preoccupation, on the part of the public and its elected representatives, with the need to control inputs and regulate processes obscures or overtakes each of these objectives.

What is the likelihood of success in the movement toward flexibility in personnel matters? We can get an indication by considering four reforms — some proposed, some actually in place.

**Less Centralization of Control and Oversight.** Greater flexibility involving inputs would mean giving line managers greater control over the traditional functions of personnel job design, classification, recruitment, and selection. The first kind of flexibility — less centralized control and oversight of basic personnel functions — is exemplified in a recent reform proposal regarding position classification, one of the cornerstones of the merit system. The National Academy of Public Administration (NAPA) has proposed reordering work along organizational lines, not individual positions (Cayer, 1992). The current federal system has 459 occupations grouped into 22 categories. NAPA has proposed 10 occupational families grouped according to similarities in "career progression, basic skills, recruitment, training, and performance management" (Cayer, 1992, p. 219).

This proposal has far-reaching implications for public personnel management. It offers greater discretion to agencies and managers in configuring work forces according to management needs. It also offers agencies and managers the opportunity to change work-force configuration within broad position classifications and pay scales as circumstances warrant. Thus broader classification and pay banding can afford managers and agencies greater discretion in managing the work force. Theoretically, this proposal could be implemented without complete compromising of concerns for accountability, if an appropriate accountability mechanism is available.

What are the prospects for this proposal? It makes sense as a reform that would bring greater flexibility to the "inputs" level, but mistrust of government remains too great. As currently configured, the proposal provides managers too much discretion and gives rise to the fear that it may lead to new forms of patronage. Both aspects render the proposal unlikely to be adopted. For this proposal to succeed, the reform must include creating or triggering an accountability mechanism that would suit the movement toward more managerial discretion. But it must also include regulatory enhancements that would satisfy those reluctant to give line managers too much power. Such a compromise, by working for a more significant shift toward greater trust in government, might then give reformers an opportunity to increase the chances for further reforms. The same dynamic applies to pay classifications. If reformers can work hard to shift the dominant accountability system, then the proposal may stand a chance.

***Fewer and Less Detailed Rules and Regulations.*** Flexibility demands greater discretion for agency managers in determining how best to meet regulatory requirements (for example, to promote and protect the rights of employees). The Americans with Disabilities Act (ADA) of 1990 is recent legislation with substantial implications for personnel management in both the public and the private sector. The ADA prohibits discrimination in employment against otherwise qualified applicants and requires that reasonable accommodations in employment conditions be made for individuals with disabilities. Unlike previous legislation in this area of employee rights, the ADA does not preimpose the kinds of regulatory details that bind managers in other ways. In fact, it allows them greater flexibility.

The public management arena is quite used to seeing legal accountability mechanisms invoked in the area of employment discrimination, through oversight and monitoring or through court rulings. In fact, the role of the courts in public management continues to expand (see Chapter Seven of this volume). Will this habit — relying on legal rulings to impose accountability — change as employers gain more experience with the ADA? This is unclear, but it is probably unlikely.

In theory, ADA implementation should be seen as an opportunity to process issues under an outcomes-oriented mandate involving relatively nonroutinized tasks. Decisions about what kinds of job skills are essential to the positions in question, how much accommodation is necessary, and whether such accommodation is reasonable are unspecified in the legislation. Under the ADA, those matters are all left to the discretion of the managers on the scene. In theory, hence, implementation of the ADA could rely primarily on a professional accountability mechanism. The source of control is internal, the degree of control is low, and the managerial strategy is based more on outcomes — improved employment opportunities for individuals with disabilities — than on compliance.

When management's discretionary decision making about reasonable accommodations is in question, the legal accountability system is the likely recourse. Under such conditions, the boundaries of reasonable accommodations will be tested through litigation.

Thus the primary vehicle for ADA enforcement — the courts — will prove to be the problem for this move toward flexibility. Historically, the courts have not accepted anything but solutions that meet legal accountability requirements, nor are they likely to do otherwise. After a series of court rulings has been made, a de facto set of strict regulations will emerge through legal precedent, thus eliminating much of the flexibility the law seems to give. The fact that the courts will be the final arbiter of what is reasonable suggests that the long-term prospects for the ADA do not include its success as a means of increasing flexibility in the public service.

*Greater Empowerment of Line Personnel.* Greater discretion for line managers in allocating outputs (for example, such rewards as promotions, salary increases, and bonuses) has been granted under the Civil Service Reform Act of 1978 and the 1984 Performance Management and Recognition System. One of these initiatives is the bonus system that was put in place for the SES under the CSRA. In theory, this provision grants discretion to managers in rewarding their employees with bonuses as they see fit. Both initiatives stand as examples of reforms that allow for a nonnetherworld use of outputs (that is, flexible pay systems for top-level bureaucrats), but both have been failures (Shafritz, Riccucci, Rosenbloom, and Hyde, 1992).

The Performance Management and Recognition System was subject to politicization by the Reagan and Bush administrations and to intense scrutiny by the media. The public reaction to recent news stories involving bonuses given by (and to) outgoing Bush administration cabinet members offers an object lesson in perceived or real abuses that result from too much discretion. Even if these cases prove to have been within the bounds of the law, public reaction indicates just how vulnerable these and similar flexibility reforms are to the dominant position and pervasive power of the bureaucratic and regulatory accountability systems. Not only does this threaten reforms, it may also come to be regarded as a basis for reinforcing efforts to control and regulate the bureaucracy through even tighter accountability mechanisms. The reactionary consequences are clear. As a result, the prospects for greater flexibility in this area seem bleak.

*Greater Deference to the Capacity of Professionals.* Greater deference to managers and workers in the use of human resources is manifested in one of the currently "hot" managerial models, total quality management (TQM). TQM aims to increase the flexibility and productivity of all government operations, including personnel management. There has been much debate about how transferable TQM principles are from the private sector to the public sector. Various TQM reformulations are being undertaken in a variety of public agencies at all levels of government. Swiss (1992) proposes a reformed TQM that captures client feedback, performance tracking, continuous improvement, and worker participation. For the most part, these reformulations are being pursued in an accountability context that emphasizes bureaucratic and legal mechanisms.

TQM, even in the modified form Swiss proposes, fundamentally challenges the conventional individualistic approach to work design and performance evaluation that is widely used in government. TQM also challenges conventional accountability mechanisms regarding work design and performance evaluation, which emphasize individual effort and extensive scrutiny of individual performance by supervisors. This input-oriented approach fits well with the category of a bureaucratic accountability system. Its most common manifestation is the annual individual performance appraisal.

TQM, as proposed, emphasizes highly participative, client-centered work processes that keep the focus on a general outcome—customer satisfaction. TQM is better suited to professional accountability mechanisms, with an emphasis on increasing productivity and improving results. From the perspective of accountability, the prognosis for TQM depends on how likely the American polity and government leaders are to move the dominant accountability mechanism away from bureaucratic controls and toward more discretion, under a professional model. The required changes in how people are hired, rewarded, and regulated would be radical. As Light (1993, p. 18) notes, "Whatever the merits of [TQM], the federal government is not a private entity. No matter how much government managers want to manage, the public demands bureaucratic accountability."

## The Prospects and the Challenges of Greater Flexibility

The challenge of public personnel management remains the same: getting and retaining high-quality employees and holding them accountable for their performance. Rourke (1992,

p. 544) notes the consensus on the need to control the bureaucracy: "In the day of the administrative state, controlling bureaucracy has become one of the highest imperatives of democratic politics." The trend in most of these reforms is away from
bureaucratic and legalistic accountability mechanisms, and
toward professional and political accountability mechanisms
where the emphasis is more on trust, outputs, and outcomes.

The challenge of public management is to structure employees' and agencies' accountability in such a way that sufficient
attention is paid to the appropriate strategy and the nature of
the core task. The probability of successfully incorporating or
sustaining some efforts, such as TQM, may be high in the short
term because the environmental context has created enough
"heat" to light a fire under these reforms (Walters, 1992). To
the extent that we introduce reforms that are blind to these accountability dynamics, we run the risk of being lulled into com-
placency by short-term success. But the long-term success of
such reforms will be influenced by the dynamics of accountability. If the reforms are contrary to the dominant accountability systems, and if no adjustments in accountability systems are
made, then the prognosis for long-term success is poor. Unless
we structure relationships and expectations and attune them to
the appropriate accountability mechanisms, the reforms are
likely to be eroded by long-standing accountability dynamics.

Short-term adoption of flexible reforms may be a possibility these days because civil service reform is now a "hot" item,
a popular thing to do (Walters, 1992). Accountability dynamics
may not appear significant in the short-run process of adopting
personnel reforms, but the accountability dynamics will be significant in the long term. We see the equivalent at the federal
level in the Clinton administration's efforts to "sell" the idea of
shared sacrifice as a way of dealing with the national government's budget crisis. President Clinton may manage to succeed
in selling sacrifice to the populace, but if budgetary dynamics
remain unchanged, then the chance of fundamental long-term
reform in our budget outcomes is unlikely.

Increased flexibility in the public service raises a number of accountability and human resources policy questions. The

most fundamental one involves the tension between flexibility in personnel practices and equal treatment for all employees. The tradition of employment in the public sector, with its strong emphasis on equal treatment of employees, tends to result in personnel policies that are rigid and inflexible. The challenge for public officials is to design personnel policies that are flexible yet not subject to abuse and charges of favoritism or discrimination — reforms that do not completely sacrifice accountability. The challenge for elected officials is to find the political will to pass legislation that endorses this kind of flexibility.

## References

Ban, C. "Research and Demonstrations Under CSRA: Is Innovation Possible?" In P. W. Ingraham and D. H. Rosenbloom (eds.), *The Promise and Paradox of Civil Service Reform.* Pittsburgh, Pa.: University of Pittsburgh Press, 1992.

Ban, C., and Ingraham, P. W. "Short-Timers: Political Appointee Mobility and Its Impact on Political-Career Relations in the Reagan Administration." *Administration and Society,* 1990, *22,* 106–124.

Barnard, C. I. *The Functions of the Executive.* Cambridge, Mass.: Harvard University Press, 1938.

Barzelay, M., and Armajani, B. *Breaking Through Bureaucracy: A New Vision for Managing Government.* Berkeley: University of California Press, 1992.

Bowsher, C. A. "Meeting the New American Management Challenge in a Federal Agency: Lessons from the General Accounting Office." *Public Administration Review,* 1992, *52*(1), 3–7.

Caiden, G. F. "The Problem of Ensuring the Public Accountability." In J. G. Jabbra and O. P. Dwivedi (eds.), *Public Service Accountability: A Comparative Perspective.* West Hartford, Conn.: Kumarian Press, 1988.

Cayer, N. J. "Classification in the Federal Service: New Looks at Alternative Approaches." *Public Administration Review,* 1992, *52*(2), 217–220.

Dubnick, M. J. "Deregulation and the Prospects for Administrative Reform." In J. DiIulio (ed.), *Deregulating Bureaucracy.* Washington, D.C.: Brookings Institution, 1994.

Dubnick, M. J., and Romzek, B. S. *American Public Administration: Politics and the Management of Expectations.* New York: Macmillan, 1991.

Dubnick, M. J., and Romzek, B. S. "Accountability and the Centrality of Expectations in American Public Administration." *Research in Public Administration,* 1993, *2,* 37–78.

Durant, R. F. *The Administrative Presidency Revisited: Public Lands, the BLM, and the Reagan Revolution.* Albany: State University of New York Press, 1992.

Emery, F. E., and Trist, E. L. "The Causal Texture of Organizational Environments." *Human Relations,* 1965, *18*(1), 21–32.

Fay, C., Risher, H., and Hempel, P. "Locality Pay: Balancing Theory and Practice." *Public Personnel Management,* 1991, *20*(4), 397–408.

Finer, H. "Administrative Responsibility and Democratic Government." *Public Administration Review,* 1941, *1,* 335–350.

Fried, R. C. *Performance in American Bureaucracy.* Boston: Little, Brown, 1976.

Friedrich, C. J. "Public Policy and the Nature of Administrative Responsibility." In C. J. Friedrich and E. S. Mason (eds.), *Public Policy.* Cambridge, Mass.: Harvard University Press, 1940.

Glenn, R. M. "Performance Appraisal: An Unnerving Yet Useful Process." *Public Personnel Management,* 1990, *19*(1), 1–10.

Goodnow, F. J. *Comparative Administrative Law: An Analysis of the Administrative Systems, National and Local, of the United States, England, France and Germany.* New York: G. P. Putnam, 1893.

Gray, A., and Jenkins, W. I. *Administrative Politics in British Government.* Sussex, England: Wheatsheaf Books, 1985.

Gruber, J. *Controlling Bureaucracies: Dilemmas in Democratic Governance.* Berkeley: University of California Press, 1987.

Hargrove, E. C., and Glidewell, J. C. *Impossible Jobs in Public Management.* Lawrence: University Press of Kansas, 1990.

Heclo, H. *A Government of Strangers: Executive Politics in Washington.* Washington, D.C.: Brookings Institution, 1977.

Hood, C. C. *The Limits of Administration.* New York: Wiley, 1976.

Ingraham, P. W., and Rosenbloom, D. H. "Political Foundation of the American Federal Service: Rebuilding a Crumbling Base." *Public Administration Review,* 1990, *50*(2), 210–219.

Ingraham, P. W., and Rosenbloom, D. H. (eds.). *The Promise and Paradox of Civil Service Reform.* Pittsburgh, Pa.: University of Pittsburgh Press, 1992.

Kaufman, H. "Administrative Decentralization and Political Power." *Public Administration Review,* 1969, *29*(1), 3–15.

Kellough, J. E., and Rosenbloom, D. H. "Representative Bureaucracy and the EEOC: Did Civil Service Reform Make a Difference?" in P. W. Ingraham and D. H. Rosenbloom (eds.), *The Promise and Paradox of Civil Service Reform.* Pittsburgh, Pa.: University of Pittsburgh Press, 1992.

Kilmann, R. H. *Beyond the Quick Fix: Managing Five Tracks to Organizational Success.* San Francisco: Jossey-Bass, 1984.

Klingner, D., and Nalbandian, J. *Public Personnel Management: Contexts and Strategies.* (3rd ed.) Englewood Cliffs, N.J.: Prentice-Hall, 1993.

Krislov, S., and Rosenbloom, D. *Representative Bureaucracy and the American Political System.* New York: Praeger, 1981.

Levine, C. H. *The Unfinished Agenda for Civil Service Reform: Implications of the Grace Commission Report.* Washington, D.C.: Brookings Institution, 1985.

Levine, C. H., and Kleeman, R. S. "The Quiet Crisis in the American Public Service." In P. W. Ingraham and D. F. Kettl (eds.), *Agenda for Excellence: Public Service in America.* Chatham, N.J.: Chatham House, 1992.

Levine, C. H., Peters, B. G., and Thompson, F. J. *Public Administration: Challenges, Choices, Consequences.* Glenview, Ill.: Scott, Foresman, 1990.

Light, P. *Monitoring Government: Inspectors General and the Search for Accountability.* Washington, D.C.: Brookings Institution, 1993.

McGregor, E. B., Jr. "Symposium: The Public Service as Institution." *Public Administration Review,* 1982, *42*(4), 304–320.

Macy, J. W., Jr. "The Future of the Institution." *Public Administration Review,* 1982, *42*(4), 308–310.

Mainzer, L. C. *Political Bureaucracy: The American Public Service.* Glenview, Ill.: Scott, Foresman, 1973.

March, J. G., and Simon, H. A. *Organizations.* New York: Wiley, 1958.

Meier, K. *Politics and the Bureaucracy: Policymaking in the Fourth Branch of Government.* (3rd ed.) Pacific Grove, Calif.: Brooks/ Cole, 1993.

Mintzberg, H. *Structuring Organizations.* Englewood Cliffs, N.J.: Prentice-Hall, 1979.

Mosher, F. *Democracy and the Public Service.* (2nd ed.) New York: Oxford University Press, 1982.

Nalbandian, J., and Klingner, D. "The Politics of Public Personnel Administration: Towards Theoretical Understanding." *Public Administration Review,* 1981, *41*(5), 541–549.

National Commission on the Public Service (Volcker Commission). *Leadership for America: Rebuilding the Public Service.* Washington, D.C.: National Commission on the Public Service, 1989.

Newland, C. A. "A Midterm Appraisal—The Reagan Presidency: Limited Government and Political Administration." *Public Administration Review,* 1983, *43*(1), 1–21.

Nigro, L. G. "Personnel *for* and Personnel *by* Public Administrators: Bridging the Gap." In N. B. Lynn and A. Wildavsky (eds.), *Public Administration: The State of the Discipline.* Chatham, N.J.: Chatham House, 1990.

Organisation for Economic Co-operation and Development. *Flexible Personnel Management in the Public Service.* Paris: Organisation for Economic Co-operation and Development, 1990.

Osborne, D., and Gaebler, T. *Reinventing Government: How the Entrepreneurial Spirit Is Transforming the Public Sector.* Reading, Mass.: Addison-Wesley, 1992.

President's Private Sector Survey on Cost Control (Grace Commission). *War on Waste.* New York: Macmillan, 1984.

Rainey, H. "Perceptions of the Incentives in Business and Government: Implications for Civil Service Reform." *Public Administration Review,* 1979, *39*(4), 440–448.

Romzek, B. S. "Balancing Work and Nonwork Obligations." In C. Ban and N. Riccucci (eds.), *Public Personnel Manage-*

*ment: Current Concerns, Future Challenges.* New York: Longman, 1992.

Romzek, B. S., and Dubnick, M. J. "Accountability in the Public Sector: Lessons from the *Challenger* Tragedy." *Public Administration Review,* 1987, *47*(3), 227–239.

Romzek, B. S., and Dubnick, M. J. "Institutional, Organizational, and Individual Levels of Accountability: The Los Angeles Police Department and the Rodney King Beating." In B. Bozeman (ed.), *Proceedings of the National Public Management Research Conference.* Syracuse, N.Y.: The Maxwell School, Syracuse University, 1991.

Rosenbloom, D. *Federal Service and the Constitution: The Development of Public Employment Relationships.* Ithaca, N.Y.: Cornell University Press, 1971a.

Rosenbloom, D. "Some Political Implications of the Drift Toward a Liberation of Federal Employees." *Public Administration Review,* 1971b, *31*(4), 420–426.

Rosenbloom, D. "The Bill of Rights and the Ongoing Administrative Revolution." *Public Administration Quarterly,* 1994, *16,* 294–302.

Rourke, F. E. "Responsiveness and Neutral Competence in American Bureaucracy." *Public Administration Review,* 1992, *52*(6), 539–546.

Shafritz, J. M., Riccucci, N. M., Rosenbloom, D. H., and Hyde, A. C. *Personnel Management in Government: Politics and Process.* (4th ed.) New York: Marcel Dekker, 1992.

Simon, H. A. *Administrative Behavior.* New York: Free Press, 1957.

Skowronek, S. *Building A New American State: The Expansion of National Administrative Capacities, 1977–1920.* Cambridge, England: Cambridge University Press, 1982.

Stillman, R. J. II. *Preface to Public Administration: A Search for Themes and Direction.* New York: St. Martin's Press, 1991.

Summer, C. E. *Strategic Business Behavior in Business and Government.* Boston: Little, Brown, 1980.

Swiss, J. E. "Adapting Total Quality Management (TQM) to Government." *Public Administration Review,* 1992, *52*(4), 356–362.

Thompson, J. D. *Organizations in Action: Social Science Bases of Administrative Theory.* New York: McGraw-Hill, 1967.

Waldo, D. *The Administrative State: A Study of the Political Theory of American Public Administration.* (2nd ed.) New York: Holmes and Meier, 1984.

Walters, J. "How Not to Reform Civil Service." *Governing,* 1992, *6*(2), 30–34.

Wheat, E. M. "The Activist Auditor: A New Player in State and Local Politics." *Public Administration Review,* 1991, *51*(5), 385–392.

White, L. D. *The Republican Era, 1869–1901: A Study in Administrative History.* New York: Macmillan, 1958.

Wilson, J. Q. *Bureaucracy: What Government Agencies Do and Why They Do It.* New York: Basic Books, 1989.

Yates, D. *Bureaucratic Democracy.* Cambridge, Mass.: Harvard University Press, 1982.

# 12

# New Visions of Government and the Public Service

## B. Guy Peters

Waldo (1968) once wrote that public administration has had so many identity crises that the life of the average adolescent appears idyllic in comparison. Waldo was discussing public administration as an academic discipline, but the contemporary practice of public administration displays much of the same uncertainty. The questions of practice concern the structure of government, management of those structures, and the proper role of public administration in governance. Many of the old certainties about government and the role of the public service are now either totally altered or subject to severe questioning.

    At least three of the old chestnuts that have guided our thinking about the public service in the process of governance are simply no longer as canonical as they once were. The first of these principles is the assumption of an apolitical civil service, and associated with it is the politics-administration dichotomy and the concept of "neutral competence" (Kaufman, 1956) within the civil service. It is increasingly clear that civil servants do have significant (if not dominant) policy roles in most contemporary governments (Peters, 1992), and that governance is probably better because they do.

The problem then becomes how to structure government in ways that recognize the reality, even the desirability, of the enhanced policy roles for civil servants while also preserving the requirements of democratic accountability. This is a difficult balance for the designers of government institutions to achieve, especially given the historical legacy of thinking about the neutrality of the civil service in Anglo-American democracies and public demands for enhanced accountability (Gruber, 1987; Day and Klein, 1987). Furthermore, political leaders have come to recognize the growing policy role of civil servants and, in response, often have acted to try to minimize that role (Ingraham, 1987; Aberbach and Rockman, 1988). Therefore, the struggle over competence to make policy is now more obvious to those working within government, as well as to citizens on the outside. The politicization of the role of the civil service, if not the members of the civil service themselves, may make the delicate balance of policy competence all the more difficult to achieve.

A second significant change in assumptions about government relevant to this discussion is a decline in the assumption of hierarchical and rule-based management within the public service, and in the authority of civil servants to implement and enforce regulations outside the public service. The neat Weberian model of management does not apply to public organizations to the extent that it once did. In its place stand a variety of alternative sources of power and authority. The market may be an increasingly significant standard against which to compare the structure and performance of government organizations (Lan and Rosenbloom, 1992; Hood, 1990; Boston, 1991). While the inherent differences between the public and private sectors are crucial to understanding governance (Allison, 1986), even governments on the political left have sought to utilize a number of market-based reforms in their structures and performance. (The most radical use of the variety of market-based reforms available to government was implemented by the Labour government of New Zealand.)

An alternative to the market model, as well as to traditional models of bureaucracy, is the "dialectic" or participatory organization. This model has been discussed by scholars for a number of years, but governmental organizations are being placed under increasing pressure to accommodate the interests of lower-level employees, as well as those of clients, into their decision-making processes (Barzelay and Armajani, 1992). This change in management is at once a manipulative mechanism for increasing efficiency and a genuine moral commitment to participation (Thomas, 1993). Contemporary public organizations may also be expected to negotiate societal compliance with their decisions, and with contracts for service delivery, rather than directly implement programs through law and other authoritative means. Finally, civil servants increasingly may be expected to make their own decisions about what constitutes the public interest and must at times make judgments that may go against the stated policies and desires of their political masters. (This autonomous role is not unfamiliar in the United States but is extremely unusual and threatening in Westminster systems. The Ponting affair in Britain and the Al-Mashat case in Canada are examples of the importance of this change in the norms of governing in Westminster governments; see Chapman, 1993.) All these changes make the role of civil service managers even more difficult than it was before, and they make the role of civil servants within governments all the more ambiguous.

The third change in the assumptions about governance and the public bureaucracy concerns the permanence and stability of the organizations within government. Joining a public organization is sometimes conceptualized as similar to joining a Japanese corporation: it is seen as lifetime employment. The permanence of public organizations is frequently overestimated (Peters and Hogwood, 1988) but has been an important partial truth about government. Increasingly, this pattern of permanence is being attacked. Increased recognition of the dysfunctions of permanence, and the recognition that many of the most significant social and economic problems currently exist in the interstices of existing organizations, have led to discussions of alternative forms of governmental organization. The character of the alternative organizational structures remains somewhat inchoate at present, but the discussion has begun. In particular, ideas about task forces, "czars," interdepartmental committees, and similar structures have generated options for thinking about a more flexible pattern of governance. (This pattern is already used rather widely in several European systems; see, for example, Fournier, 1987, and his discussion of coordination within French government.) Further, not only are the organizations of government considered somewhat less permanent than in the past, the personnel commitments of government have also come to be considered less permanent.

Rather than looking back to these vestiges of the past, this chapter will attempt to be prospective and to examine alternative paths of development for the public service. I will develop several alternative models of the state that appear to be emerging and then look at the implications of these models for the civil service. Except for the market model, these alternatives have not been articulated in any comprehensive fashion, and I will have to extract these almost as ideal types from academic and practical discussions of governing. Further, there is some similarity of analysis and prescription across some of these models, although the meanings attached may be quite different (Roth, 1987). They all have the effect, however, of "hollowing" out the state and making it, and particularly the public service, a less significant actor in society. This discussion will concentrate on these developments in governance within the United States but will also make some comparative allusions. What is perhaps most interesting in the comparative analysis is the extent to which the alternative visions have appeared more strongly and clearly in official documents than in scholarly writings in many countries. (Obvious examples are statements of the public-choice approach in New Zealand and of the participatory model in Canada.) Although focused on alternatives, this chapter will also argue that one possible model is a vigorous restatement of the status quo ante and its less manifestly political and policy role for the civil service. For many civil servants, and probably for even more politicians, the "old-time religion" may still be the best way to run a government.

## Visions of the State and Governance

Few governments in the Western world have remained untouched by the wave of reform that has swept through the public sector over the past several decades. The reforms undertaken in most political systems may have been unprecedented, but they also have tended to be rather piecemeal and unsystematic (Savoie and Peters, forthcoming). This absence of clear visions and integrated strategies may explain, in part, why the results of the reforms have tended to disappoint so many of their advocates (Caiden, 1990). What I will attempt to do in this chapter, therefore, is to explicate several more integrated visions of possible futures for the state bureaucracy. The nature of each image will in turn influence the manner in which governance could be practiced under such a regime. If the implications of these alternative visions are more fully explored and understood and contrasted with the conventional wisdom about governance, then there is some possibility, although no guarantee, of more effective planned change in government.

My concern here with alternative visions does not mean that any of these schemes is superior to the traditional model of the civil service in governance. I tend to think that is not the case, but I do think that continuing reform in government is likely. If reform is to occur, it is more likely to be effective if it is systematic and integrated. We should also remain cognizant, however, of the internal contradictions of some of these approaches. It may be that, like Simon's discussion (1957) of the "proverbs of administration," our thinking about the complexities of the public service, even when guided by a relatively strong set of theoretical assumptions, tends toward situational rather than systematic remedies.

As we look at these several alternatives to the traditional system of governance, we will be looking at the implications and prescriptions of each vision for several aspects of governing. The first of these aspects is structure: How should the public sector be organized? The second issue is personnel: How should the members of the public sector be recruited, motivated, and managed? The third issue is the policy process: What should the role of the career public service be in the policy process, and, more generally, how should government seek to influence the private sector?

## The Market Model

The most familiar of the alternatives to the traditional model of administration, and seemingly the most popular among politicians, is the *market model* of administration. The development of this model has several intellectual roots. The first is the analysis of the failings of conventional bureaucracies made by such scholars as Niskanen (1971), Tullock (1965), Moe (1984, 1989), Ostrom (1986), and a host of other devotees of public choice (Bendor, 1990). They have argued that because of the self-interest of the members of the organizations, especially the "bureau chiefs" at the apex, public bureaucracies have tended to expand at an unjustifiable rate and to charge their sponsors (read "legislatures") too much for the services produced. The permanence of bureaucrats and their monopoly of information have been said to put them at a competitive advantage in dealings with legislatures. The root of any failings in the public sector, as seen from this perspective, is the self-interest of bureaucrats. This characteristic of bureaucrats does not differentiate them from other individuals; the problem is the assumption that members of the public service will necessarily act in the public interest.

The second intellectual root of the market approach to governance in the public sector is generic management and its ally, the "new public management" (Pollitt, 1990; Massey, 1993). This corpus of analysis functions under the assumption that management is management, no matter where it takes place, and that instruments used to organize and motivate personnel are as applicable to the public sector as to the private sector. Thus, rather than deploring the absence of a sense of the public interest, as the public-choice literature often appears to do, this approach to the public sector assumes the lack of any meaningful difference between the two sectors and then builds a series of management recommendations on that assumed similarity.

At a relatively high intellectual plane, the recommendations of this variant of managerial thinking may be based on the ubiquity of principal-agent relationships (Perrow, 1986) and the applicability of transaction-cost analysis (Williamson, 1975; Calista, 1989) in organizations, whether they are public or private. At a lower level of academic development, generic management is often the accepted doctrine of outsiders who want to export their favorite management techniques to the public sector. (And they usually want to export these techniques at a profit.) At both levels of conceptualization, the approach has been criticized by insiders (scholars and practitioners) who consider management in the public sector to be a distinctive form of activity.

*Structure.* The market approach assumes that one of the principal problems with the traditional structure of the public sector is a reliance on large, monopolistic departments that receive little direction from the environment. The size and complexity of government organizations, combined with their delivery of unpriced goods and services, is seen (especially by students of public choice) to be the root of a good deal of the (perceived) inefficiency and ineffectiveness of government. These structural difficulties are accentuated by the emphasis on formal rules and authority as guides for action in traditional public organizations, rather than a dependence on either market signals (Rose, 1989) or the entrepreneurial spirit of individuals.

The prescriptions arising from this diagnosis of the source of problems in public organizations are rather obvious. One of the central elements of reform is the decentralization of policy and implementation decisions. This decentralization can be accomplished through the splitting up of large departments into smaller "agencies," through the assigning of functions to lower levels of government, or through the use of private or quasi-private organizations to deliver public services. This advice is particularly applicable when the good or service in question is marketable. In the most extreme versions of this approach, government would create multiple, competitive organizations to supply the same goods and services, with the expectation that the same competitive mechanisms presumed to work in the private sector would also work in the public sector.

This advice, to divide large departments into smaller segments, is less applicable to the United States than it has been to government in other developed democracies. We do not have to go through the exercise of creating large numbers of agencies and corporate bodies, as in the United Kingdom, New Zealand, and the Netherlands (Davies and Willman, 1992; Boston, 1991). The cabinet departments in the United States traditionally have granted substantial autonomy to their component agencies, and those organizations have been able to act somewhat autonomously. Of course, the admonitions of market proponents about the relationship of these agencies to market forces have not been followed very often; thus they have been autonomous more in a political sense than in the sense of operating as quasi-firms supplying goods and services in the marketplace. For the United States, the structural recommendations have been more in the direction of creating private and quasi-private organizations that will provide the services once provided by government. Full privatization has been more significant at the state and local levels, but contracting and other instruments for introducing market forces have been significant at the federal level.

This approach has some structural recommendations at the "micro" level of organizations, as well as for the "macro" level of entire departments. An emphasis on entrepreneurial activity and individual responsibility tends to press for relatively flat organizations, with little of the layering that traditional public organizations tend to consider essential to control and consistency in decisions. Advocates of this approach tend to presume that the leader of the organization, as well as the "bottom line" resulting from the organization's dealings with the external environment, will be more effective than a hierarchy in producing appropriate decisions. This observation points to the importance of relatively integrated (as opposed to piecemeal) reforms. Structural changes without associated changes in management are unlikely to produce the benefits presumed by theoretical presuppositions.

*Management.* The managerial implications of the market model also should be rather obvious. If workers in the public sector are considered to be very much the same as workers in the private sector, then the same managerial techniques should apply. This would mean that some of the cherished traditions of personnel management in government would have to be modified. These changes are already under way in a number of personnel areas, most obviously in the rewards for public officials' participation in government. One of the traditions of public personnel systems has been that individuals in the same grade of the civil service would be paid the same amount. This tradition is being replaced with a merit principle, which says that people should be paid more in line with what they could earn in the market and that better performance should be rewarded with better pay, regardless of any differences that may emerge between workers.

The emphasis on differential rewards for differential performance is especially important at the top managerial level of the small, relatively autonomous agencies created as a part of this approach. In several of the reward schemes already implemented, managers are hired under contracts that contain specific performance standards. If the agency manager and his or her organization achieve those standards, the manager is eligible for full pay (and perhaps bonuses); if the organization does not reach these goals, then the manager may lose pay or be fired. In this model of the public sector, the manager is an entrepreneur who is responsible for what happens in the agency and is rewarded accordingly. Lower echelons within these organizations may be rewarded under similar contractual arrangements based on performance standards. The managerialist reward system in the United States, implemented as part of the Civil Service Reform Act of 1978, is similar in its dependence on bonuses at the upper echelons (and on the possibility of dismissal). Merit pay also has been implemented at lower echelons. One of the greatest difficulties with these programs in the United States has been the failure of political leaders to fund the bonuses and other incentives contained in the plans.

There reward schemes depend on the capacity of government to measure the performance of its employees and their organizations. Any number of studies have demonstrated the severe difficulties encountered in attempting to perform this seemingly simple managerial task (Metcalfe and Richards, 1990; Boston, 1992), especially if performance is to be measured at the output or impact level, rather than merely at the activity level. This measurement problem means, then, either that performance contracts and effective managerialism will be limited to the relatively few agencies or other parts of government providing marketable or otherwise measurable services, or that it must depend on specious measures of performance. In either case, the capacity to implement this aspect of the market vision of the public sector appears at least a bit suspect.

We should also note that these managerialist trends are not neutral in their effects on the perceived role of the public service. Measuring performance is substantially easier, if still difficult, for the managerial and service-delivery functions of the civil service. It is much more difficult to measure for the policy-advice functions. As a result of this difficulty, adoption of managerialist performance evaluations and pay schemes will tend to introduce some bias in the direction of a more managerial and less policy-based role for civil servants, both because of changes in the signals coming from evaluators above and because the evaluated may decide that they can maximize their own rewards by playing the managerial game.

*Policy Making.* The final aspect of the marketized vision of the state that we will examine here is the conceptualization of how public policy should be made. In particular, we will be concerned with the appropriate role of the career public servant in making policy.

A fundamental contradiction appears to reside at the heart of the role that this vision assigns to the bureaucracy. On the one hand, the market approach advocates decentralizing bureaucratic functions to multiple, "entrepreneurial" agencies that would be expected to make autonomous decisions. These decisions presumably would be based either on signals received from the market or on the judgment of the entrepreneurial leaders of the organization. Breaking the bonds of bureaucracy is meant to liberate decision making and produce more risk taking and innovation. On the other hand, the practitioners who have advocated this approach have expected these quasi-autonomous organizations to comply with the policy and ideological directives coming from above. One consistent observation about the Reagan, Thatcher, and Mulroney governments, and about other, similar regimes, is that they attempted to impose their own views on the civil service. Bureaucrats were seen as too committed to the growth of their own organizations, as well as perhaps too committed to serving their narrow clientele rather than "the public interest." Attempts at politicization are by no means new, but they were more overt during the past decade. Defenders of the traditional view have seen politicization as the erosion of one of the most important features of merit systems and the civil service. In some ways, however, this is merely a reaffirmation of the traditional view that civil servants should be "on tap but not on top," and that political leaders are responsible for policy. Whether or not this is part of the traditional conceptualization, there is some inconsistency, and bureaucrats are having what may be unreasonable demands placed on them.

Even if that apparent inconsistency could be resolved, additional problems for policy making would arise from the application of this approach. One of the most important of these is the problem of coordination and control. The rather radical decentralization of policy making to more autonomous organizations provides relatively little opportunity for either senior bureaucrats or politicians to coordinate policy. One critique of the traditional approach to governance has been that, de facto, independence of the bureaucracy thwarts consistency across policies and often produces destructive competition (Allard, 1990). The market approach appears to exalt such competition and potential inconsistency, so long as actions conform to the political ideals of those political leaders. It is perhaps too much to believe that the leaders of autonomous agencies would be content to be managers of those organizations and not become concerned with policy.

Finally, at a more conceptual level, there is the problem of the role of the citizen. The market model tends to conceptualize the recipients of government programs, and the public more generally, as *consumers*. This is at once empowering and demeaning of the public. As a beneficial change, this conception provides the citizen with the same expectation of services that he or she has from a private sector firm. (Those of us who deal regularly with airlines and Blue Cross–Blue Shield may consider being treated like the customer of a private concern to be a threat.) Changes such as the Citizen's Charter in Britain and PS 2000 in Canada have many of these elements of consumerism in them (Lovell, 1992). Nevertheless, the citizen is now little more than a consumer, and his or her role as the holder of rights and a legal status vis-à-vis the state appears somewhat diminished. Government may be more than buying and selling and probably should be more. If it is reduced to that level, then the citizen is a less significant figure in political theory than he or she is usually thought to be.

*Summary.* As noted, the market vision has been the most popular alternative view of the state and of government. It tends to consider public sector agencies as facing the same managerial and service-delivery tasks as organizations would in the private sector, and as being amenable to the same techniques for performing those tasks. It assumes that if the rule-based authority structure usually associated with bureaucracy is removed or deemphasized, then there can be a flowering of the creative and administrative talent of individuals working in the public sector. Although it is usually associated with the political right, some devotees of this approach believe that its successful implementation would result in a more effective and efficient public sector, whether the latter is delivering defense or social services.

### The Participatory State

The second alternative view of the state I will discuss here is almost the antithesis of the market approach, in terms of the political ideologies of most of its advocates, but in some instances the analyses and recommendations appear remarkably similar. I have called this approach the *participatory state,* but it has been discussed with a number of different names. An alternative characterization might be the *empowerment state,* in which groups (presumably) excluded under more hierarchical models would be permitted greater organizational involvement (Kernaghan, 1992). Like the market approach, this approach considers the hierarchical, rule-based organization usually encountered in the public sector to be a severe impediment to effective management and governance. Nevertheless, rather than concentrate attention on the upper echelons of leaders in an organization, who are the protoentrepreneurs within government, this approach concentrates on the lower echelons, or workers, as well as on the clients of the organization.

The fundamental assumptions of this approach are that there is a great deal of energy and talent being underutilized at the lower echelons of hierarchies, and that the workers and clients closest to the actual production of goods and services in the public sector have the greatest amount of information about the programs. It is assumed that if those ideas and talents were harnessed, government would work better. Therefore, the general prescription is greater participation and involvement on the part of those groups within government that are commonly excluded from decision making. Somewhat predictably, the advocates of this approach tend to come more from the political left, although some on the right, interested in empowerment of and self-management by clients, also advocate versions of this approach. (Jack Kemp as secretary of Housing and Urban Development is one such right-wing advocate.)

The intellectual roots of this approach are also somewhat diverse. There is one body of literature that argues that involvement and participation are the best ways to motivate individual employees, even if these are somewhat manipulative. Another strand of literature argues that the lower echelons of public organizations are central to the effective functioning of those organizations, and as a simple reality the role of "street-level bureaucrats" needs to be recognized. At a higher intellectual level, there are various strands of literature on "discursive democracy" and the like that argue for the enhanced participation of clients and workers in the identification and clarification of problems within organizations.

*Structure.* The structural implications of this approach are somewhat less clear than for the public-choice approach. For this approach, process appears more important than the structures within which the processes occur. At one level, the formal patterns of organization may be irrelevant if there are other opportunities for workers and clients to participate in decisions. There are, however, structural reforms that may make participation easier; therefore, this approach is not entirely silent on the issue of the design of public organizations. In considering both participation and decision making, we need to note the extent to which the enhanced participation of one group — either lower-echelon employees or clients — may minimize the impact of the other.

The most obvious implication for structure is that, very much as in the public-choice approach, public organizations would be much flatter and have fewer tiers between top and bottom. If indeed the lower echelons are perceived as having a great deal to offer in decision making, and if they are highly motivated to provide good services, then hierarchical control is merely an impediment to good performance in an organization. The alternative implication, however, is that if clients and lower-echelon employees are given substantial involvement in making decisions, then there may be a need for greater control from above, to ensure that public laws and financial restraints are adhered to faithfully.

One of the other structural implications of the participatory approach to governing is that there may have to be a variety of structures to channel participation. This is especially true for the participation of clients but may also be true for lower-level employees whose involvement in decision making has been less than what this approach envisions. As governments have come to implement programs of participation for clients and workers alike, a variety of councils, advisory groups, and the like, have come into being. It is interesting that much of what is defined as the rights of participation, even though defined as citizenship rights, is in practice the rights of consumers. Again, this brings the participatory approach closer to the market approach than might be expected from the political ideologies of their typical adherents.

*Management.* The participatory approach to governance contains somewhat more obvious implications for management than for structure in the public sector. The basic premise is that governmental organizations function better if lower-level workers and perhaps clients as well are included more directly in managerial decisions. At one level, such involvement could be considered manipulative, with top management exchanging a bit of participation for greater productivity and loyalty from workers. Early "human relations" management did have some of this manipulative character, but the more contemporary advocates of participation have been more ideological and believe in the human as well as the organizational importance of participation. Even then, however, there may be something of a manipulative element in thinking that the overall governance of society can be enhanced through permitting and encouraging greater social "discourse" in the process of making decisions.

Perhaps the most important feature of the participatory approach is its attempt to involve societal interests more explicitly in governance. We should remember, however, that these managerial ideologies are by no means the first theoretical justifications of enhanced participation. The neocorporatist and corporate pluralist literature represents another very strong strand of thinking about how to gain the advantages of the knowledge, and quiescence, of social groups (Olsen, 1986). The difference may be that this level of legitimate involvement of social interests is now becoming popular in countries with an Anglo-American political cultural legacy, as well as in countries with a more Continental legacy. Thus, while the market model may denigrate the role of the citizen, this model appears to enhance the role of the citizen and to attempt an inducement of democratic participation by means other than voting.

*Policy Making.* The implications for policy making are for a bottom-up versus a top-down version of the policy process (this language is usually reserved for the implementation process but can also be applied to the process more generally). That is, this version does not assume that governments can govern best by making decisions in a centralized fashion and then implementing them through laws and relatively rigid hierarchies. Rather, the vision is one of decentralized decision making. This is true both in the sense of the lower echelons having substantial if not determinate impact on policy decisions and in the sense of organizations themselves having a great deal of control over the decisions that determine their own fates. The assumption is also that decisions made in this manner will be objectively better, given the presumably greater information possessed by the lower levels of the organization. In its emphasis on decentralization, the participatory approach shares a good deal with the theorists (if not always the practitioners) of the public-choice approach.

Given this concern with the involvement of lower-echelon workers, the participatory approach is almost silent on the involvement of top-echelon bureaucrats — those usually referred to as being at the decision-making level — in policy selection. One possible implication would be that political leaders, having somewhat greater involvement with the public, may be more suitable conduits for participatory input into decisions. But if communication within an organization is even moderately efficient, the lower echelons should be able to send messages to the top that would then have an influence on policy. In either case, the design question is really how those usually excluded from decisions can have an impact on those decisions, and there is no simple answer.

The other perspective that the participatory model may have on policy making involves the realistic statement that the lower echelons of the bureaucracy do have a major impact on policy in almost any political system (Lipsky, 1980; Adler and Asquith, 1981). Most decisions in government are not made by political leaders or even by the upper echelons of the civil service. Rather, they are made by the lower echelons — the street-level bureaucrats — who have to make numerous decisions about particular cases every day. Not only are those decisions crucial to the actual determinations of citizens' claims against the state for services, they are also crucial to popular perceptions of government. For most people, government is the policeman, or the tax collector, or the safety inspector, and the interactions between citizen and representative of the state may shape the public's ideas about what government does and what it thinks about its citizens. Thus a participatory emphasis in governance may make government more popular with clients, if not necessarily more efficient in delivering services.

*Summary.* The participatory model is not as well articulated as the public-choice model. Still, it is possible to extract some of the implications of this vision for the role of the civil service in governing society, as well as for the nature of governance itself. The participatory approach is ideologically very different from that of public choice, both in its vision and in its assumptions about human behavior in organizations. Even with those differences, the prescriptions for design in the two approaches are not all that dissimilar. In particular, the principal prescription is for decentralization and for some transfer of power to the lower echelons of the organization, as well as to the clients of the organization. Further, this model recognizes the role of the bureaucracy in making public policy, just as the public-choice approach does, although this model considers such involvement more positively.

Although the prescriptions are not dissimilar to those of public choice, the meaning attached to designs for governance are markedly different. Decentralization in the participatory model, rather than being a means of creating competition among service providers so that a market can work, is intended primarily to channel control to a different set of bureaucrats, or to clients. This could be thought to be the very type of capture that the public-choice model seeks to avert (Macey, 1992). Likewise, the involvement of lower-level bureaucrats in decisions is considered positively, but the alternative is seen to be domination by upper-level bureaucrats, rather than by political leaders. In this model, both of those elites are seen as equally antithetical to the interests of clients, rather than as each other's competitor for power.

## The Temporary Organization

The third alternative to the traditional model of government organization will be discussed as the *temporary organization*. As already noted, joining a government organization often has been conceptualized as accepting lifetime employment (assuming that the individual wants to remain). Likewise, forming an organization is usually thought of as creating a permanent entity, no matter how transient the reasons for the structure may appear (Kaufman, 1976). This permanence is often overstated, but it tends to guide thinking about the formation and management of the public sector.

The dysfunctions of permanence, both of employment and of the organizations themselves, are well known, and governments have begun to address them. This is the least clearly articulated of the three approaches to administration, but these ideas and practices do appear to be emerging in a number of governments. Permanence has come to be considered as the source of excessive conservatism of policies, and as the source of commitment to the organization more than to the policies being administered by the organization — organizations embody interests. (Interestingly, some of the public-choice literature has been seeking means of designing organizations that will be conservative and will preserve the same policies over time; see McCubbins, Noll, and Weingast, 1989.) Individuals who work for an organization may be more concerned with keeping their jobs and keeping the organization healthy in budgetary terms than with doing anything in particular. Further, this emphasis on permanence tends to lock in certain conceptions of policy, and even of what the real policy problems are. In all, despite some obvious attractions, permanent governmental structures may present significant problems for effective and efficient governance.

In addition to recognition of the dysfunctions of permanence, the changing nature of governance problems and of the labor market has tended to produce movement away from permanence. First, an increasing number of significant problems that government confronts fall between the cracks of the existing organizations. For example, although we have the Drug

Enforcement Agency, a large number of agencies—the Coast Guard, the Department of Defense, the Customs Bureau, the FBI, among others—are also involved in the "war on drugs." This widened involvement of agencies in policies has already created a fourth or fifth or nth "branch" of government that attempts to coordinate and control the existing organizations and policies. I would argue that the policy space and the organizational space for government are already well populated (Hogwood and Peters, 1983), and any new initiatives are likely to confront existing actors.

The other pressure creating impermanence in government organizations is the fundamental transformation of the labor market in most industrialized societies, with much less full-time and permanent employment and an increasing level of part-time and temporary employment. Government has already begun to adjust to these broader economic changes and has found more part-time employment to be a way of saving money and enhancing organizational flexibility. Thus, even when there is a permanent organization per se, the members of the organization may themselves be transients. This is certainly a shift from the tradition of government employment and has important managerial and policy implications.

*Structure.* The fundamental advice that this approach offers is for alternative structural arrangements within government. Rather than relying exclusively on the traditional forms of departments, agencies, and bureaus, which perceive themselves as having virtually permanent claims on particular policy spaces, this approach would seek some flexibility in and, frequently, termination of existing organizations. Indeed, state and local governments have already made moves in this direction, with "sunset laws" and other devices that force relatively frequent reconsideration of the existence of their organizations. This would be done to prevent the ossification that can afflict permanent organizations. Further, it might be expected to allow government to respond more rapidly to changing social and economic conditions. For example, there might be less resistance to creating organizations intended to respond to novel circumstances if there were some assurance that these organizations would be terminated when their tasks were completed. Moreover, the ability to create and then destroy organizations might appeal to fiscal conservatives and critics who argue that permanence and bureaucratic monopolies create excessive costs, along with policy rigidities. In fact, in many ways, the organizational universe emerging from this approach would not be dissimilar to the "agencies" being created by advocates of the market approach, with the added factor that these organizations would be subject to rapid change.

As well as being structurally impermanent, these organizations might not be populated to a large extent by full-time employees who (at least in the United States) would spend most or all of their careers within the same organization. This change in career patterns is already occurring in government. For example, the proportion of total work hours put in by federal employees has been creeping up gradually since the 1960s and appears likely to continue increasing. Predictions based on almost all studies of the labor market say that the trend toward temporary employment will continue in almost all segments of the economy. This trend may be applauded by fiscal conservatives who want to save money in the public sector, but it may do damage to other conservative values concerning the accountability of the civil service and its stability as a source of advice and values in an otherwise rapidly changing government.

*Management.* The manifest managerial implications of the temporary state are rather clear, but the latent implications are perhaps more interesting and more important. At the manifest level, this approach stresses the ability of managers to adjust their work-force requirements very flexibly. As noted, this can be used as a means of saving a good deal of money for government, as well as mitigating some of the public perceptions of wastefulness and empire building on the part of governmental organizations. Further, this approach may permit governments to respond more quickly and effectively to crises or to rapidly increased demands for service, although the potential benefits tend to be discussed less than the cost-cutting effects.

The latent implications of this approach are some diminution of employees' commitment to their employers and, with that, a potential threat to the values and ethos of the public service. It now may appear somewhat idealistic to discuss the commitment of civil servants to their organizations and to the principle of public service. Nevertheless, there is some evidence that civil servants have been motivated by these values, and that many of them would like to continue being so motivated. Putting more public sector jobs on a temporary and part-time basis will almost certainly diminish the commitment that employees feel to their jobs and will also tend to minimize their motivation for excellent performance on the job. Further, temporary status may make the civil service values of probity, accountability, and responsibility all the more difficult to enforce. In short, we could argue that a good deal may be sacrificed to gain some reduction in expenditures.

*Policy Making.* As mentioned, this is the least developed of the alternative approaches to the role of the public service in governance. In particular, this approach has little to say directly about the role of the public service in making public policy. We can, however, attempt to explore the logical implications for an active policy role for the civil service. These implications seem potentially contradictory, with some pointing toward an enhanced role for the civil service and others appearing to reaffirm an older wisdom, that of the political dominance of the elected classes over policy, with civil servants in a subordinate position.

On the one hand, with so much emphasis on the fragility of organizations in government, the traditional sources of organizational power in a common culture and of commitment to the existing policies would be diminished. The old bureaucratic structures had both the advantage and the disadvantage of stable personnel and, with them, stable policies. The permanent personnel gave a great deal of direction to policy and provided an experiential knowledge base for the construction of any new policy initiatives. On the other hand, such stability has been a barrier to innovations that might go beyond the conventional wisdom about what is feasible in the policy area (Majone, 1989).

Absence of mortmain may permit political leaders to have a stronger role in altering policies than otherwise might be possible. A group of radical reformers, such as the Thatcherites or the "Reaganauts," would be pleased to have less of an organizational inheritance to counteract.

Nevertheless, not all the pressures for this approach go toward making the life of political leaders easier. By removing the anchor of large, stable organizations beneath them, the elite members of the civil service may be able to develop their own policy ideas more autonomously. To some extent, the conception of the Senior Executive Service in the United States was that of a free-floating resource that could be used in a variety of managerial and policy-advice situations. Without large permanent organizations to encumber them in the exercise of their own conceptions of good policy, these senior officials may be able to become creative forces in policy development.

## Can We Go Home Again?

We have now looked at several alternative movements away from the traditional model of administration in the public sector. Some of these models are already being implemented. Others are only in the nascent stages (if that far along in their development). In each case, implicit or explicit comparisons have been made with the traditional model of administration, with its clear separation of roles between administration and politics, its hierarchical management style and structure, and its (largely) permanent organizations and career civil servants.

The obvious question is whether those in government, even if they wanted to, could ever return to the comfortable system that is now past. To some degree, the emphasis on management, on the political reliability of the civil service, on the empowerment of staff and clients, and on flexibility presses toward an alteration in the tacit bargain that has existed among the participants in governance. Both sides can gain some advantages from this change, although the advantages appear to run mostly in the direction of politicians and secondarily to the previously disadvantaged tiers within organizations. Similarly, the principal disadvantages appear to accrue to the senior levels of the civil service. Politically, then, returning to the status quo ante may be impossible.

If there is to be a return to the bureaucratic Garden of Eden, then there will have to be a strong restatement of the desirability of such a move, given that the public service is not the most probable natural constituency for such a move. Therefore, there will have to be political activity to produce the movement. This can be justified in part through the traditional values of neutrality and competence in the civil service, and through the need to stress such values as public service, rather than thinking of government as providing services like those of any "other" business. The end of Republican hegemony in the United States, and the waning of market ideology in a number of other Western countries, may initiate public discourse on ideas of public service in a way not possible recently. Indeed, the Major government in Britain is substantially less ideological than the Thatcher government before it, the Tories have lost in Canada, and the right-leaning Schluter government has been turned out of office in Denmark.

The governance role of public administration is perhaps the most significant aspect of any reassertion of the role of the public service. Again, we must contrast the role of the civil service, as contained in the "ideology" of the traditional model of governance, with the reality of the civil service's role in the model as it evolved in practice. The existence of a powerful and entrenched civil service created, in essence, the conditions for a strong policy role for that bureaucracy. Although the market model in particular would appear to give somewhat enhanced power to the civil service, any redistribution of power would be in the civil service's managerial role, rather than in its role as policy maker and adviser. In fact, the practice of the market model has been to attempt to centralize power in political leaders and limit the autonomy of the presumably entrepreneurial actors created by reforms.

Nevertheless, the traditional model of the public service and its role in government is more than merely a rationalization for civil servants to make policy. It is also a statement of basic values about such matters as accountability and responsibility, on which the alternatives, and the market model in particular, have little to say. The concept of a permanent and professional civil service that provides policy advice, as well as management, is seen by the advocates of the traditional model as almost indispensable to good government, and as embodying the means of providing citizens (and their politicians) with a way to receive both the best advice and the best service. To its critics, the permanence of the bureaucracy is a severe problem. To its advocates, it is the source of stability and reliability and is the best means of ensuring that government can be held accountable for its actions.

Up to this point, we have been discussing these models as distinct alternatives for organizing the entire public sector. Another way to consider this set of options is to think of the possible desirable matches between particular governmental tasks and alternative forms of organizing (Wilson, 1989). It may well be that for the provision of certain marketable services, the market model is adequate and desirable, while the same model would be totally inappropriate for many social services (education being one commonly discussed exception). Likewise, the participatory model would be well suited to urban planning or environmental issues but would produce difficulties for many criminal justice programs. The temporary model probably would suit such complex issues as drug-law enforcement, as well as such transient concerns as disaster relief. Attempts at full-blown contingency theories for public administration do appear to have generated relatively few benefits, but we should still think about ways of making the punishment fit the crime.

The purpose of this chapter is not so much to force choices among alternative visions of governance as to make the available choices more evident. To the extent that these alternative models have been implemented (particularly the market model), they have been put forward as much for ideological reasons as from a thorough consideration of their relative merits. Each of the alternatives does have merits but may also impose costs on society and on the actors in government. Any choice of paradigm for administration is unlikely to be optimal, but we should be clear about what we receive and what we sacrifice when we make judgments about governance.

## References

Aberbach, J. D., and Rockman, B. A. "Mandates or Mandarins? Control and Discretion in the Modern Administrative State." *Public Administration Review*, 1988, *48*, 607–612.

Adler, M., and Asquith, S. *Discretion and Power.* London: Heinemann, 1981.

Allard, C. K. *Command, Control and the Common Defense.* New Haven, Conn.: Yale University Press, 1990.

Allison, G. T. "Public and Private Management: Are They Fundamentally Alike in All Unimportant Respects?" In F. S. Lane (ed.), *Current Issues in Public Administration.* (3rd. ed.) New York: St. Martin's Press, 1986.

Barzelay, M., and Armajani, B. J. *Breaking Through Bureaucracy: A New Vision for Managing Government.* Berkeley: University of California Press, 1992.

Bendor, J. "Formal Models of Bureaucracy: A Review." In N. Lynn and A. Wildavsky (eds.), *Public Administration: The State of the Discipline.* Chatham, N.J.: Chatham House, 1990.

Boston, J. "The Theoretical Underpinnings of State Restructuring in New Zealand." In J. Boston and others (eds.), *Reshaping the State.* Oxford, England: Oxford University Press, 1991.

Boston, J. "Assessing the Performance of Departmental Chief Executives: Perspectives from New Zealand." *Public Administration*, 1992, *70*, 405–428.

Caiden, G. F. *Administrative Reform Comes of Age.* Berlin: Aldine de Gruyter, 1990.

Calista, D. J. "A Transaction-Cost Analysis of Implementation." In D. Palumbo and D. J. Calista (eds.), *Implementation Theory.* Lexington, Mass.: Lexington Books, 1989.

Chapman, R. A. "Reasons of State and the Public Interest: A British Variant of the Problem of Dirty Hands." In R. A. Chapman (ed.), *Ethics in Public Service.* Edinburgh, Scotland: University of Edinburgh Press, 1993.

Davies, A., and Willman, J. *What Next? Agencies, Departments and the Civil Service.* London: Institute for Public Policy Research, 1992.

Day, P., and Klein, R. *Accountabilities.* London: Tavistock, 1987.

Fournier, J. *Le Travail gouvernementale.* Paris: Presses Universitaires Françaises, 1987.

Gruber, J. *Controlling Bureaucracies: Dilemmas in Democratic Governance.* Berkeley: University of California Press, 1987.

Hogwood, B. W., and Peters, B. G. *Policy Dynamics.* Brighton, England: Harvester, 1983.

Hood, C. "De-Sir Humphreying the Westminster Model of Bureaucracy." *Governance,* 1990, *3,* 205–214.

Ingraham, P. W. "Building Bridges or Burning Them? The President, the Appointees and the Bureaucracy." *Public Administration Review,* 1987, *47,* 425–435.

Kaufman, H. "Emerging Doctrines of Public Administration." *American Political Science Review,* 1956, *50,* 1059–1073.

Kaufman, H. *Are Government Organizations Immortal?* Washington, D.C.: Brookings Institution, 1976.

Kernaghan, K. "Empowerment and Public Administration: Revolutionary Advance or Passing Fancy?" *Canadian Public Administration,* 1992, *35,* 194–214.

Lan, Z., and Rosenbloom, D. H. "Public Administration in Transition?" *Public Administration Review,* 1992, *52,* 535–537.

Lipsky, M. *Street-Level Bureaucracy.* New York: Russell Sage Foundation, 1980.

Lovell, R. "The Citizen's Charter: The Cultural Challenge." *Public Administration,* 1992, *70,* 395–404.

McCubbins, M. D., Noll, R. G., and Weingast, B. R. "Structure and Process, Politics and Policy: Administrative Arrangements and the Political Control of Agencies." *Virginia Law Review,* 1989, *75,* 431–482.

Macey, J. R. "Organizational Design and Political Control of Regulatory Agencies." *Journal of Law, Economics and Organization,* 1992, *8,* 93–110.

Majone, G. *Evidence, Argument and Persuasion in the Policy Process.* New Haven, Conn.: Yale University Press, 1989.

Massey, A. *Managing the Public Sector.* Aldershot, England: Edward Elgar, 1993.

Metcalfe, L., and Richards, S. *Improving Public Management.* (2nd ed.) Newbury Park, Calif.: Sage, 1990.

Moe, T. "The New Economics of Organizations." *American Journal of Political Science,* 1984, *28,* 739–777.

Moe, T. "The Politics of Bureaucratic Structure." In J. E. Chubb and P. E. Peterson (eds.), *Can the Government Govern?* Washington, D.C.: Brookings Institution, 1989.

Niskanen, W. *Bureaucracy and Representative Government.* Hawthorne, N.Y.: Aldine, 1971.

Olsen, J. P. *Organized Democracy.* Oslo, Norway: Universitetsforlaget, 1986.

Ostrom, E. "An Agenda for the Study of Institutions." *Public Choice,* 1986, *48,* 3–25.

Perrow, C. "Economic Theories of Organization." *Theory and Society,* 1986, *15,* 11–45.

Peters, B. G. "Public Policy and Public Bureaucracy." In D. Ashford (ed.), *History and Context in Comparative Public Policy.* Pittsburgh, Pa.: University of Pittsburgh Press, 1992.

Peters, B. G., and Hogwood, B. W. "Births, Deaths and Marriages: Organizational Change in the U.S. Federal Bureaucracy." *American Journal of Public Administration,* 1988, *18,* 119–133.

Pollitt, C. *Managerialism and the Public Service.* Oxford, England: Basil Blackwell, 1990.

Rose, R. "Charges as Contested Signals." *Journal of Public Policy,* 1989, *9,* 261–286.

Roth, P. A. *Meaning and Method in the Social Sciences.* Ithaca, N.Y.: Cornell University Press, 1987.

Savoie, D., and Peters, B. G. "Diagnosis and Remedy in the Reform of Government." In D. Savoie and P. Thomas (eds.), *Administrative Reform in Canada,* forthcoming.

Simon, H. A. *Administrative Behavior.* New York: Free Press, 1957.

Thomas, J. C. "Public Involvement and Government Effectiveness." *Administration and Society,* 1993, *24,* 444–469.

Tullock, G. *The Politics of Bureaucracy.* Washington, D.C.: Public Affairs Press, 1965.

Waldo, D. "Scope of the Theory of Public Administration." *Annals of the American Academy of Political and Social Sciences,* 1968, *8,* 1–26.

Williamson, O. E. *Markets and Hierarchies.* New York: Free Press, 1975.

Wilson, J. Q. *Bureaucracy: What Government Agencies Do and Why They Do It.* New York: Basic Books, 1989.

# Conclusion

# The Challenges Facing American Public Service

*Barbara S. Romzek*
*Patricia W. Ingraham*

The recent round of government-bashing and the concomitant erosion of confidence in governmental institutions has created a kind of "blow it up" quality in many reform proposals. The Clinton administration, with its renewed emphasis on government as a problem solver, has emphasized reinvention and greatly improved performance as a condition of new responsibility. Even among strong advocates of the public service, there is widespread consensus that a great deal needs to be fixed.

The report of the National Performance Review (1993) makes hundreds of specific recommendations for changes in the federal government. The National Commission on the Public Service (1989) and the National Commission on the State and Local Public Service (1993) identify numerous challenges facing all levels of the American public service.

While there is wide consensus on the need for change, there is less agreement about the nature of the changes and the ways to initiate them. The normative implications of redesigning the public service will be most appropriately addressed by elected officials, but design issues must be informed by research on the public service. The challenge the research community faces is to provide insight into the design and implementation issues confronting this ambitious and essential reconsideration of government operations. The research in this volume yields important insights into the task of reforming the public service. Any transfer of insights from the reinvention model to reform of the American public service must carefully consider issues of environmental complexity, organizational capacity, workforce vitality, and governance.

## Environmental Complexity

In the midst of this fundamental rethinking of the role of government we find the implicit recognition that some aspects of government are indispensable. There are some problems, such as national security, that only governments can handle. There are other functions, such as conducting criminal trials and elections, that only governments should handle. In this era of breathtaking changes in nation-states, some things still stay the same. The need for any government to have an administrative capacity that maintains political systems has not diminished over time. Instead, most governments experience increased need for administrative capacity to handle system maintenance. Newly formed nation-states in Eastern Europe and Asia must grapple with questions of national defense, international trade, and currency exchanges, as well as with such internal functions as mail delivery, tax collection, bank regulation, and (in democracies) the administrative machinery for conducting elections and ensuring the rights and privileges of citizenship.

At the time of this writing, the state of Israel and the Palestinian Liberation Organization have agreed on self-rule for Palestinians living in Gaza and on the West Bank. This agreement has been widely hailed as a breakthrough in extremely long-standing tensions in the Middle East. Because of the historical intractability of the problem, the agreement surprised nearly everyone, and media coverage has been widespread. In the midst of all the coverage, the impending challenges of setting up administrative systems (for traffic control, elections, and so on) have been mentioned, if at all, as an afterthought. Yet such domestic maintenance will be central to peace in the region, as well as to the quality of life and self-governance for Palestinian residents.

Governments are still needed, but there has been a broad rethinking of the role of governments and of the employees who work for them. The chapters in this book demonstrate that modern public organizations are "caught," to a considerable extent, in the interstices of our constitutional principle of the separation of powers. While the environment of government has changed, Rosenbloom and Ross (Chapter Six) remind us that the fundamental political relationships embodied in American public administration reflect efforts by legislatures and chief executives to achieve dominance over administrative agencies and operations. O'Leary (Chapter Seven) notes that the courts are having more impact on public management. Many specified administrative procedures, often decried as unnecessary, are in fact important mechanisms for accountability. The president, Congress, and the courts proceed as if each institution wielded unilateral and hierarchical authority over public organizations. A similar dynamic is played out among chief executives, legislative bodies, and courts in state and local governments. Each of the powers sees accountability as responsiveness to its particular direction.

This tension between continuity and change creates enormous challenges, of which public agencies, public employees, and government reformers must be aware. One challenge involves the dramatically expanded scope and complexity of the environment in which public organizations operate. Several authors in this book (Rainey, Chapter Five; Romzek and Dubnick, Chapter Eleven) note the complexity of this environment for the public sector, as well as the diverse and conflicting values, expectations, and goals of public agencies and employees. Such complexity requires a comprehensive approach; partial solutions or "tinkering" will not be adequate and may confound problems of responsiveness and efficiency.

Organizations such as the Environmental Protection Agency must make long-term environmental decisions for which there are no clear answers. Agencies like the U.S. Departments of Housing and Urban Development, Health and Human Services, and Labor operate in arenas where the problems are not clear and piecemeal programs have been inadequate. State and local governments, facing increasing challenges due to unfunded mandates, must find new ways to solve old problems that were previously handled with the aid of the federal government. And they must find ways to solve new problems in an era of shrinking resources. These challenges underscore the need for what Kettl (Chapter One) calls *learning organizations,* agencies whose boundaries are permeable and flexible enough to predict and provide for new levels of complexity and uncertainty.

## Organizational Capacity

Governmental operations have not adapted successfully to the changing context. Administrative structures and policies designed for a centralized command-and-control operation are incapable of success in a rapidly changing environment. Entrepreneurial organizations, which go back to basics and put their customers first, cut red tape, and empower employees, have been identified as a solution (National Performance Review, 1993). The challenge facing leaders in American public management is how to make the transition. What steps are necessary to shift successfully from the present cumbersome, risk-averse management systems to the more flexible, responsive, empowered, and committed work force that is widely recognized as necessary for the next century?

One step is to reverse the loss of organizational capacity. Staff cutbacks and the erosion of the esteem of the public service have resulted in a loss of staff expertise. O'Leary (Chapter Seven) notes that increases in unfunded mandates have resulted in an increase in the use of consultants from outside government.

Government no longer has a monopoly on information, and agencies face disincentives to learn. In these circumstances, agencies develop cultures that discourage innovation.

The issue of privatization has been popular in the United States for some time as a way to reduce the role of government and to decrease the costs of government. The challenge facing government in the face of privatization is how to maintain a level of skill and expertise adequate to effectively solve future problems that do not lend themselves to contracting by a third party. Regardless of the specific functions and services government retains, it will be imperative that government develop strategies that allow it to keep a skilled, expert, and motivated work force. In doing so, government must design processes and procedures that afford the necessary flexibility and support to facilitate government reform.

Kettl, like Milward (Chapter Two), notes that as policy decisions to privatize have resulted in the delegation of public service provision to the private sector, government has not increased its capacity for contract management. Privatization may remove service provision from the governmental arena, but it does not necessarily remove the political and governmental concern about equitable service delivery. Such situations result in very tenuous accountability patterns for private sector contractors and place government in a vulnerable situation with respect to solving problems in areas that require special expertise. Kettl suggests that an important step toward regaining this capacity in government is for organizations to put themselves in a learning mode.

Light (Chapter Three) notes that innovation in government too often occurs in spite of organization cultures that discourage innovation and offer few incentives for learning. Changing structures, reenergizing organizational cultures, removing impediments to interorganizational collaboration, rethinking assumptions about employees' motivation and performance, designing jobs and reward systems that encourage innovation and reform — these are just a few of the fundamental reinvention challenges.

It is also clear that the traditional function of the central personnel office, as organizational "police," will shift toward a function more closely identified with organizational facilitation and management. This challenges not only traditional norms of accountability but also past practices related to equity and fairness inside the organization. Of equal significance, it opens the door to reconsideration of entrance requirements and the role of politics in the process. Consideration of these tenuous balances must also be a part of reinvention.

## Work-Force Vitality

Reinvention is not a simple task and cannot be approached in simplistic ways when its focus is the vitality of the public work force. Cooper (Chapter Four), Wise (Chapter Ten), and Perry (Chapter Eight) note that public employees occupy a special place in our democratic society: they have a special character (more demographically diverse), a special mission (the public interest), and special needs and rights (as employees of government).

The prevailing political environment can have dramatic effects on the structure, image, and functioning of the American public service. The current context of the public service presents problems for developing and sustaining the links between government employees and the organizations for which they work. The commitment of public employees to public service has been eroded by environmental factors ranging from political rhetoric to program management. Many initiatives intended to improve such links have focused on fostering investment ties rather than on employees' commitment (Romzek, 1990).

The long-term vitality of the public sector requires serious consideration of the needs of public employees if we hope to tap their energies and creativity in reinventing government. Organizational cultures and the dynamics of internal labor markets have the potential to advance the values of the political system, through an emphasis on managerial discretion for work-force deployment. Public service positions need to be redesigned with incentives for entrepreneurship that do not encourage risk-averse behavior or completely sacrifice accountability.

Cooper focuses particularly on the issue of whether public employment is a right or a privilege. The answer to that question has fundamental consequences for management of the public service in a democratic system. The questions facing the public service are these: Recognizing that public employment is a privilege, how do we protect those rights that public employees do have? How do we grant greater managerial discretion in work-force deployment and avoid what Cooper calls the "due-process quagmire"?

The Senior Executive Service (SES) within the federal government was designed to tap these talented and experienced administrators, as necessary, to advance the president's policy agendas. So far, the SES has not lived up to its potential, partly because it has not forged any trusting alliances between political appointees and career SES members (see Sanders, Chapter Nine). Therefore, SES members have not been deployed as a systemwide human resource, and they (as well as political appointees) express disappointment at the unrealized potential of the SES. The promise of the SES still exists. The challenge is to find ways to overcome agency-based parochialism and tap this talent pool for governmentwide policy agendas. To do this, a concerted effort must be made by top officials to evoke a change in the culture of the public service, so that the emphasis is on the common purposes of government, not on parochial agency missions. Agency-based and individually focused goals should not be downplayed. What is needed instead is firm, sustained articulation by chief executives of how these separate goals contribute to the common purposes of government.

One aspect of the changing environment that affects the public service is the increasing diversity of our labor pool. Wise notes that the management of work-force diversity, with its emphasis on efficiency and flexibility, will require a shift away from the legalistic protection of individual rights that characterizes traditional public personnel management. Programs that promote upward mobility and access to elite positions through internal labor markets are one way to maximize the benefits of diversity.

Wise also observes that pay-for-performance plans, which

have been popular since the Civil Service Reform Act of 1978, have ignored the public service component of government employment. Both Wise and Perry note an erosion of the normative underpinnings for public service. The result is a loss in status and legitimacy for government service, a diminution in the idea that working for the public interest is valuable and honorable.

Quite clearly, the public service of the future will be less centralized, with more opportunity for autonomy in structure and processes. That change cannot occur without consideration and reconciliation of the issues that will be raised for accountability. A newly energized public service will find ways to cultivate and reward entrepreneurial activity. This shift must occur in the context of a shared vision for the organization and its programs, both among branches of government and between elected officials and career civil servants. The future public service must recognize that public employment is a privilege, but that some basic employee rights must continue to be protected.

## Governance

Successful governance requires a public service staffed by people who approach their duties with an emphasis on common purposes and collaboration, rather than on parochial mandates. Milward (Chapter Two) reminds us that government organizations exist to make the kinds of trade-offs that the prudent manager of a business enterprise would not make.

For many reasons — related to conflicting demands, limited resources, contracting, and "hollowed-out" government, the tidy public organizations perceived by courts, legislatures, and chief executives are no longer the norm. The reinvention challenge for democratic governance is to design flexible, responsive, entrepreneurial organizations staffed by energetic, committed, and creative employees while ensuring that these energies are directed toward appropriate democratic goals and values. This will require a change in the culture of the government agencies for which these individuals work. Collaboration must be encouraged and rewarded, not merely tolerated or discouraged.

Romzek and Dubnick (Chapter Eleven) explore the challenge of reconciling flexibility with accountability in public personnel management. They note that the American system of government relies on multiple accountability mechanisms to hold public employees responsible for their performance. The most common ones involve highly detailed scrutiny of personnel practices and decisions by actors internal to the organization (supervisors) and external to it (courts and legislatures). The two-way nature of these accountability relationships is often overlooked. This circumstance affords public employees the opportunity to influence which accountability mechanism will be used to measure their performance.

The unresolved tension in public accountability mechanisms for the American public service is between procedural flexibility and equal treatment. Current management literature emphasizes the need for flexibility and managerial discretion to respond quickly and effectively to rapidly changing organizational tasks and environments. If we do away with rigid and inflexible public personnel systems in the interest of entrepreneurial public management, how can we ensure that accountability will not be lost in the change? We are reminded of the many World War II–era books and movies that featured a character who was a master of "midnight requisitions." If we believe the popular media, such entrepreneurial behavior was greatly appreciated by the character's unit and tolerated by officials at headquarters. It remains to be seen whether the American public will accept similarly unorthodox practices from public administrators during peacetime.

How can we tap the potential of the public service to help solve societal problems without opening the system up to political favoritism or other unequal treatment? A successful rethinking of the public service will require expectations to be attuned to the accountability mechanisms appropriate for assigned tasks. Flexibility will be needed in accountability mechanisms, too. Multiple accountability mechanisms will have to accompany diverse and multiple expectations and tasks.

Peters (Chapter Twelve) articulates alternative visions of the state and the assumptions embedded in those visions. He notes that the traditional model makes some basic statements about accountability and responsibilities, with a permanent and professional civil service providing policy advice as well as management. His suggestion for the mixed use of models, as suited to organizational tasks, meshes with Romzek and Dubnick's prescription to attune primary accountability mechanisms to the task at hand.

With these calls for change comes a new recognition: only government can make the decisions and mold the policies that are increasingly central to maintaining an acceptable quality of life for all citizens, international competitiveness for the nation and its products, and a future that for many will be better than today.

Finally, it is important to note, as Peters does, that there are many models of change and many paths to reform. Not all governments can or should change in the same way. Just as one size does not fit all, prescriptions for reform and the change process itself must be tailored to the realities of the organization and to its capabilities. This, too, causes change to be more complex and more difficult. Future reforms must proceed from a base that is both better informed about and more understanding of the particular demands of change in the public sector and the public service.

## Challenges and Choices

The challenge of democratic governance in the future is formidable. The American governance system faces new problems, which require new solutions at a time when governmental capacity to fund any such reforms is constrained. We simply do not have the luxury of throwing money at these problems. Solutions must emphasize "thinking smarter" and working better with the resources at hand.

The fundamental issues of what government does and how it does it must be combined with the democratic issues of politics, responsiveness, and accountability if reinventing and reform are to succeed. This makes the job much, much harder. Rosenbloom and Ross (Chapter Six) remind us that public

administrative arrangements are inextricably bound up with issues of political power, the character of the polity, and our concept of citizenship. Failure to consider democratic issues in the
reform process will only reinvent problems, not solve them.

Government can still fulfill the roles of problem solver and
guardian of the public interest. To do so effectively, our governance system will need leadership to reenergize the public service and focus attention on an integrative management approach
that contributes to common purposes and surmounts narrow
special interests. Such leadership must come from top elected
officials. As Frederickson (1993) notes, proposed reforms in
governmental operations will not find long-term success unless
there are corresponding reforms in the behavior and politics of
elected officials. Frederickson calls for special care in resisting
the tendency to define difficult policy or political issues as management issues, assign unfunded mandates to lower levels of
government, and obscure the true costs of government programs
by passing the obligation on to future generations. Of course,
elected officials cannot accomplish these reforms alone. Success
will depend on support for such a transformation from leaders
in the public service.

The original design of the American public service was
intended to solve the problem of employees who lacked skills
and had acquired their jobs through political patronage. Today the public service faces different problems: inflexibility, eroding capacity and legitimacy, and overemphasis on process rather
than on outcomes. Design reforms that will realize the full potential for effective public service are critically important.

The report of the National Performance Review (1993)
raises time-honored questions in American governance: Is the
public service part of the problem or part of the solution? How
do we ensure that government reforms in the direction of decentralization, autonomy, and variation do not further erode
the weak sense of common purpose that characterizes the public service in the 1990s?

Whatever the common purposes that government ultimately pursues, a skilled, expert, and motivated public service
work force will be essential for success. Success for government

in the 1990s and beyond will necessitate accommodating greater managerial discretion, increased administrative responsiveness, and continued protections against political abuse. In addition, flexibility in managing the public service must be accompanied by reforms that cultivate and reward entrepreneurial activities.

More broadly, the American polity needs to identify the tasks of government that are indispensable to sustaining our commitment to democratic governance. In making systemic reforms, we must recognize that our public service must accommodate all the values (some of which are incompatible) that our system of governance expects to sustain. How do we cut red tape and increase managerial discretion without eroding accountability? How do we empower employees to get results and at the same time ensure that they direct their energies toward desired goals and missions? How do we go back to basics without undermining the capacity for governance? What kinds of expertise, and how much, must government keep inside, and how much can it afford to contract out? When services are contracted out, what kind of contract-management capacity must be developed or maintained?

A citizen is not the same as a customer. Governmental change and reform must be cognizant of democratic demands, as well as of the more mundane challenges of organizational change. How do we reconcile the "customer first" approach of reinvention with the citizen sovereignty that forms the basis of our republic? As always, the responsibility for successful governmental reform rests ultimately with our elected officials, but a revitalized public service can be an important partner.

## References

Frederickson, H. G. "The Seven Principles of Total Quality Politics." *Government Executive,* 1993, *25*(12), 42–43.

National Commission on the Public Service (Volcker Commission). *Leadership for America: Rebuilding the Public Service.* Washington, D.C.: National Commission on the Public Service, 1989.

National Commission on the State and Local Public Service.

*Hard Truths/Tough Choices: An Agenda for State and Local Reform.* Albany, N.Y.: Nelson A. Rockefeller Institute of Government, 1993.

National Performance Review. *From Red Tape to Results: Creating a Government That Works Better and Costs Less.* Washington, D.C.: U.S. Government Printing Office, 1993.

Romzek, B. S. "Employee Investment and Commitment: The Ties That Bind." *Public Administration Review,* 1990, *50,* 374–382.

# Name Index

## A

Aberbach, J. D., 296, 319
Acs, Z. J., 68, 87
Adams, J. Q., 147, 265
Adler, M., 310, 319
Allard, C. K., 305, 319
Allerton, W. S., 168, 182, 187
Allison, G. T., 296, 319
Allred, S., 94, 113
Angle, H. L., 203, 209
Appleby, P. H., 26, 37, 151, 163
Armajani, B. J., 23, 38, 161, 163, 268, 289, 297, 319
Arnold, M. S., 245, 252, 256
Arnold, R., 155, 156, 163
Aronson, S., 146, 163
Asquith, S., 310, 319
Audretch, D., 68, 87

## B

Bacher, R. N., 205, 214
Backoff, R. W., 131, 139
Balfour, D., 198, 209
Ballard, J., 66, 87
Ban, C., 171, 187, 277, 280, 289
Bardach, E., 157, 163
Barnard, C. I., 33, 34, 37, 205, 209, 272, 289
Baron, J. N., 192, 195, 205, 213
Barton, E., 122, 138
Barzelay, M., 23, 38, 161, 163, 268, 289, 297, 319
Bass, B. M., 133, 137
Baum, L., 171, 187
Bazelon, D. L., 168, 188
Bendor, J., 300, 319
Bennett, C., 69, 87
Bennis, W., 133, 137

Beyer, J. M., 133, 139
Beyna, L. S., 124, 138
Blais, A., 24, 38
Blinder, A., 66, 68, 87
Boston, J., 296, 302, 304, 319
Bowsher, C. A., 43, 281, 289
Boyle, R., 244, 251, 256
Bozeman, B., 195, 209
Brandl, J., 63n
Brennan, W. J., Jr., 95, 102
Broder, D., 44
Brownlow, L., 154, 163
Brudney, J. L., 197, 206, 208, 209
Brumback, G. B., 191n, 203, 209
Bryson, J. M., 131, 137
Buchanan, B., II, 203, 209
Buitendam, A., 240, 256
Burns, J. M., 207, 210
Burton, L., 108, 113
Bush, G.H.W., 158

C

Caiden, G. F., 269, 289, 299, 319
Calista, D. J., 301, 319
Cameron, K., 127n, 137
Campbell, A., 217, 237
Campbell, J. P., 128n, 137
Canon, B. C., 174, 188–189
Cappelli, P., 253, 256
Carnevale, A. B., 194, 210
Carroll, J., 158, 162, 166
Carroll, P. B., 120, 137
Carter, S., 69, 87
Cascio, W. F., 253, 256
Cayer, N. J., 283, 289
Chapman, R. A., 297, 319
Chayes, A., 170, 172, 188
Chisholm, D., 42, 60
Cleveland, H., 30, 35, 38
Clinton, W. J., 199, 206, 288
Consolini, P. M., 26, 39
Cooper, P. J., 17, 90, 95, 114, 142,
    173, 188, 327, 328
Cotton, J. L., 68, 87
Cowherd, D. M., 254, 257
Czarniawska, B., 192, 200, 210

D

Daft, R. L., 128, 129, 137
Dahl, R., 151, 157, 163

Damanpour, F., 66–67, 87
Danhof, C. H., 25, 27, 38
Darman, R., 45
Davies, A., 302, 319
Davis-Blake, A., 195, 210
Day, P., 296, 319
Deci, E. L., 181, 188
Devanna, M. A., 204, 210
Dion, S., 24, 38
DiPrete, T. A., 247, 257
Doeringer, P., 247, 257
Doig, J. W., 134, 135, 137, 149, 163
Donahue, J. D., 25, 38
Donnelly, J., 154, 163
Downs, A., 22, 38
Downs, G. W., 124, 125, 137
Doying, R., 69, 87
Drucker, P. S., 195, 210
Dubnick, M. J., 8, 14, 260, 263,
    268, 269, 272, 273, 279, 281,
    289–290, 293, 324, 330, 331
Dudrow, J., 69, 87
Durant, R. F., 280, 290

E

Eaton, D., 150, 163
Eisenhower, D. D., 158
Ekland-Olson, S., 185, 188
Else, B., 57, 61
Emery, F. E., 22, 38, 274, 290
Etzioni, A., 162, 163
Evanisko, M., 67, 88
Ezrahi, Y., 28–29, 38

F

Fay, C., 268, 290
Figueiredo, C., 69, 87
Finer, H., 263, 269, 290
Fiol, C. M., 21, 38
Fiorina, M., 155, 158, 160, 163–164
Fisher, L., 109, 114, 168, 184, 188
Fisher, R., 162, 164
Fiss, O. M., 172, 188
Fombrun, C., 204, 210
Ford, G. R., 156, 158
Fournier, J., 298, 320
Franklin, G., 155, 156, 165
Federickson, H. G., 42–43, 60, 158,
    164, 332, 333

Freeman, J., 68, 88
Fried, R. C., 138, 266, 290
Friedrich, C. J., 263, 269, 290
Frug, G. E., 170, 172, 188

**G**

Gaebler, T., 2, 13, 35, 39, 146,
  147, 156, 157, 159, 165, 194,
  212, 216, 237, 264, 268, 292
Galbraith, J. R., 65, 88
Gardner, J. W., 207, 210
Garvey, G., 195, 210
Garvin, D., 67, 88
Glazer, M. P., 203, 210
Glazer, N., 179, 188
Glazer, P. M., 203, 210
Glenn, R. M., 268, 290
Glick, H. R., 175, 188
Glidewell, J. C., 272, 290
Golden, O., 66, 82, 88
Golembiewski, R. T., 204, 210
Goodings, R., 68, 88
Goodnow, F. J., 149, 156, 164, 269,
  290
Goodsell, C., 119, 138, 146, 160,
  164
Gore, A., 2, 159
Gray, A., 269, 290
Gruber, J., 263, 269, 290, 296, 320
Guetzkow, H., 22, 38
Gulick, L., 151, 164, 220, 237
Gutek, B. A., 122, 138

**H**

Hale, G. E., 168, 182, 184, 188
Hale, M. M., 241, 257
Hall, D. T., 194, 214
Hamilton, A., 147–148
Hannan, M., 68, 88
Hanrahan, J. D., 46–47, 60
Hargrove, E. C., 134, 135, 137,
  272, 290
Harris, M., 193, 210
Hartzell, B., 69, 87
Hastings, A. H., 124, 138
Haveman, H., 68, 88
Hayami, K., 68, 89
Heclo, H., 226, 237, 266, 290
Hedberg, B., 21, 38

Helling, L., 191$n$
Hempel, P., 268, 290
Herring, E., 157, 164
Higgins, C., 68, 88
Hirschman, A. O., 207, 210
Hofstadter, R., 151, 164
Hogwood, B. W., 297, 313, 320,
  321
Hole, D., 69, 87
Holmes, O. W., 90–91, 92
Hood, C. C., 270, 271, 291, 296,
  320
Horowitz, D. L., 168, 172, 176,
  177, 182, 188
Howell, J., 68, 88
Hyde, A., 169, 171, 180–181, 190,
  274, 276, 286, 293

**I**

Ilsley, P. J., 206, 210
Ingraham, P. W., 1, 4, 5, 13, 68,
  88, 18, 123, 138, 146, 164, 200,
  210, 227, 237, 239$n$, 264, 265,
  266, 268, 276, 277, 280, 281,
  289, 291, 296, 320, 322
Ingram, H., 44, 60
Iscoe, I., 183–184, 189

**J**

Jabes, J., 199, 210
Jackson, A., 147, 149, 164, 265
Jamieson, D., 194, 211
Jefferson, T., 146
Jenkins, W. I., 269, 290
Johnson, C. A., 171, 174, 178,
  188–189
Johnson, G., 206, 211
Johnson, L. B., 155
Johnston, W. B., 193, 211

**K**

Kahn, J. D., 97, 98, 114
Kahn, R. L., 32, 38, 122, 138
Kalkstein, H., 66, 89
Kanter, D. L., 193, 211
Kanter, R. M., 68, 88
Kaplan, E., 97, 114
Katz, D., 32, 38, 122, 138

Katzell, R. A., 193, 211
Kaufman, H., 264, 266, 291, 296,
   312, 320
Kellman, S., 69, 88
Kellough, J. E., 279, 291
Kelly, R. M., 241, 257
Kemeny, J. G., 19–20, 38
Kemp, J., 307
Kennedy, P., 118, 138
Kernaghan, K., 307, 320
Kerr, C., 193, 211
Kettl, D. F., 9, 12, 13, 16, 19, 25,
   38, 43, 46, 59, 60, 121, 138,
   194, 211, 242, 325, 326
Kilmann, R. H., 272, 291
Kimberly, J., 67, 88
King, J. B., 252
King, R., 273
Kleeman, R. S., 267, 268, 291
Klein, H. J., 136, 138
Klein, J. I., 136, 138
Klein, R., 296, 319
Klingner, D., 266, 274, 277, 280,
   291, 292
Knight, J. P., 227, 237
Knoke, D., 203, 208, 211
Koenig, H., 168n, 170, 189
Kraemer, K. L., 4, 14, 195, 213
Kravchuk, R., 158, 164
Krislov, S., 263, 269, 291
Krueger, R., 69, 88

L

Lambright, W. H., 135, 138
Lan, Z., 146, 159, 164, 296, 320
Landau, M., 42, 60
Lane, L. M., 197, 211
LaPorte, T. R., 26, 39
Larkey, P. D., 124, 125, 137
Lawler, E. E., III, 66, 89, 204, 211
Lawless, M. W., 42, 60
Lazarus, H., 66, 89
Lee, R. D., Jr., 117, 138
Leemans, A. M., 199, 211
Lengnick-Hall, C. A., 204, 211
Lengnick-Hall, M. A., 204, 211
Levine, C. H., 194, 211, 264, 267,
   268, 276, 291
Levine, D., 66, 89

Levine, D. I., 254, 257
Lewis, E. B., 135, 138
Light, P. C., 16–17, 63, 69, 84, 89,
   276, 287, 291, 326
Lindblom, C., 145, 164
Lipset, S. M., 122, 138, 193, 212
Lipsky, M., 56, 61, 157, 164, 206,
   214, 310, 320
Loden, M., 194, 212
Lovell, R., 306, 320
Lowi, T., 155, 156, 164
Lyles, M. A., 21, 38

M

McConnell, G., 156, 164
McCubbins, M. D., 312, 320
Macey, J. R., 311, 320
McGregor, E. B., Jr., 195, 204,
   212, 264, 291
Macy, J. W., Jr., 265, 291
Madison, J., 44
Madonna, 120–121
Mainzer, L. C., 281, 292
Majone, G., 315, 320
Major, J., 317
March, J. G., 21, 22, 33, 39, 202,
   212, 277, 292
Marshall, T., 95, 101–102
Martin, S. J., 185, 188
Mascarenhas, R., 162, 164
Mashaw, J., 170, 189
Massey, A., 300, 320
Mayer, R., 155, 165
Meier, K., 266, 292
Melnick, R. S., 168, 170, 181, 189
Metcalfe, L., 304, 320
Miles, R. E., 42, 60
Miles, R. H., 170–171, 189
Milkovich, T. G., 4, 13, 200, 204,
   212
Miller, G. E., 183–184, 189
Milward, H. B., 16, 41, 43, 57, 58,
   61, 119, 138, 326, 329
Mintzberg, H., 220, 237, 277, 292
Mirvis, P. H., 193, 211
Moe, T., 300, 320–321
Molnar, J. J., 126, 128, 139
Monroe, J., 147
Monti, D. J., 170, 189

Moore, R. A., 42, 60
Mosher, F. C., 44, 61, 149–150,
    152, 165, 263, 269, 292
Mowday, R. T., 191, 212
Mulroney, B., 1, 305

**N**

Nadler, D., 68, 89
Nalbandian, J., 169, 189, 266, 274,
    277, 280, 291, 292
Nanus, B., 133, 137
Nau, H. R., 118, 139
Newburg, A., 234, 237
Newland, C. A., 280, 292
Nickel, J., 66, 89
Nigro, L. G., 273, 277, 292
Niskanen, W. A., 24, 39, 300, 321
Nixon, R. M., 158
Noll, R. G., 312, 320
Nutt, P. C., 131, 139

**O**

O'Leary, R., 142, 168, 169, 170,
    173, 174, 175, 176, 177, 178,
    179, 180, 181, 183, 184, 185,
    189, 190, 324, 325
Oleszek, W., 158, 165
Olsen, J. P., 21, 39, 202, 212, 309,
    321
O'Mara, J., 194, 211
Osborne, D., 2, 13, 35, 39, 146,
    147, 156, 157, 159, 165, 194,
    212, 216, 237, 264, 268, 292
Ospina, S., 191n
Osterman, P., 250, 252, 257
Ostrom, E., 300, 321
Ostrom, V., 151, 165
Outshoorn, J., 241, 257

**P**

Paine, T., 59, 165
Parker, A. H., 193, 211
Perot, R., 160
Perrow, C., 26, 39, 301, 321
Perry, J. L., 4, 14, 19n, 68, 89,
    142, 191, 195, 200, 201, 202,
    203, 204, 209, 213, 229, 230,

237, 239n, 243, 254, 257, 327,
    329
Peters, B. G., 197, 198, 199, 200,
    213, 260–261, 276, 291, 295,
    296, 297, 299, 313, 320, 321,
    330–331
Peters, T. J., 41, 61, 66, 89, 134,
    139, 236, 237
Pfeffer, J., 68, 89, 179–180, 190,
    192, 195, 205, 213
Pinder, C., 136, 139
Piore, M., 247, 257
Pollitt, C., 300, 321
Porter, J. W., 22, 39
Porter, L. W., 191, 202, 212, 213
Powell, L. F., Jr., 95, 99
Pressman, J., 145, 156, 165
Price, D. K., 25, 29, 39
Provan, K. G., 43, 57, 58, 61
Publius, 148, 165

**Q**

Quarrey, M., 66, 89
Quinn, R. E., 130, 139

**R**

Rahm, D., 195, 209
Rainey, H. G., 4, 9–10, 14, 17, 59,
    115, 119, 138, 171, 185, 190,
    220, 237, 281, 292, 324
Reagan, R., 1, 95, 158
Rehnquist, W. H., 99–100, 101,
    102, 103
Riccucci, N. M., 171, 187, 274,
    276, 286, 293
Richards, S., 304, 320
Richardson, J., 147, 165
Ripley, R., 155, 156, 165
Risher, H., 268, 290
Roberts, K. H., 22, 39
Roberts, N. C., 66, 89
Rockman, B. A., 296, 319
Rogers, D. L., 126, 128, 139
Rohr, J. A., 109, 114, 149, 151,
    152, 153, 165
Rohrbaugh, J., 130, 139
Romzek, B. S., 1, 8, 14, 200, 201,
    204, 214, 239n, 260, 263, 267,

269, 272, 273, 279, 290,
    292-293, 322, 324, 327, 330,
    331, 334
Roosevelt, F. D., 153
Roosevelt, T., 148
Rose, R., 241, 257, 301, 321
Rosen, C., 66, 89
Rosenbloom, D. H., 118, 138, 142,
    145, 146, 147, 151, 153, 156,
    158, 159, 161, 162, 164,
    165-166, 169, 170, 171, 180-181,
    186, 190, 227, 237, 263, 264,
    265, 266, 268, 269, 274, 276,
    277, 279, 281, 286, 291, 293,
    296, 320, 324, 331-332
Rosener, J. B., 194, 212
Ross, B. H., 142, 145, 324,
    331-332
Roth, P. A., 298, 321
Rothman, D. J., 168, 190
Rothman, S. M., 168, 190
Rourke, F. E., 25, 39, 263,
    287-288, 293
Ruttan, V., 68, 89

**S**

Salamon, L. M., 25, 39, 44, 61
Salancik, G. R., 68, 89, 179-180,
    190
Sampson, C. L., 117, 118, 139
Sanders, R. P., 142-143, 215, 328
Savas, E. S., 42, 61
Savoie, D., 299, 321
Scalia, A., 91, 95, 96, 97-98, 102,
    103, 105
Schein, E. H., 69, 89, 133, 139,
    229, 237
Schluter, P., 317
Schneider, W., 122, 138, 193, 212
Schuh, G. E., 63n
Schuler, R. S., 229, 238
Schurz, C., 150, 166
Seashore, S. E., 126, 140
Seidman, H., 145, 156, 166
Sekaran, U., 194, 214
Senge, P. M., 34, 39, 68, 89
Shafritz, J. M., 145, 166, 169, 171,
    180-181, 190, 274, 276, 286, 293
Sherwood-Fabre, L., 132, 139

Siahpush, M. S., 240, 257
Simon, H. A., 22, 33, 39, 151, 166,
    272, 277, 292, 293, 299, 321
Skowronek, S., 146, 166, 264, 265,
    293
Smith, D. G., 94, 114
Smith, L. J., 43, 58, 61
Smith, S., 241, 257
Smith, S. R., 43, 56, 61, 206,
    214
Smith, W., 66, 89
Snow, C. C., 42, 60
Steers, R. M., 191, 212
Stevens, J. P., 91, 110
Stillman, R. J., II, 146, 166, 266,
    293
Storing, H., 149, 166
Straussman, J., 168, 170, 182, 189,
    190
Summer, C. E., 272, 293
Swenson, D., 69, 87
Swiss, J. E., 287, 293
Sylvia, R. D., 171, 190

**T**

Thatcher, M., 1, 305, 316, 317
Thomas, J. C., 297, 321
Thomas, L., 178
Thompson, F. J., 276, 291
Thompson, J. D., 22, 32, 39, 180,
    190, 274, 294
Thompson, V., 158, 161, 166
Tichy, N. M., 116, 132, 139, 204,
    210
Trent, D., 66, 87
Trice, H. M., 133, 139
Trist, E. L., 22, 38, 274, 290
Truman, H. S., 158
Tuchman, B. W., 31, 39
Tullock, G., 300, 321
Tushman, M. L., 22, 40, 68, 89
Tusi, A. S., 129, 139
Tyson, L. D., 66, 89

**U**

Urwick, L., 151, 164
Ury, W., 162, 164
Uzzi, B., 195, 210

### V

Van de Ven, A., 68, 89
Van Riper, P., 149, 150, 166
Venti, S. F., 241, 258

### W

Wagner, J., III, 68, 88
Wald, M., 97, 98, 114
Waldo, D., 145, 151, 156, 166–167, 265, 294, 295, 321
Walters, J., 288, 294
Walton, R. E., 203, 214
Wamsley, G. L., 119, 140, 159, 167
Warren, K., 156, 167
Wasby, S. L., 170, 190
Washington, G., 265
Waterman, R. H., Jr., 134, 139
Weber, M., 23, 24, 25, 29, 32, 36, 40, 296
Wechsler, B., 198, 209
Weingast, B. R., 312, 320
Wheat, E. M., 270, 294
White, B. R., 94
White, L. D., 146, 149, 150, 167, 264, 294
Wholey, J. S., 123, 140
Wigdor, A. K., 4, 13, 200, 204, 212
Wildavsky, A., 145, 156, 165, 167

Williams, L. G., 97, 114
Williamson, O. E., 301, 321
Willman, J., 302, 319
Wilson, J. Q., 134, 140, 276, 277, 294, 318, 321
Wilson, W., 3, 14, 23–24, 25, 40, 147–148, 149, 150–151, 167, 191, 214
Wise, C., 168, 169, 170, 173, 174, 175, 176, 177, 185, 189, 190
Wise, C. R., 42, 62
Wise, L. R., 143, 191$n$, 194, 201, 203, 213, 214, 239, 243, 244, 245, 246, 255, 257, 258, 327, 328–329
Wolch, J. R., 43, 62
Wolf, J. F., 197, 198, 205, 211, 214
Wood, R. C., 168, 170, 174, 175, 190
Wray, L., 80–82, 84
Wright-Izak, C., 203, 208, 211

### Y

Yarbrough, T. E., 168, 175, 190
Yates, D., 263, 269, 294
Yuchtman, E., 126, 140

### Z

Zussman, D., 199, 210

# Subject Index

## A

Accountability: and administrative theory, 162; aspects of, 6–7, 263–294; background on, 263–264; challenges for, 265–268, 330; choice for mechanisms for, 272–273; and contracting, 9–10, 107; and core tasks, 273, 277–278; dynamics of, 288; and ecological context, 267–268, 272, 278–279, 288; and flexibility, 280–287; future for, 287–289; and managerial strategy, 272–273, 274–277; mechanisms of, 269–287; patterns for, 274–280; and values, 266–267
*Adler* v. *Board of Education,* 92, 112
Administration, public: aspects of, 145–167; background on, 145–146; and divided government, 158–159; education for, 161–162; expertise of, and courts, 181–182; institutional foundations for, 152–158; issues critical to, 161–163; and micromanagement, 154–155; neopopulist, 159–160; and politics-administration dichotomy, 147–152, 161; prehistory of, 146–147; reforms in, 148–149
Administrative Procedure Act (APA) of 1946, 150, 153, 155, 156
Advisory Commission on Intergovernmental Relations, 56
Affirmative action, and accountability, 279–280
*AFSCME Local 2477* v. *Billington,* 101, 112

Agencies, and Congress, 153-154,
   155-156, 160
Alabama, courts and personnel man-
   agement in, 169, 170-171
American with Disabilities Act
   (ADA) of 1990, 284-286
Apple, subcontracting by, 41-42
*Arnett* v. *Kennedy,* 99, 100, 112
Association for Retarded Citizens,
   75, 84
Audits, for contracting, 27-28, 45,
   55-56
Authority: administrative, and
   courts, 179-181; lack of, 7-8;
   paradox of public, 20-23, 33

                    B

*Barkoo* v. *Melby,* 95, 112
Birmingham, Alabama, personnel
   management in, 169
*Bishop* v. *Wood,* 100, 112
Blue Cross-Blue Shield, 306
*Board of Regents* v. *Roth,* 99, 112
Boeing, subcontracting by, 41-42
Boston, school desegregation case in,
   174, 175
*Branti* v. *Finkel,* 96, 112
*Broadrick* v. *Oklahoma,* 96, 112
*Brown* v. *Houston Independent School
   District,* 101, 112
Brownlow Committee, 152, 167
Budgetary power, and courts,
   184-185
Bureaucratic accountability,
   270-271, 273, 277, 279-280, 282
Bureaucracy: barriers to learning
   by, 23-31; and hollow state, 58;
   learning by, 31-35; and organi-
   zational functions, 8-9; and orga-
   nizational learning, 23-26
Bush administration, 42, 44, 45,
   196, 286

                    C

*Camara* v. *Municipal Court,* 97, 112
Canada: governance of, 1, 297, 298,
   305, 306, 317; PS 2000 in, 306;
   senior executives in, 228

Carter administration, 45, 121, 195,
   196
Central Intelligence Agency (CIA), 96
*Challenger,* 31, 273
Change. *See* Innovation; Reform
Chernobyl disaster, 31
Civil service. *See* Public organiza-
   tions
Civil Service Reform Act (CSRA) of
   1978; and accountability, 277,
   280, 286; and reward system,
   3-4, 200, 303, 329; and senior
   executives, 216, 217, 244
Clean Air Act, 180, 181
*Cleveland Board of Education* v. *Louder-
   mill,* 99, 100-101, 112
Clinton administration: and account-
   ability, 288; and employee ties,
   196; and issues of reform, 2, 4,
   11, 322; and organizational
   learning, 20
*Clinton Police Department Bargaining
   Unit* v. *City of Clinton,* 101, 112
*Cobb* v. *Village of Oakwood,* 101, 112
Commitment strategy: and employee
   ties, 201-207; for senior executives, 231
Commonwealth of Independent
   States, communicating with, 11, 325
Communication, for organizational
   learning, 22, 33
*Connick* v. *Myers,* 94, 112
Constitution: Fifth Amendment to,
   179; First Amendment to, 92,
   94, 98, 101, 111, 169; Fourth
   Amendment to, 97-98; Preamble
   to, 162; Sixteenth Amendment
   to, 149
Context: and accountability,
   267-268, 272, 278-279, 288;
   complex, for public organizations, 323-325; of employee ties,
   193-195; and innovation, 68, 70,
   72, 73, 75-77; for management,
   4-8; strategic, for senior executives, 229-230
Contracting out: and accountability,
   9-10, 107; aspects of, 41-62; auditing and evaluating, 27-28, 45,
   55-56; challenges of, 11-12;

dimensions of, 46–49; and employee rights, 106–108; and employee ties, 194, 195, 197, 199; and governance, 302; and lobbying, 58–59; and organizational learning, 25, 27–28; personnel in, 49–54; and policy directions, 27; problems of, 54–55; research needed on, 55–56

Control: degree of, 270; and flexibility, 283–284; and policy making, 305; sources of, 269–270

Core tasks, and accountability, 273, 277–278

*Cornelius* v. *NAACP Legal Defense and Education Fund,* 112

Courts: and administrative authority, 179–181; and administrative expertise, 181–182; aspects of employee rights to, 90–114; background on, 90–92, 168–170; and budgetary power, 184–185; and deference paradox, 111; and external control of organizations, 170–172; findings of, 172–186; and fund redistribution, 182–184; future agenda for, 186–187; and implementation, 174–176; issues for, 92–102; and judicial supervision of organizations, 172–174; in partnership with personnel management, 168–190; and personnel administration, 104–111; and policy issues, 177–179; restrictions by, 102–104; and staff morale, 185–186; and unintended consequences, 176–177

*Crain* v. *Board of Police Commissioners,* 95, 112

Culture: and employee ties, 204–205; and personnel administration, 133–135; for senior executives, 228–229, 232

Cynicism, growth of, 193

**D**

*D'Acquisto* v. *Washington,* 101, 112

Dakota County, Minnesota: analysis of innovation in, 67, 69, 72–85; Community Services in, 75, 77–81, 86–87; context in, 72, 73, 75–77; Developmental Disabilities Account Management Program in, 69, 75, 81, 82, 83, 84; leadership in, 74, 80–83; linkage systems in, 74–75, 83–85; overview of, 85–87; Project Fast Forward (FF) in, 69, 75–76, 77, 79, 82, 85–86; structure in, 73, 77–79

Decision of 1789, 146

Defense Contract Audit Agency, 45

Demographics: and accountability, 267; and employee ties, 193–194, 197, 198–199

Denmark, governance of, 317

Diversity: in administrative theory, 146–147; in work force, 240–241, 251

*Dodds* v. *Childers,* 95, 112

Drug Enforcement Agency, 312–313

Drug testing, and employee rights, 97–98

*Duchesne* v. *Williams,* 101, 112

Due process, and employee rights, 98–101, 111

**E**

Educational institutions, and effectiveness, 127, 129

*EEOC* v. *Wyoming,* 110, 112

Effectiveness, organizational, 125–126, 128

Efficiency, valued, 266

*Elrod* v. *Burns,* 96, 112

Employee-organization linkages: aspects of, 191–214; background on, 191–192; changes in, 192; and commitment strategy, 201–207; concept of, 191–192; context of, 193–195; effects on, 195–199; issues for future, 207–209; and reinvigorated public service, 199–207

Employees: court impact on rights of, 90–114; courts and morale of, 185–186; development of, and internal labor market, 250; part-time, 197; temporary and inter-

nal labor market, 244–246,
252–253
Employment Act of 1946, 150,
154
Employment relationships, changes
in, 195–197, 208
Empowerment: for managers, 286;
in participatory governance, 307;
and personnel administration,
133–135; for senior executives,
234–236
Environment. *See* Context
Equal employment opportunity
(EEO), and internal labor market, 241, 255
Equal Employment Opportunity
Commission, 267, 277, 280
Exchange theory, for motivation,
135–136
Expertise: administrative, 181–182;
external, for learning organizations, 26–28; professional, 267,
286–288
Exxon *Valdez*, 52

**F**

Fair Labor Standards Act, 109–110,
169
Farmers Home Administration, 43
Federal Advisory Committee Act of
1972, 156
Federal Bureau of Investigation
(FBI), 313
Federal Employees Pay Comparabil-
ity Act of 1990, 48
Federal Labor Relations Authority,
267
Federalists, and administrative the-
ory, 146, 147–148
Flexibility: future for, 287–289; need
for, 280–282; in personnel,
283–287
Flexiplace, and employee ties, 197,
198–199
France: governance of, 298; senior
executives in, 228
*Frank* v. *Maryland,* 97, 112
Freedom of Information Act, 46,
155–156

**G**

Gainsharing, and employee ties,
202–203
*Garcia* v. *San Antonio Metropolitan
Transit Authority,* 109–110, 112,
169, 187
*Garner* v. *Board of Public Works,* 92,
112
*Garraghty* v. *Jordon,* 101, 112
*Givhan* v. *Western Line Consolidated
School District,* 94, 112
Glass ceiling, for senior executives,
226, 233
Globalization, and employee ties, 194
Goal model, of organizations,
126–128
*Goldberg* v. *Kelly,* 99, 112
*Goldman* v. *Weinberger,* 102, 112
Governance: and accountability,
263–294; alternative visions of,
299–316; aspects of, 259–321;
challenges for, 329–331; changes
in, 295–299; management for,
303–304, 309, 314–315; market
model of, 296–297, 300–306,
318; overview of, 259–261; participatory model of, 297,
306–311, 318; policy making for,
304–306, 309–311, 315–316; and
public service, 295–321; research
needed on, 56–59; return to
traditional forms of, 316–318;
structures for, 301–303, 308–309,
313–314; summaries on, 306,
311; temporary organization
model of, 297–298, 312–316, 318
Government by proxy: and contracting, 44; and employee ties, 194;
and organizational learning, 25,
36; and privatization, 9–10
Grace Commission, 4, 264, 292
*Grusendorf* v. *City of Oklahoma City,*
102, 112

**H**

*Harmon* v. *Thornburgh,* 98, 112
Harris County, Texas, employee
rights in, 95

*Hartness* v. *Bush*, 98, 113

Hatch Act, 96

*Hodel* v. *Virginia Surface Mining Association*, 110, 113

Hollow state: background on, 41–42; concept of, 42–44; and contracting, 41–62; dimensions of, 44–46; implications of, 57–58; and privatization, 9–10; research needed on, 55–59

House Committee on Government Operations, 28, 36, 38

Human resource management: and employee ties, 204; and internal labor market, 239–258; for organizational learning, 37; for senior executives, 218–225, 231, 235–236

**I**

IBM, accounting issues at, 120

Implementation: administrative focus on, 156–157; and courts, 174–176

Importance, paradox of, 120–121

Information, and organizational learning, 24, 32–34

Innovation: aspects of encouraging, 63–89; barriers to, 63–65, 70–72; case study of, 67, 69, 72–85; and context, 68, 70, 72, 73, 75–77; factors related to, 66, 68–69, 73–75; faith in, 87; and leadership, 68, 71, 74, 80–83; and linkage systems, 68–69, 71–72, 74–75, 83–85; overview of, 85–87; and structure, 68, 70–71, 73, 77–79; tendencies toward, 65–67. *See also* Reform

Internal labor market (ILM); aspects of, 239–258; background on, 239–242; balance for, 255–256; challenges to, 243–246; concept of, 239; implications for, 246–255; and job security, 251–253; and mobility, 241–242, 246–247, 249–251, 256; and rank-in-person or in-position, 244, 247–248; and reward sys-

tem, 243–244, 253–255; status and position rules in, 246–248; and temporary employees, 244–246, 252–253

Internal process models, of organizations, 128–129

Investment strategy, and employee ties, 200–201

Israel, and administrative systems, 323–324

**J**

Job Corps, 123

Job evaluation, and internal labor market, 247, 248

Job security, and internal labor market, 251–253

**K**

Kansas City, Missouri, school desegregation case in, 173, 174, 175, 176, 177

*Kelley* v. *Johnson*, 101, 113

*Keyishian* v. *Board of Regents*, 93, 113

Knowledge: decentralized, 29–31; power of, 34–35

**L**

Labor market. *See* Internal labor market

Law: and employee rights, 90–114; and personnel management, 168–190; rule of, valued, 267

Leadership: dual, in public organizations, 5–6; and employee ties, 206–207; and innovation, 68, 71, 74, 80–83; and personnel administration, 133–135; transformational, 133, 332

Learning organizations: aspects of, 19–40; background on, 19–20; challenges to, 23–31; concept of, 21; implications of, 35–37; need for, 11, 31; and paradox of authority, 20–23; propositions on, 31–35

Legal accountability, 270–271, 277–278, 280, 282, 285

Legislative Reorganization Act of
    1946, 150, 153
Life-style issues, and employee
    rights, 101–102
Linkages, and innovation, 68–69,
    71–72, 74–75, 83–85. *See also*
    Employee-organization linkages
Los Angeles Police Department, 273
Loyalties, and contracting, 54

**M**

*McAuliffe* v. *Mayor of New Bedford,*
    91, 113
McKnight Foundation, 75, 77, 82, 85
Malcolm Baldrige Quality Award,
    67
Management: and administrative
    theory, 145–167; aspects of,
    141–259; balance in, 143; for
    diversity, 251; and employee ties,
    191–214; empowerment for, 286;
    environment of, 4–8; for gover-
    nance, 303–304, 309, 314–315;
    hierarchical, 296–297; and inter-
    nal labor market, 239–258;
    micro-, 154–155; overview of,
    141–143; of senior executives,
    215–238; strategy of, and ac-
    countability, 272–273, 274–277;
    Theory X for, 104, 106
Market model, for governance,
    296–297, 300–306, 318
*Marshall* v. *Barlow's Inc.*, 97, 113
*Martin* v. *Wilks,* 169, 187
*Maryland* v. *Wirtz,* 110, 113
Massachusetts: employee rights in,
    90–91; school desegregation in,
    174, 175
Massachusetts Institute of Technol-
    ogy (MIT), earnings at, 120
*Mathews* v. *Eldridge,* 99, 113
MCI, subcontracting by, 41–42
Medicaid and Medicare, 25, 27
Minnesota: Department of Human
    Services of, 76; innovation case
    study in, 67, 69, 72–85
Minnesota, University of, Hubert
    Humphrey Institute of Public
    Affairs at, 63n

Missouri, school desegregation case
    in, 173, 174, 175, 176, 177
*Missouri* v. *Jenkins,* 185, 187
Mobility: and internal labor market,
    241–242, 246–247, 249–251, 256;
    of senior executives, 224–225,
    226–227, 232, 236
Model Cities, 25
Monopoly, and organizational learn-
    ing, 24–25
*Monsanto* v. *Acting Administrator,* 179, 187
Motivation: court impact on, 181;
    and employee ties, 201, 203,
    205–206; norm-based and affec-
    tive factors in, 201, 243; and per-
    sonnel administration, 135–137
*Mt. Healthy Board of Education* v.
    *Doyle,* 94, 113

**N**

National Academy of Public Ad-
    ministration (NAPA): and ac-
    countability, 283; and employee
    ties, 203, 212; and internal labor
    market, 248, 255, 257; and
    senior executives, 224, 227, 228,
    229, 230, 232, 237
National Aeronautics and Space Ad-
    ministration (NASA), 8, 45, 273
*National Association of Letter Carriers* v.
    *Civil Service Commission,* 96, 113
National Association of Schools of
    Public Affairs and Administra-
    tion, 161
National Commission on the Public
    Service (Volcker Commission):
    and accountability, 268, 292; and
    administrative theory, 159, 165;
    and employee ties, 192, 193, 197,
    198, 212; and issues of reform, 2,
    13, 322, 333; and senior execu-
    tives, 226, 237
National Commission on the State
    and Local Public Service: and
    employee ties, 202, 212; and is-
    sues of reform, 2, 13, 322,
    333–334
*National League of Cities* v. *Usery,*
    109–110, 113

National Performance Review: and administrative theory, 159, 160; and employee ties, 197, 200, 212; and issues of reform, 2, 4, 322, 325, 332, 334

*National Treasury Employees* v. *Von Raab,* 97, 98, 113

Netherlands, governance of, 302

Netherworld, and personnel management, 276, 278, 280

Network organizations. *See* Contracting out

Networks, and organizational learning, 35, 36–37

New Bedford, Massachusetts, employee rights in, 90–91

New Deal, and administrative theory, 150

New York Bureau of Municipal Research, 149

New Zealand, governance of, 297, 298, 302

Nike, as hollow corporation, 41

Nuclear Regulatory Commission (NRC), 20

**O**

*O'Connor* v. *Ortega,* 97, 113

Organisation for Economic Cooperation and Development, 279, 292

Organization theory, and personnel administration, 116, 125–130

Organizational learning. *See* Learning organization

Organizations. *See* Public organizations

**P**

PACER SHARE, 202

Palestinian Liberation Organization, and administrative systems, 323–324

Participatory model, for governance, 297, 306–311, 318

Patronage functions, in personnel management, 278

Pay for performance: and employee ties, 200–201; and internal labor market, 243–244, 253–255; and market model, 303–304; and private sector, 4

Pendleton Act of 1883, 150

Pennsylvania: court impact in, 178; employee rights in, 101

Performance Management and Recognition System, 136, 200, 213, 255, 286

Permanence, dysfunctions of, 312

*Perry* v. *Sindermann,* 91, 93, 113

*Perry Education Association* v. *Perry Local Educators' Association,* 96, 113

Personnel administration: and accountability, 263–294; aspects of, 115–140; assessing, 118–119; background on, 115–117; blaming in, 122; courts in partnership with, 104–111, 168–190; defending, 122–123; developments for, 130–137; discretion and authority lacking for, 7–8; effectiveness of, 118–125; flexibility in, 280–289; fragmentation in, 124; future agenda for, 186–187; implications of court decisions for, 108–111, 173–174, 176–182, 184–186; and internal labor market, 239–258; issues of reforming, 2, 12; measuring, 119–120; and motivation, 135–137; netherworld in, 276, 278, 280; and organization theory, 116, 125–130; and performance, 117–118; and pessimism, 124–125; and politics, 123; and self-promotion, 123; and values conflicts, 120–122, 130

Philadelphia, employee rights in, 101

*Pickering* v. *Board of Education,* 93, 94, 113

Policy making: and civil servants, 296, 304–305; and contracting, 27, 58–59; for governance, 304–306, 309–311, 315–316

Political accountability, 270–271, 273, 278, 280

Political responsiveness, valued, 266

Politicization: and accountability,

286; and employee ties, 198; and
governance forms, 305; and job
security, 252
Politics-administration dichotomy:
perdurability of, 151–152; in personnel, 123; politics of, 147–151
Presidential Management Intern
Program, 206
President's Committee on Administrative Management (Brownlow
Committee), 152, 167
President's Private Sector Survey on
Cost Control (Grace Commission), 4, 264, 292
Press freedoms, and employee
rights, 96
Private sector, models of success
from, 3–4, 200
Privatization: challenges of, 11–12;
and governance, 302; and implications of contracting out, 41–62;
irony of, 59; and legitimacy issues, 56–57; and organizational
capacity, 326; and organizational
functioning, 9–10
Professional accountability, 270–271,
273, 278, 285, 287
Professional blinders, and organizational learning, 29
Professional expertise, valued, 267,
286–287
Progressive movement: and administrative theory, 147, 148–149,
157–158, 159, 160, 161; and organizational learning, 23–24, 29
Psychological attachments, and employee ties, 197–199, 200–201,
208
Public administration. See Administration, public
Public forum doctrine, and employee rights, 96
Public organizations: accountability
in, 6–7, 263–294; activities of,
15–140; capacity of, 325–327;
challenges of, 322–334; changing
nature of, 9; choices for,
331–333; and contracting out,
41–62; court control of, 170–174;
employee linkages with, 191–214;

employee rights in, 90–114; environmental complexity for,
323–325; functions of, 8–10; and
governance, 259–321, 329–331;
innovation in, 63–89; issues of
reforming, 1–2; learning by,
19–40; management environment
of, 4–8; management of change
in, 141–259; overview of, 15–17;
permanence of, 297–298, 312;
personnel administration in,
115–140; reinvigorated, 199–207;
and work-force vitality, 327–329
Public-private partnerships, and organizational learning, 25

Q

Quality movement: and accountability, 286–287; and reward system,
202

R

Rank, in person or in position, 244,
247–248
Rankin v. McPherson, 94–95, 113, 114
Reagan administration: and accountability, 280, 286; and employee ties, 196; and governance,
305, 316; and issues for reform,
4; and personnel administration,
123; and privatization, 42, 44, 45
Reform: background on, 1–3;
challenges for, 10–13, 322–334;
and continuity, 324–325; defining
agenda for, 3–10; and governance, 259–321; issues of, 1–14;
management environment of,
4–8; responsibilities of, 17;
themes of, 15. See also Innovation
Reorganization Act of 1939, 152
Resolution Trust Corporation, 56
Reward systems: congruent,
201–204; and internal labor market, 243–244, 253–255; and market model, 303–304
Right-privilege dichotomy, and employee rights, 91–92, 95, 96, 97,
98, 99–100, 102, 104–108

Risk management, and employee rights, 105–106
Roper Organization, 193
*Roosevelt Campobello International Park Commission* v. *United States Environmental Protection Agency*, 181, 187
Rules and regulations, and flexibility, 284–286
*Rust* v. *Sullivan*, 95
*Rutan* v. *Republican Party of Illinois*, 91, 96, 102, 113, 169, 187

**S**

Sacramento Air Logistics Center, Directorate of Distribution of, 202–203
*Schaper* v. *City of Huntsville*, 101, 113
Science, declining confidence in, 28–29
Searches, administrative, and employee rights, 97
Senior Executive Service (SES): and accountability, 267, 280, 282, 286; analysis of, 215–238; background on, 215–216; career paths in, 224–225; challenges to, 328; development and management of, 227; empowerment for, 234–236; and executive resource management, 218–225, 231, 235–236; and governance, 316; limitations of, 225–228; managerial activities of, 220; and mobility, 224–225, 226–227, 232, 236; and personnel administration, 121, 123; political management activities in, 222–223; in practice, 218–225; promise of, 216–218; protection in, 233–234; rank-in-person in, 244; reinventing, 228–234; role of, 142–143, 218; and search committees, 232; self-image in, 220–221; strategic context for, 229–230
Senior Executives Association (SEA), 219; Professional Development League of, 215n
Service implementation networks. *See* Contracting out

Shadow state, 43
*Shelton* v. *Tucker*, 93, 96, 113
*Sherbert* v. *Verner*, 93, 113
*Sierra Club* v. *Ruckelshaus*, 180, 187
*Snepp* v. *United States*, 96, 113
Social equity, and administrative theory, 158
Social good, and employee ties, 205
Social overhead, in contracting, 107
Social Security Administration, 273
Socialization, and employee ties, 205–206
Special needs doctrine, and employee rights, 105, 109
Speech: freedom of, and employee rights, 92–97; of public concerns, 94–95
Stakeholder models, of organizations, 129
*Stanley* v. *Illinois*, 99, 113
Strategic planning, and personnel administration, 131–133
Structures: for governance, 301–303, 308–309, 313–314; and innovation, 68, 70–71, 73, 77–79
Sweden, rank-in-person in, 244
Systems, linkage, and innovation, 68–69, 71–72, 74–75, 83–85
Systems-resource models, of organizations, 126, 128

**T**

Temporary organization model, for governance, 297–298, 312–316, 318
Tenure at Office Act of 1820, 146–147
Texas: Department of Mental Health of, 183; employee rights in, 95
Three Mile Island, 19–20, 31
Tort Claims Act of 1946, 150, 153–154

**U**

Unconditional conditions doctrine, and employee rights, 93, 95, 96, 98

Union of Soviet Socialist Republics, communication with former states of, 11, 325

United Kingdom: Citizen's Charter in, 306; governance of, 1, 297, 302, 305, 306, 316, 317; senior executives in, 228

*United Public Workers* v. *Mitchell*, 92, 96, 113

U.S. Air Force, 102, 202–203

U.S. Bureau of the Budget, 30

U.S. Civil Service Commission, 196n, 267

U.S. Coast Guard, 313

U.S. Customs Service, 98, 313

U.S. Department of Defense, 313

U.S. Department of Energy (DOE): challenges for, 11, 16, 325; contracting by, 9, 44, 45, 47–48, 50; and organizational learning, 21, 27

U.S. Department of Health and Human Services, 95, 132, 139

U.S. Department of Housing and Urban Development, 11, 307, 325

U.S. Department of State, 11, 229, 233, 278, 325

U.S. Department of the Navy, 277

U.S. Department of the Treasury, 132, 139

U.S. Department of Transportation (DOT), 27, 47–48, 51

U.S. Environmental Protection Agency (EPA): challenges for, 11, 16, 325; and contracting, 45, 46, 47, 49, 50–55, 61; court impact on, 175, 177, 178, 179–180, 181, 182–183, 184, 185–186; Office of General Counsel at, 179; and organizational learning, 21, 27; Science Advisory Board at, 180

U.S. Forest Service, 278

U.S. General Accounting Office (GAO): and contracting, 43, 47, 48n, 49, 50n, 51n, 55; 61; and organizational learning, 20–21, 27, 40; and personnel administration, 125, 140; and reward systems, 255, 257; and senior executives, 230, 238

U.S. General Services Administration, 223

U.S. Merit Systems Protection Board, 118, 137, 140, 267

U.S. Office of Federal Procurement Policy, 47, 61

U.S. Office of Management and Budget (OMB): and contracting, 45, 61; and organizational learning, 27, 35–36, 40; and senior executives, 223, 230–231, 234

U.S. Office of Personnel Management (OPM): and employee ties, 196n, 199, 214; and personnel administration, 118, 124, 136; and senior executives, 223, 225, 227, 230, 231–232, 238; and temporary workers, 252

U.S. Postal Service, 273

U.S. Supreme Court, 91–113, 169

**V**

Values: and accountability, 266–267; and personnel administration, 120–122, 130

Vendors. *See* Contracting out

Veterans Administration, 219

Virginia, court impact in, 182

Virtual corporation, 42

Volcker Commission. *See* National Commission on the Public Service

Volunteers, and employee ties, 197, 206

**W**

Walter-Logan Act of 1940, 152–153

*Wieman* v. *Updegraff*, 93, 113

Work ethic: changing, 193; and contracting, 52–53

Work force: capacity of, 242; configuration of, 284; core and peripheral, 252; diversity in, 240–241, 251; vitality of, 327–329. *See also* Internal labor market

*Wyatt* v. *Stickney*, 170–171, 175, 187